THE PHILOSOPHY
OF EXISTENTIALISM

THE PHILOSOPHY
OF
EXISTENTIALISM

JEAN-PAUL SARTRE

Edited and with a Foreword by Wade Baskin

INTEGRATED MEDIA

NEW YORK

"The Roots of Existentialism: An Introduction," translated from *Petite Histoire de "L'Existentialisme"* by Forrest Williams and Stanley Maron, 1949.

"The Humanism of Existentialism," translated from *L'Existentialisme Est un Humanisme* by Bernard Frechtman, 1947.

"The Problem of Nothingness," translated from *L'Être et le Néant* by Hazel E. Barnes, 1956.

"The Emotions: Outline of a Theory," translated from *Esquisse d'une Théorie des Emotions* by Bernard Frechtman, 1948.

"The Role of the Image in Mental Life," translated from *L'Imaginaire*, 1948.

"What Is Writing?" translated from *Qu'est-ce que la Littérature?* by Bernard Frechtman, 1949.

"Essays in Aesthetics": "The Venetian Pariah" appeared as "*Le Sésquestre de Venice*" in *Les Temps Modernes*, November 1957; "The Paintings of Giacometti" appeared in *Les Temps Modernes*, June, 1954; "The Mobiles of Calder" and "The Quest for the Absolute" were first published in *Les Temps Modernes* and later in *Situations III*, Paris, Gallimard, 1948; all translated by Wade Baskin, 1963.

Cover design by Angela Goddard

ISBN 978-1-4804-4456-0

Philosophical Library
www.philosophicallibrary.com

This 2015 edition distributed by Open Road Integrated Media
345 Hudson Street
New York, NY 10014
www.openroadmedia.com

CONTENTS

FOREWORD

The vast ethical and political implications of the existential situation—the absurdity of human life, man's gnawing anguish, his solitude, and his alienation—have dominated the thinking of Jean-Paul Sartre for almost three decades. His recent refusal to accept the Nobel Prize for Literature caused astonishment only among those who look upon existentialism as nothing more than a philosophy based on disillusionment and despair and thrust into prominence at the close of World War II. Such an act is of course wholly consonant with the views expressed in the very works on which the award was to be based.

It has been said that existentialism is not a disciplined philosophical system but a label for revolts, in diverse guises, against traditional philosophy. Though Sartre never represented himself as an "existentialist," journalists seized upon the epithet, first suggested by Gabriel Marcel, and linked it inseparably to the name of the man whose views gained ascendancy during France's darkest hour. No one is better qualified than Jean Wahl, the author of the first essay in this collection of representative essays, to explain the roots of existential thought. It was in 1946 that the eminent Professor of Philosophy summarized for his colleagues the history of the particular form of revolt which he classed as existential. The broad popularity of Sartre's views and the lack of familiarity with their humanistic, religious, and aesthetic origins are responsible for much misunderstanding. Professor Wahl's introductory essay should provide the reader with a basis for clarification.

The other essays in the collection point up a maxim set down in 1943 in Sartre's monumental work *Being and Nothingness*: "The being of an existent is never to reveal itself completely." The first of the essays by Sartre, "The Humanism of Existentialism," is a brilliant exposition intended for a general audience. Though it is not in any sense a definitive statement of his position, it is a partial revelation of his thought at a crucial moment in its evolution, a revelation that will be complete only when the last word has been said. It is at the same time a refutation of the prevalent notion that recognition of the absurdity of life can culminate in despair. It reveals that his revolt has not forced him to break completely with the tradition established by Christian and non-Christian thinkers who accepted man's alienation and solitude even while proclaiming his basic goodness and his responsibility to himself as well as to others. The essay has a permanent place in the history of his quest for a new morality.

Sartre's essays on nothingness, on the emotions, and on the image contain the essentials of his metaphysical speculations. He begins his investigation of phenomenological ontology—the description of the structure of being in the dramatic moment of experience—by studying the act of nihilation through which being is split into something (man) conscious of his not being something else: the for-itself and the in-itself, or that which is and that which is not. His emphasis on the role of nothingness in our perception of the world is a unique contribution to philosophical thought. It enables him to advance his most significant ethical tenet: to live "authentically" we must be conscious of our freedom to choose and concerned with the effect our choice will have on all men. Like Faust, we achieve "salvation" only through utter commitment, through continuous striving toward a projected goal.

"What Is Writing?" assumes new significance in the light of Sartre's recently published autobiography, *The Words*, which advances a partial answer to the question that concludes the essay: "*Why* does one write?"

Sartre's approach to aesthetics is as ingenious and as original as his approach to metaphysics and to ethics. His four essays evidence his concern over fundamental issues relating to the nature of art as well as to the formation and function of the artist in the existential situation. In questioning art he stirs once again the dust of metaphysical speculations. Here as in all his other writings we sense a spirit of dedication and a sincere desire on the part of the writer to effect a change in the life of the reader. Each of the three artists studied, because he embodies contradictions and confronts enigmas, presents Sartre with a challenge and affords him the opportunity to illustrate his theories. Tintoretto is the product of class contradictions and has to achieve self-affirmation through deceit. Giacometti is obsessed by his alienation in a world of things accessible only through their appearances and has to discover how to paint emptiness. Calder works on the borderland between freedom and control and has to discover how to imbue something immobile with movement.

The essays on aesthetics also provide us with a host of striking images and intimate asides: the definition of genius as "a conflict between a finite presence and an infinite absence"; the description of Tintoretto's paintings as a "passionate love affair" between a city and her rejected suitor; allusions to the uniqueness of touch and the significance of the Other's look; having to learn anew to live "at a respectable distance" from others after World War II ended; fright on boarding a plane as it relates to his love of beauty and his abhorrence of ugliness; the expressed hope that Giacometti will one day paint an illusion that will cause us to experience the "same shock that we feel on returning late and seeing a stranger walking toward us in the dark."

Nothing in these essays is beyond the grasp of the general reader interested in learning from the source the ideas of the most controversial thinker of our time. In fact, on many occasions he too will feel a shock of recognition—a feeling that what he is reading is not something new but something long anticipated.

Wade Baskin
Southeastern State College

THE ROOTS OF EXISTENTIALISM

An Introduction by Jean Wahl

One day not long ago, as I was leaving a café in Paris, I passed a group of students, one of whom stepped up to me and said: "*Sûrement, Monsieur est existentialiste!*"

I denied that I was an existentialist. Why? I had not stopped to consider, but doubtless I felt that terms suffixed by *ist* usually conceal vague generalities.

The subject of existentialism, or philosophy of existence, has begun to receive as much attention in New York as in Paris. Sartre has written an article for *Vogue;* a friend informs me that *Mademoiselle*, a magazine for teen-age young ladies, has featured an article on existentialist literature; and Marvin Farber has written in his periodical that Heidegger constitutes an international menace. The philosophy of existence has become, not only a European problem, but a world problem.

It is no less of a problem to define this philosophy satisfactorily. The word "existence," in the philosophic connotation which it has today, was first used by Kierkegaard. But may we call Kierkegaard an existentialist, or even a philosopher of existence? He had no desire to be a philosopher, and least of all, a philosopher with a fixed doctrine. In our own times, Heidegger has opposed what he terms "existentialism," and Jaspers has asserted that "existentialism" is the death of the philosophy of existence! So that it seems only right to restrict our application of the term "existentialism" to those who willingly accept it, to those whom we might call The Philosophical School of Paris, i.e., Sartre, Simone de Beauvoir, Merleau-Ponty. But we still have not found a definition of the term.

We face another difficulty in the paradox that the manner in which most of us speak of the philosophy of existence partakes of what Heidegger calls "the domain of the inauthentic." We speak of the philosophy of existence; this is precisely what Heidegger, and Sartre as well, would like to avoid since we are concerned with questions which, strictly speaking, belong to solitary meditation and cannot be subjects of discourse. And yet we are gathered here today to discuss these questions . . .*

To begin with, we must contrast the philosophy of existence to the classical conceptions of philosophy to be found in, say, Plato, Spinoza, and Hegel. For Plato, philosophy was the search for Essence, because Essence is immutable. Spinoza sought access to an eternal life which is beatitude. Generally speaking, the philosopher has wished to rise above the realm of Becoming and find a truth universal and eternal. He has generally operated—or so he believed—solely by reasoning. One might say that the last philosopher of this kind was Hegel, who carried farthest this effort to understand the world rationally. On the other hand, Hegel differed from the others by his insistence upon Becoming and the importance which he assigned to this notion. Already, in this sense, he had diverged from the tradition of Plato, Descartes, Spinoza, and many others. Nevertheless, Hegel believed in a universal reason. He tells us that our thoughts and

---

* The substance of the text was originally delivered in a lecture in 1946 in France at a meeting of the *Club Maintenant*. The slightly revised form translated here was prepared by the author himself.—Tr.

feelings have meaning solely because each thought, each feeling, is bound to our personality, which itself has meaning only because it takes place in a history and a state, at a specific epoch in the evolution of the universal Idea. To understand anything that happens in our inner life we must go to the totality which is our self, thence to the larger totality which is the human species, and finally to the totality which is the absolute Idea. This is the conception which Kierkegaard, whom we may call the founder of the philosophy of existence, came forward to contradict.

Opposing the pursuit of objectivity and the passion for totality which he found in Hegel, Kierkegaard proposed the notion that truth lies in subjectivity; that true existence is achieved by intensity of feeling. To consider him merely as a part of a whole would be to negate him. "One might say," he wrote, "that I am the moment of individuality, but I refuse to be a paragraph in a system." To the objective thinker he opposes the subjective thinker, or, rather, what he calls the individual, the unique. By dint of knowledge, Kierkegaard says, we have forgotten what it is to exist. His principal enemy was the expositor of a system, i.e., the professor.

The existent individual, as Kierkegaard defines him, is first of all he who is in an infinite relationship with himself and has an infinite interest in himself and his destiny. Secondly, the existent individual always feels himself to be in Becoming, with a task before him; and applying this idea to Christianity, Kierkegaard says: one is not a Christian—one becomes a Christian. It is a matter of sustained effort. Thirdly, the existent individual is impassioned, impassioned with a passionate thought; he is inspired; he is a kind of incarnation of the infinite in the finite. This passion which animates the existent (and this brings us to the fourth characteristic) is what Kierkegaard calls "the passion of freedom."

The notions of choice and decision have an importance of the first order in the philosophy of Kierkegaard. Each decision is a risk, for the existent feels himself surrounded by and filled with uncertainty; nevertheless, he decides. Note that what we have just said concerning the existent's mode of thinking and being discloses the object of his thought: the infinite; for with such infinite passion one can only desire the infinite. Thus, the *how* of the quest gives the goal; and, since we are in contact with this infinite, our decisions will always be decisions between the All and the Nothing, like those of Ibsen's Brand. Under the influence of these passions and decisions, the existent will ceaselessly strive to simplify himself, to return to original and authentic experience.

But so far we have dwelt only on the subjectivistic aspect of Kierkegaard's philosophy. For him, as for the other philosophers whom we will consider, there is no subjective without a certain *rapport* with a being. "The existence of a Christian is contact with Being," he wrote in 1854 in his Journal. The existent must always feel himself in the presence of God and reintegrate into Christian thought this notion of being in front of God. But to feel oneself before God is to feel oneself a sinner. Thus, it is by sin, and particularly by consciousness of sin, that one enters the religious life. But once in the religious sphere, one has still to progress, by a sort of spiritual voyage, from a religion which stays close to philosophy to the highest stage of religion. In the highest stage of religion, reason is scandalized, for we meet with the affirmation of the incarnation in the idea of the birth of the eternal being at a certain place and a certain moment in history.

The existent individual, then, will be he who has this intensity of feeling because he is in contact with something outside of himself. He will undergo a kind of crucifixion of the understanding. He will be essentially anxious, and infinitely interested in respect to his existence because an eternity of pains or an eternity of joys depend upon his relation with God. Thus, he will be in relation with what Kierkegaard calls "the absolute Other": a God who, though protective, is absolutely heterogeneous to the individual; an infinite love which, no doubt, embraces us, but which we feel to be other than ourself because in our fundamental individuality and sinfulness we are opposed to it.

We have noted two ways by which Kierkegaard opposed Hegel: by the emphasis laid upon subjectivity, and by the importance assigned to intensity of individual feeling. We must add to these distinctions Kierkegaard's insistence upon the idea of Possibility. For Hegel, the world is the necessary unfolding of the eternal Idea, and freedom is necessity understood. For Kierkegaard, on the contrary, there are real possibilities, and any philosophy which denies them is oppressive, suffocating. Moreover, the idea of Possibility is linked to the idea of Time, and we may contrast Kierkegaardian time, with all its ruptures and discontinuities, to the logical unwinding of Hegelian time, just as the subjective and passionate dialectic of Kierkegaard has been contrasted to the Hegelian dialectic.

Naturally, the ideas of Kierkegaard pose many problems. On the one hand, is there not a tendency in Kierkegaard to rationalize and explain the paradox by presenting it as the union of the finite and the infinite? And although he purports to present us with a scandal to reason, does he not thereby diminish to some extent the element of scandal? On the other hand, Kierkegaard himself realized that the coming of Christ into the world did not constitute the supreme paradox, which would have been reached only if no one had perceived the coming of God. "I meditate on this question," wrote Kierkegaard, "and my spirit loses its way." Let us add that the paradox exists only for him who dwells below; for the blessed, that is to say, for those who see the truth, the paradox vanishes. In short, this entire construction exists only from an "earthbound" point of view. But perhaps this does not constitute a genuine objection. In a general way it is very difficult to determine whether such observations are objections or whether, by accentuating the paradox, they reinforce the Kierkegaardian conception. We could say the same in regard to questions brought out by the relations between Subjectivity and History (the intensity of the subjective feeling being paradoxically founded upon an objective historical fact), and by the relations between Eternity and History (for, if the moment of incarnation is an eternal moment, the paradox threatens to vanish).

Without a doubt we could trace the history of the philosophy of existence back to Schelling, a philosopher whom Kierkegaard knew, and to the battle waged by Schelling, near the end of his life, against Hegel. To Hegelianism Schelling opposed what he called his "positive philosophy" or his "affirmation of incomprehensible contingency." We may even find in the writings of the young Hegel certain features which are not dissimilar to Kierkegaardian thought; but we must be wary of attributing too much historical importance to the youthful Hegel. Moreover, even the quasi-Kierkegaardian elements which did infiltrate into Hegel's philosophy lost in transit their character of subjective protestation.

We could even trace the philosophy of existence back to Kant, who demonstrated that we cannot conclude existence from essence and thus opposed the ontological proof. Existence ceased to be perfection, and became position. In this sense, we may say that Kant begins a new period in philosophy. Or we may go back to Pascal and Saint Augustine, who replaced pure speculation with a kind of thinking closer to the person, the individual. It remains no less true, however, that we are able to recognize and understand these early prefigurations of the philosophy of existence only because a Kierkegaard existed.

The second major event in the history of the philosophy of existence occurred when two German philosophers, Jaspers and Heidegger, translated the reflections of Kierkegaard into more intellectual terms.

We may consider the philosophy of Jaspers as a sort of secularization and generalization of the philosophy of Kierkegaard. In the philosophy of Jaspers we are no longer referred to Jesus, but rather, to a background of our existence of which we may glimpse only scattered regions. Humanity has multiple activities, and each of us has multiple possibilities. But we develop one, we sacrifice another, and we never attain to that Absolute which Hegel prided himself on being able to reach through the unwinding of the Idea to its necessary conclusion. The absolute, in jaspers' philosophy, is "something hidden," revealing itself in fugitive fragments, in scattered flashes like intermittent strokes of lightning. We have the sensation of a night into which our thought or non-thought plunges. Consequently, we are doomed to "shipwreck," *naufrage;* our thought fails utterly, yet fulfills itself in this very disaster by sensing the background of Being from which everything springs.

We know that this background is something real; we derive our reality from it; yet we cannot construe it, and as existents we cannot even express ourselves completely. But in this awareness of defeat, which comes most vividly to us in situations in which we are strained to the utmost, we fully realize ourselves. Whether it be in human drama or in scientific discovery, we sense that there is something other than ourselves, something which exceeds us; and we assert ourselves in our existence by our relation with this transcendence. In this respect, we find in Kierkegaard and Jaspers the same connections between existence and transcendence. To this transcendence, no longer called Jesus (save in some recent writings), Jaspers has given the name *Umgreifend* or "All-enveloping," the other-than-us which encompasses us.

Jaspers senses deeply those values which escape language, science, and objectivity; and the antithesis resident in our experience of transcendence. He also endeavors to complement the Kierkegaardian and Nietzschean intuitions with the profound feeling of human communication and human historicity. For him, we are not isolated, as Kierkegaard would have us isolated. Communication, a struggling love with other persons, is at the core of his system.

Communication has consistently been one of the major problems in the philosophy of existence. Indirect in Kierkegaard, direct and striving in Jaspers, divided into "authentic" and "inauthentic" in Heidegger (the authentic sphere being reserved, it seems, for poetic expression), clumsy and failing in Sartre, communication is always there—at least as a problem. Even in the absence of communication, the idea obstinately persists.

Now let us turn to Heidegger. His problem is the ancient problem of Being. He has declared that he is not a philosopher of existence, but a philosopher of Being, and that his eventual aim is ontological. Heidegger considers the problem of existence solely to introduce us to ontology, because the only form of Being with which we are truly in contact (according to Heidegger) is the being of man. To be sure, there are other forms of Being for Heidegger: there is what he calls "the being of things seen," or scenes; there is the being of tools and instruments; there is the being of mathematical forms; there is the being of animals; but only man truly exists. Animals live, mathematical things subsist, implements remain at our disposal, and scenes manifest themselves; but none of these things exists.

In order that we ourselves may truly exist, rather than remain in the sphere of things-seen and things-used, we must quit the inauthentic sphere of existence. Ordinarily, due to our own laziness and the pressure of society, we remain in an everyday world, where we are not really in contact with ourselves. This everyday world is the domain of what Heidegger calls "the anyone"*—or what we might call "the domain of Everyman"—where we are interchangeable with each other. In this domain of "anyone," we are not conscious of our own existence. And an awareness of ourselves as existents is attainable only by traversing certain experiences, like that of anguish, which put us in the presence of the background of Nothingness from which Being erupts.

Kierkegaard insisted upon the experience of anguish, which he compared to dizziness, as a revelation of the possibilities which lie beyond. The Heideggerian anguish, however, does not lead to "mere possibilities," which are partial and relative non-entities, but to Nothingness itself. Through anguish we sense this Nothingness, from which erupts everything that is, and into which everything threatens at every instant to crumble and collapse. This attempt to give reality to an absolute Nothingness (even were we to consider it mistaken) is one of Heidegger's most interesting ventures.

Naturally, this Nothingness is difficult to characterize. We cannot even say that it *is*, and Heidegger has invented a

---

* In German, *das Man.—Tr.*

word, *Nichten* ("naughten"), to characterize its action. Nothingness "naughtens" itself and everything else. It is an active Nothingness which causes the world which erupts from it to tremble to the foundations. One might say that it is the negative foundation of Being, from which Being detaches itself by a sort of rupture. Let us remark parenthetically that in a postscript to the tract in which Heidegger discloses his theory of Nothingness, he tells us that this Nothingness, differing from each and every particular thing which *is*, can be none other, at bottom, than Being itself—for, he argues, what is there different from each thing that *is*, if not Being? Thus, we reach by a different route the identification which Hegel had effected between Being and Non-Being. And this might suggest many problems, e.g., how can one say that it is solely through anguish that Being reveals itself, and that it is into Being that everything may collapse?

In any case, the experience of anguish reveals us to ourselves as out in the world, forlorn, without recourse or refuge. Why we are flung into the world, we do not know. This brings us to one of the fundamental assertions of the philosophy of existence: we are, without our finding any reason for our being; hence, we are existence without essence.

Obviously, we have abandoned any classical scheme, any hierarchy of realities at the top of which is God, the most perfect Being. Now we see only existents, flung for no reason upon the earth, and essences are merely constructions from existences. No doubt one may seek out essences of material things and implements, but there can be no essence of an existent individual, of man. Here we see most clearly the essence—if we may so speak!—of the philosophy of existence, as contrasted to nearly all classical philosophy, from Plato to Hegel, in which existence always derives from essence.

The existence of man, this being, flung into the world, is essentially finite. Limited by death, his existence is a "being for death," as the Kierkegaardian anguish was a "sickness unto death." Although our existence is characterized by the fact that there are things possible to us, the moment will come when there will be no more possibilities, when there will be no more "ahead of us." This is, of course, the moment of death, which Heidegger characterizes as the impossibility. It is this fact of our being in a finite and limited time which accounts for the tragic character of Anxiety.

Nevertheless, in this limited world we do accomplish a movement—or rather, movements—of transcendence; not towards God, because God does not exist (this is the principal teaching which Heidegger retains from Nietzsche), but towards the world, towards the future, and towards other people. Thus, the idea of transcendence loses its religious character and acquires, paradoxically enough, a sort of immanent character; it is a transcendence in immanence. Let us note immediately, in reply to any possible objections from those who might insist that transcendence implies in common philosophical parlance a religious affirmation, that Heidegger observes the word "transcendence" ought to denote the end towards which we are going; properly speaking, to transcend is to rise towards. Thus, a being such as God could never be a transcendent being. Only man can transcend.

Let us examine more closely these various transcendences. First, there is transcendence (or, for those who still shy away from this term: "passing beyond") towards the world. We are in-the-world, so to speak. We are naturally outside of ourselves: this is the signification, according to Heidegger, of the word "existence," which suggests an egress. By way of signifying the same idea, Heidegger says that existence is naturally *ecstatic*, in the primitive meaning of this term. Curiously enough, few philosophers have insisted upon our essential participation or relationship with the world. At the outset of his Meditations, Descartes cast doubt upon the reality of the world. Kant questioned his idea of the world. Whereas, for Heidegger, we are always "open to the world." In a brilliant passage in one of his lectures, Heidegger compared his theory to Leibniz's monadology. The monads, said Leibniz, have neither doors nor windows, each monad being entirely self-enclosed. According to Heidegger, individuals are likewise doorless and windowless, but this is true not because individuals are isolated, but because they are *outside*, in direct relation with the world—in the street, so to speak. Individuals are not "at home," because there are no homes for them.

Second, not only are we always and as a matter of course in natural relation with the world, but we are in immediate relation with other existents. And here, this theory which first presented itself as an individualism becomes an affirmation of our natural, even our metaphysical, relation with other individuals. Even in our most individual and private consciousness, even when we think we are most alone, we are not separated from others. "Without others," says Heidegger, is another mode of "with others."

Third, we go beyond ourselves towards the future. Each of us is always in front of himself. We are always planning, and we project ourselves into the plan. Man is a being who is constantly oriented towards his possibilities; the existent is a being who *has* to exist. In this connection, we may say that the time of existence begins with the future. In fact, what Heidegger calls *das Verständnis*, or Comprehension, is always stretched towards the future. And thus it is that we are always filled with anxiety or care. We are always concerned with something which is yet to come; and Being, in so far as we seize it in existence, is care and temporality.

It is clear that these three transcending movements are not quite analogous to transcendence as conceived by Kierkegaard and Jaspers, since they are transcendences within the world and paradoxically immanent to it. We surpass ourselves, but always in the circle of the intramundane.

We have been at pains to examine three movements of transcendence which enter into Heidegger's philosophy. Two more transcendences complete the list: transcendence of the existent from Nothingness ("on the substratum of Nothingness"), and transcendence from "particular things which are" towards Being (a transcendence to which we have already alluded). In summary, transcendence towards the world, towards other men, towards the future, towards Being, and transcendence out of Nothingness are the five uses of the idea of transcendence to be found in Heidegger. We may feel that in this multiplicity of meanings there are sources of ambiguity.

We have noticed that we are always ahead of ourself. On the other hand, like the One of the second hypothesis of Parmenides,* we are always "younger" than ourself. Moreover, because we are flung into the world, we find ourself with such-and-such a determinateness and such-and-such a constitution, in such-and-such a place and time. This means that we are not only our future; we are also our past. One might say that we have to find ourself—the expression "we have to" implying futurity, and the expression "ourself" implying both futurity and pastness. We have also noticed that our future is limited by the fact that at the terminus there is always death as the impossibility of possibility. Our future is again limited by

---

* Plato, *Parmenides* (Steph. 152).—Tr.

the fact that our possibilities are not abstract ones, but rather, are embedded in specific conditions not chosen by the individual.

Thus, we move ceaselessly from our future to our past, from our anticipations and plans to our memories, regrets, and remorses. This fact of being constantly in touch with both the future and the past constitutes a third term in the vocabulary of Heidegger: the third ecstasy of Time. Being both before and behind ourself, we are in the same Time as ourself. Consequently, for Heidegger the third ecstasy of Time, or the Present, is in some sense the product of the juncture of our future and our past. We may fix upon this idea as the starting point of Heideggerian ethics, from which he conceives an act of "Resolute Decision" by which we take upon ourself our past, our future, and our present, and affirm our destiny. Here, for the second time we may note, in passing, the possibility of comparing the philosophy of Heidegger with the philosophy of Nietzsche. We may also compare it, as always, with the philosophy of Kierkegaard. We may perceive the influence of Kierkegaard on Heidegger's theory of "Everyman"; on the notions of anguish, suffering, and sin; on the pre-eminence accorded to Future (a pre-eminence, to be sure, which also appears in the philosophy of Hegel); and even on the notion of a "resolute decision."

It is important for a proper understanding of Heidegger that we do not consider these notions as a series of philosophical dogmas. According to Heidegger, man, unlike other beings, interrogates himself. In fact, man *is* that being who questions, endangers, and puts at stake his very existence. We noted that the philosophy of existence is essentially the affirmation that existence has no essence (thereby going further than merely stating that essence comes after existence). But we may add, as a second characteristic of the philosophy of existence, that one's existence, because it is without essence, is the risk itself. Inasmuch as man is in-the-world, and is the being who is a philosopher in his own being, man endangers, when he questions himself, the world which he is developing, in some sense, around himself.

If we take the first Heideggerian definition of philosophy to be the endangering of Being by a being, the second definition, derived by Heidegger from his own etymological interpretation of the word "philosophy," is "the wisdom of love" (not, as usually derived, "the love of wisdom"). If we understand by wisdom the communion of ourselves with things, philosophy becomes the acknowledgement of our selves as beings-in-the-world. Philosophy becomes knowledge of the existent, not only in so far as he is oriented towards his future, as Kierkegaard defined him, but also in so far as he is in ecstatic relation with the world. From this point of view, the philosophy of Heidegger is an expansion, and in a certain sense, a negation of Kierkegaardian individualism. We must recognize the injustice of reproaching this philosophy for immuring us in ourself; on the contrary, it declares that there is no subject-object dichotomy and that the classical conception of the Subject must be exploded to reveal us as always outside of ourself— this latter phrase, indeed, ceasing to have any meaning, since there is no "ourself" to be outside of.

In putting himself in danger, man endangers the whole universe which is bound to him. In every philosophical question, the totality of the world is implicated at the same time as the existence of the individual is self-endangered and cast into a supreme gamble. Thus, we see the ideas of individuality and totality, and we may even add, the ideas of individuality and generality, constantly reuniting. In fact, Heidegger speaks not merely for one particular individual; he speaks for every individual. He is describing human existence in general. Anguish is doubtless a particular experience, but through Anguish we arrive at the general conditions of existence, or what Heidegger calls "the Existentials." In this respect the philosophy of Heidegger claims a further distinction from the philosophy of Kierkegaard, in that Kierkegaard always remains in the existential, whereas Heidegger attains Existentials, that is to say, the general characteristics of human existence. One may well ask if the notion of essence is not reinstated in the philosophy of Heidegger, and if Kierkegaard is not more consistent in his banishment of this notion. One may ask further if the search for Existentials and for Being is compatible with affirmations of existence.

Perhaps the most important question of all concerns the kind of ethical conclusions which may be drawn from these conceptions of Heidegger. Simply stated, we may say that, finding ourselves forlorn and abandoned in the world, we must shoulder our human condition and—as has already been intimated—assert our destiny. The existent is not to remain in the stage of anguish; or the stage of nausea, as it is described by Levinas and Sartre, two philosophers of existence whose reflections are linked in origin to the ideas of Heidegger. According to each of these philosophers, man can and must triumph over this experience. Man may take upon himself his own destiny, by what Heidegger calls "the Resolute Decision," which is comparable to "Repetition" in Kierkegaard and to the active consent to eternal recurrence which culminates the philosophy of Nietzsche.

Heidegger has not completed his philosophy. *Being and Time (Sein und Zeit)* is the name of his great work, and, in fact, one sees that for Heidegger the very nature of Being is constituted of temporality, and that he strives to bring Space itself into one of his moments of Time, i.e., the Present; thereby assenting, to a certain extent, to the Bergsonian theory of Space and Time. Nevertheless, one cannot say that his ontology is complete. One may even raise the question of why it is incomplete, and whether there may not be an irreducible duality between existence and the search for Being. The only way to Being is through existence. Can one found an ontology upon this existence? Such, it seems, is the Heideggerian problem.

Since the publication of *Being and Time*, Heidegger has attempted, in certain tracts, to erect a kind of philosophy more myth-like than mystic, in which he enjoins us to a communion with the earth and the world, invoking to this end the thought of Holderlin and Rilke. On the other hand, he has made a painstaking study of the idea of Truth; but there too, it seems, he is confronted with antinomies and wavers between a fundamental realism and an idealism of freedom not unlike that of Fichte.

Recalling his distinction between different forms of being, one may well ask if the being of the implement, and even the being of the scene, does not imply the human being. This question brings to the foreground the whole problem of idealism in Heidegger. No doubt, he would like to pass beyond the antinomy of idealism-realism. Nevertheless, it seems (save in certain passages of particular profundity) that he is forced to be now a realist, now an idealist, and that he does not succeed in passing beyond the domain in which these two doctrines stand in opposition, despite all his desire to do so. One might say that one of the attractions of his philosophy derives in good part from the fact that he carries far each of two great tendencies of the human spirit: the realistic tendency to insist upon things as almost impervious to the mind; the idealistic tendency, so recurrent in German philosophy, to locate everything in the mind. Thus, Heidegger will say on the one hand that truth consists in "letting things go," that truth is in things, and is a property of things, not of judgments; on the other hand, that the source of truth lies in our freedom. And at times it seems that this freedom, in turn, should be defined as the capacity to surrender to things. In the latter case, the realistic element triumphs. But the problem remains, essentially unresolved.

We can see that the philosophy of Heidegger contains a certain number of heterogeneous elements. The notion of the experience of anguish, and marked Kierkegaardian influences, lead to a definition of human existence as anxious, bent over itself, making plans. On the other hand, the Heideggerian individual is in-the-world, an idea which is foreign to Kierkegaard and may have come in part from Husserl. And we must not forget the metaphysic or ontology, and the importance assigned to the notion of Being. It is the fusion of Kierkegaardian elements, affirmations of being-in-the-world, and ontology which gives to the philosophy of Heidegger its particular tonality.

Before embarking on a critical exploration of the philosophy of Heidegger, we may notice that the first two elements in this fusion are linked. Existence is anxious, not only because it is drawn towards the future, but because it is in the world; and "the being-in-the-world" assumes the form of forlornness because experience is pervaded and gripped by anxiety. We sense in this philosophy both a tendency towards an extreme individuality and a tendency towards a deeply-felt totality.

This sketch of the philosophy of Heidegger leads to some further considerations. Taken as a whole, does not this doctrine imply a *Weltanschauung* which is negated by the doctrine itself? There is no place for God, it seems, in the philosophy of Heidegger; and yet, when he depicts us as forlorn, and even guilty, is there not—at least, in these expressions—an echo of the religious ideas among which he grew up and the religious influences which accompanied the early developments of his thought and philosophy? We might venture to say that some of the essential notions in his philosophy arise from a certain level of thought which he believed he had passed beyond. Could it be that if Heidegger were completely free of his religious presuppositions, he would cease to be Heidegger? Midway between Kierkegaard and Nietzsche, he is in the world of Nietzsche with the feelings of Kierkegaard and in the world of Kierkegaard with the feelings of Nietzsche.

In the second place, could we not conceive of a philosophy of existence linked, not solely to experiences of separation, forlornness, and profound melancholy, but also to feelings of hope and confidence? This objection to Heidegger has often been voiced by Gabriel Marcel. The Heideggerian doubtless would reply that, existence being finite and ourselves being destined for death, there is no cause for such hope and confidence. But does the thought of death reveal more of the existence and condition of Man than the thought of life? Certain passages in Sartre's *L'Être et le Néant (Being and Nothingness)* challenge Heidegger on this very point and tend to minimize the idea of death which is of first importance in the philosophy of Heidegger.

In the third place, we may question whether certain ideas have been adequately defined; in particular, the ideas of Being and Possibility. The idea of Possibility, though used by Kierkegaard, Jaspers, and Heidegger, is nowhere made precise, except perhaps in the work of Sartre. And the attempt to throw some light—a dim enough light, as it happens—upon the idea of Nothingness is, in the last analysis, more intriguing than satisfying.

Lastly, our assessment brings us to Heidegger's moral conclusions. The "resolute decision," by which we take upon ourselves our destiny, constitutes a sort of act of faith, understandable in Nietzsche as a pure act of the creative will of values, but less clearly substantiated in Heidegger. Moreover, this "resolute decision" remains extremely formal. How does one proceed from theory to practice? Heidegger himself has applied it differently at different times, doubtless according to the lessons he believed to be furnished by experience; but we cannot set aside the fact that at the time of the formation and initial triumphs of Nazism, his "resolute decision" was to follow the lead of the Nazi chiefs. This may not have been—contrary to his belief at the time and to the belief of his adversaries to this day—an absolutely logical consequence of his philosophy. But we may conclude from this evidence that the ethics of Heidegger remains purely formal, admits of several interpretations, and finally, is not an ethics at all.

We come now to the third stage in this brief history of the philosophy of existence.

Several young and able French philosophers have found in the ideas of Heidegger something fresh and significant which answers to their own feeling of anguish. There was already in France—particularly in the philosophy of Gabriel Marcel—something which could be compared to the philosophy of Jaspers and Heidegger. Furthermore, the influence of Heidegger was directly felt in France before the war—though, to be sure, in a small circle of thinkers.

The philosophy of Sartre, although containing much that

is original with him, is linked in part to the philosophy of Heidegger and in part to that of Husserl. The latter leads him into a kind of idealism which may not be completely consonant with the elements which he may have derived from Heidegger. In common with Heidegger, Sartre has "the ontological concern," the need to study the idea of Being, and also an emphasis on the idea of Nothingness, though for Sartre this latter idea is often rendered in a sense more Hegelian than Heideggerian. Sartre characterizes Being as having two forms: "in-itself" (*l'en-soi*), which is always identical with itself and corresponds to what is extended for Descartes; and "for-itself" (*le pour-soi*), which corresponds to Thought construed in Hegelian fashion as a constant movement.

Which is primary, the "in-itself" or the "for-itself"? This is one of the most difficult of all problems to resolve in the philosophy of Sartre. When he says that the "in-itself" is primary, he classifies himself as a realist; when he emphasizes the "for-itself," he classifies himself as an idealist. The "for-itself" appears to be a Nothingness, or more precisely, a nullification; following a comparison drawn by Gabriel Marcel, we might say that the "for-itself" is a kind of *trou d'air* or vent in the "in-itself." This conception is not dissimilar to Bergson's conception of consciousness as being primarily selection.

Inasmuch as these two forms of being are absolutely opposed to each other in all their characteristics, one is tempted to ask if it is proper to call both of them Being. If ontology is the science of a unique being, can there be any ontology in this ontological theory?

In the second place, one may question if there actually is something in reality which can be the "in-itself" as defined by Sartre; that is to say, something purely and uniquely itself. On this point the Hegelian theory, in which the Absolute is the development of the implicit "for-itself" towards an explicit "for-itself" seems far more satisfactory. No doubt, Sartre's affirmation of the "in-itself" responds to an epistemological concern on his part, and answered the need to affirm a reality independent of thought; but has one the right to pass from this assertion to the notion that this reality is what it is, and is uniquely so—is, in fact, something massive and stable?

On a good many points, as we have said, Sartre is an idealist. But by his insistence upon the intentionality of consciousness, by his definition of Knowledge as a "not-being," by his conception of a massive "in-itself" to which consciousness opposes itself as a Nothingness, by his affirmation of radical contingency, and by his insistence on the failure inherent in love-relationships, he seems to summarize the frequently justifiable grounds for the modern world's animadversions to idealism.

Perhaps the duality of Sartre's philosophy is one of its intrinsic characteristics, and not to be disprized. A search for justification and the impossibility of justification are recurrent *motifs* in the philosophy of Sartre. His philosophy is one of the incarnations of problematism and of the ambiguity of contemporary thought (for Man does seem, to the contemporary mind, to be ambiguous).

This is not to say that an effort by Sartre to dispel ambiguity is either inadvisable or improbable. There is the Sartre of *Nausea* and the Sartre of *The Flies*. There is the Sartre of *Morts Sans Sépultures*, which reflects divergent and contrary aspects of Sartre. There may yet be a Sartre who will go beyond ambiguity.

A few summary remarks are suggested by this brief survey of the philosophers of existence. Kierkegaard is not at all interested in ontology, and in this respect he is more existential than Heidegger or Sartre. Thus, in the history of the philosophy of existence, one goes from a consideration of existence proper to a study of Being with the help of the idea of existence. The latter method is that of Heidegger and Sartre. Nevertheless, Sartre and Heidegger differ considerably, and Sartre is closer than Heidegger to Kierkegaard. For example, Sartre criticizes the pre-eminence which Heidegger assigns to the ontological over the ontic.

We might mention, without discussing, Simone de Beauvoir and Merleau-Ponty, whose theories are similar to those of Sartre, though sometimes applied in different domains of experience. We must omit discussion of those who, like Bataille and Camus, are often classed as existentialists, but who would refuse to accept the appellation.

Let us construct a few rules-of-thumb for distinguishing between existentialists and non-existentialists. If we say: "Man is in this world, a world limited by death and experienced in anguish; is aware of himself as essentially anxious; is burdened by his solitude within the horizon of his temporality"; then we recognize the accents of Heideggerian philosophy. If we say: "Man, by opposition to the 'in-itself is the 'for-itself', is never at rest, and strives in vain towards a union of the 'in-itself and the 'for-itself'"; then we are speaking in the manner of Sartrian existentialism. If we say: "I am a thinking thing," as Descartes said; or, "The real things are Ideas," as Plato said; or, "The Ego accompanies all our representations," as Kant said; then we are moving in a sphere which is no longer that of the philosophy of existence.

The philosophy of existence reminds us, once more, of what all great philosophy has tried to teach us: that there are views of reality which cannot be completely reduced to scientific formulations. Naturally, those who are of the contrary opinion will still try to explain the philosophy of existence scientifically; for example, by economic or historical reasons. Such explanations often have some validity, but they are never completely satisfactory.

Thanks to existentialism, to be or not to be has again become the question. And this reminds us that there have been many existentialists—or, as Kierkegaard would say, many existents. We have just intimated that Hamlet was an existent. We could say the same of Pascal; of Lequier, the philosopher from whom Sartre has borrowed the dictum: "*Faire, et en faisant, se faire*"; of Carlyle; and of William James. We could say the same of Socrates' great enemy, Nietzsche. We could show that the origins of most great philosophies, like those of Plato, Descartes, and Kant, are to be found in existential reflections.

There is, however, a question which may trouble the mind, and even the existence, of the existentialist. Does he not risk destroying the very existence which he wishes above all to preserve? Jaspers rejected the term "existentialist." Kierkegaard did not wish to construct a philosophy; one may go even further, for not only would Kierkegaard have refused the name "existentialist," not only would he have rejected the term "philosopher of existence," but doubtless in his Christian humility he would have refused the name "existent." Is it for the existent to say that he exists? In short, is it, perhaps, necessary to choose between existentialism and existence? Such is the dilemma of existentialism.

At any rate, it is clear that one of the consequences of the existentialist movement and the philosophies of existence is that we have to destroy the majority of the ideas of so-called "philosophical common-sense," and of what has often been called "the eternal philosophy." In particular, we have to destroy the ideas of Essence and Substance. Philosophy—so goes the new affirmation—must cease to be philosophy of essence and must become philosophy of existence. We are observing a whole philosophical movement which dislodges previous philosophical concepts, and which tends to make more acute our subjective understanding at the same time as it makes us feel more strongly than ever our union with the world. In this sense, we are witnessing and participating in the beginning of a new mode of philosophizing.

We see that the negations advanced by the philosophers of existence imply some affirmations; in Heidegger, for example, the affirmation of our unity with the world. Doubtless we have also noticed, in reviewing rapidly the various philosophies of existence, that we find ourselves time and again before impasses. In Heidegger, for example, we do not know if his system is an idealism or a realism; if the Nothingness is Nothingness or Being. There is a similar impasse in Sartre, and on certain points a return, perhaps even a recoil, from the conceptions of Heidegger towards those of Hegel and Husserl. But these impasses need not turn us back. The permanence of the dogmatisms under whose banners the philosophy of existence is attacked are themselves reasons for reaffirming the importance and the leading role of the philosophy of existence. All great philosophies have encountered such impasses, but thought has gone ahead and somehow found a solution. Perhaps, in order to facilitate an egress from these difficulties, it will be necessary to distinguish more and more carefully among the different elements which we have enumerated, e.g., the insistence upon existence, and the insistence upon being-in-the-world. No doubt there are different levels and elements in reality; but it is only by distinguishing the various problems, levels, and elements in these philosophies of existence, and assessing their relative importance, that we will be able to gain an insight into their difficulties and possibly pass beyond them.

THE PHILOSOPHY
OF EXISTENTIALISM

Part I

THE HUMANISM OF EXISTENTIALISM

I should like on this occasion to defend existentialism against some charges which have been brought against it.

First, it has been charged with inviting people to remain in a kind of desperate quietism because, since no solutions are possible, we should have to consider action in this world as quite impossible. We should then end up in a philosophy of contemplation; and since contemplation is a luxury, we come in the end to a bourgeois philosophy. The communists in particular have made these charges.

On the other hand, we have been charged with dwelling on human degradation, with pointing up everywhere the sordid, shady, and slimy, and neglecting the gracious and beautiful, the bright side of human nature; for example, according to Mlle. Mercier, a Catholic critic, with forgetting the smile of the child. Both sides charge us with having ignored human solidarity, with considering man as an isolated being. The communists say that the main reason for this is that we take pure subjectivity, the Cartesian *I think*, as our starting point; in other words, the moment in which man becomes fully aware of what it means to him to be an isolated being; as a result, we are unable to return to a state of solidarity with the men who are not ourselves, a state which we can never reach in the *cogito*.

From the Christian standpoint, we are charged with denying the reality and seriousness of human undertakings, since, if we reject God's commandments and the eternal verities, there no longer remains anything but pure caprice, with everyone permitted to do as he pleases and incapable, from his own point of view, of condemning the points of view and acts of others.

I shall today try to answer these different charges. Many people are going to be surprised at what is said here about humanism. We shall try to see in what sense it is to be understood. In any case, what can be said from the very beginning is that by existentialism we mean a doctrine which makes human life possible and, in addition, declares that every truth and every action implies a human setting and a human subjectivity.

As is generally known, the basic charge against us is that we put the emphasis on the dark side of human life. Someone recently told me of a lady who, when she let slip a vulgar word in a moment of irritation, excused herself by saying, "I guess I'm becoming an existentialist." Consequently, existentialism is regarded as something ugly; that is why we are said to be naturalists; and if we are, it is rather surprising that in this day and age we cause so much more alarm and scandal than does naturalism, properly so called. The kind of person who can take in his stride such a novel as Zola's *The Earth* is disgusted as soon as he starts reading an existentialist novel; the kind of person who is resigned to the wisdom of the ages—which is pretty sad—finds us even sadder. Yet, what can be more disillusioning than saying "true charity begins at home" or "a scoundrel will always return evil for good"?

We know the commonplace remarks made when this subject comes up, remarks which always add up to the same thing: we shouldn't struggle against the powers-that-be; we shouldn't resist authority; we shouldn't try to rise above our station; any action which doesn't conform to authority is romantic; any effort not based on past experience is doomed to failure; experience shows that man's bent is always toward trouble, that there must be a strong hand to hold him in check, if not, there will be anarchy. There are still people who go on mumbling these melancholy old saws, the people who say, "It's only human!" whenever a more or less repugnant act is pointed out to them, the people who glut themselves on *chansons réalistes*; these are the people who accuse existentialism of being too gloomy, and to such an extent that I wonder whether they are complaining about it, not for its pessimism, but much rather its optimism. Can it be that what really scares them in the doctrine I shall try to present here is that it leaves to man a possibility of choice? To answer this question, we must re-examine it on a strictly philosophical plane. What is meant by the term *existentialism*?

Most people who use the word would be rather embarrassed if they had to explain it, since, now that the word is all the rage, even the work of a musician or painter is being called existentialist. A gossip columnist in *Clartés* signs himself *The Existentialist*, so that by this time the word has been so stretched and has taken on so broad a meaning, that it no longer means anything at all. It seems that for want of an advanced-guard doctrine analogous to surrealism, the kind of people who are eager for scandal and flurry turn to this philosophy which in other respects does not at all serve their purposes in this sphere.

Actually, it is the least scandalous, the most austere of doctrines. It is intended strictly for specialists and philosophers. Yet it can be defined easily. What complicates matters is that there are two kinds of existentialists; first, those who are

Christian, among whom I would include Jaspers and Gabriel Marcel, both Catholic; and on the other hand the atheistic existentialists among whom I class Heidegger, and then the French existentialists and myself. What they have in common is that they think that existence precedes essence, or, if you prefer, that subjectivity must be the starting point.

Just what does that mean? Let us consider some object that is manufactured, for example, a book or a paper-cutter: here is an object which has been made by an artisan whose inspiration came from a concept. He referred to the concept of what a paper-cutter is and likewise to a known method of production, which is part of the concept, something which is, by and large, a routine. Thus, the paper-cutter is at once an object produced in a certain way and, on the other hand, one having a specific use; and one can not postulate a man who produces a paper-cutter but does not know what it is used for. Therefore, let us say that, for the paper-cutter, essence—that is, the ensemble of both the production routines and the properties which enable it to be both produced and defined—precedes existence. Thus, the presence of the paper-cutter or book in front of me is determined. Therefore, we have here a technical view of the world whereby it can be said that production precedes existence.

When we conceive God as the Creator, He is generally thought of as a superior sort of artisan. Whatever doctrine we may be considering, whether one like that of Descartes or that of Leibniz, we always grant that will more or less follows understanding or, at the very least, accompanies it, and that when God creates He knows exactly what He is creating. Thus, the concept of man in the mind of God is comparable to the concept of a paper-cutter in the mind of the manufacturer, and, following certain techniques and a conception, God produces man, just as the artisan, following a definition and a technique, makes a paper-cutter. Thus, the individual man is the realization of a certain concept in the divine intelligence.

In the eighteenth century, the atheism of the *philosophers* discarded the idea of God, but not so much for the notion that essence precedes existence. To a certain extent, this idea is found everywhere; we find it in Diderot, in Voltaire, and even in Kant. Man has a human nature; this human nature, which is the concept of the human, is found in all men, which means that each man is a particular example of a universal concept, man. In Kant, the result of this universality is that the wild-man, the natural man, as well as the bourgeois, are circumscribed by the same definition and have the same basic qualities. Thus, here too the essence of man precedes the historical existence that we find in nature.

Atheistic existentialism, which I represent, is more coherent. It states that if God does not exist, there is at least one being in whom existence precedes essence, a being who exists before he can be defined by any concept, and that this being is man, or, as Heidegger says, human reality. What is meant here by saying that existence precedes essence? It means that, first of all, man exists, turns up, appears on the scene, and, only afterwards, defines himself. If man, as the existentialist conceives him, is indefinable, it is because at first he is nothing. Only afterward will he be something, and he himself will have made what he will be. Thus, there is no human nature, since there is no God to conceive it. Not only is man what he conceives himself to be, but he is also only what he wills himself to be after this thrust toward existence.

Man is nothing else but what he makes of himself. Such is the first principle of existentialism. It is also what is called subjectivity, the name we are labeled with when charges are brought against us. But what do we mean by this, if not that man has a greater dignity than a stone or table? For we mean that man first exists, that is, that man first of all is the being who hurls himself toward a future and who is conscious of imagining himself as being in the future. Man is at the start a plan which is aware of itself, rather than a patch of moss, a piece of garbage, or a cauliflower; nothing exists prior to this plan; there is nothing in heaven; man will be what he will have planned to be. Not what he will want to be. Because by the word "will" we generally mean a conscious decision, which is subsequent to what we have already made of ourselves. I may want to belong to a political party, write a book, get married; but all that is only a manifestation of an earlier, more spontaneous choice that is called "will." But if existence really does precede essence, man is responsible for what he is. Thus, existentialism's first move is to make every man aware of what he is and to make the full responsibility of his existence rest on him. And when we say that a man is responsible for himself, we do not only mean that he is responsible for his own individuality, but that he is responsible for all men.

The word subjectivism has two meanings, and our opponents play on the two. Subjectivism means, on the one hand, that an individual chooses and makes himself; and, on the other, that it is impossible for man to transcend human subjectivity. The second of these is the essential meaning of existentialism. When we say that man chooses his own self, we mean that every one of us does likewise; but we also mean by that that in making this choice he also chooses all men. In fact, in creating the man that we want to be, there is not a single one of our acts which does not at the same time create an image of man as we think he ought to be. To choose to be this or that is to affirm at the same time the value of what we choose, because we can never choose evil. We always choose the good, and nothing can be good for us without being good for all.

If, on the other hand, existence precedes essence, and if we grant that we exist and fashion our image at one and the same time, the image is valid for everybody and for our whole age. Thus, our responsibility is much greater than we might have supposed, because it involves all mankind. If I am a working-man and choose to join a Christian trade-union rather than be a communist, and if by being a member I want to show that the best thing for man is resignation, that the kingdom of man is not of this world, I am not only involving my own case—I want to be resigned for everyone. As a result, my action has involved all humanity. To take a more individual matter, if I want to marry, to have children; even if this marriage depends solely on my own circumstances or passion or wish, I am involving all humanity in monogamy and not merely myself. Therefore, I am responsible for myself and for everyone else. I am creating a certain image of man of my own choosing. In choosing myself, I choose man.

This helps us understand what the actual content is of such rather grandiloquent words as anguish, forlornness, despair. As you will see, it's all quite simple.

First, what is meant by anguish? The existentialists say at once that man is anguish. What that means is this: the man who involves himself and who realizes that he is not only the person he chooses to be, but also a lawmaker who is, at the same time, choosing all mankind as well as himself, can not help escape the feeling of his total and deep responsibility. Of course, there are many people who are not anxious; but we claim that they are hiding their anxiety, that they are flee-ing from it. Certainly, many people believe that when they do something, they themselves are the only ones involved, and when someone says to them, "What if everyone acted that way?" they shrug their shoulders and answer, "Everyone doesn't act that way." But really, one should always ask himself, "What would happen if everybody looked at things that way?" There is no escaping this disturbing thought except by a kind of double-dealing. A man who lies and makes excuses for himself by saying "Not everybody does that," is someone with an uneasy conscience, because the act of lying implies that a universal value is conferred upon the lie.

Anguish is evident even when it conceals itself. This is the anguish that Kierkegaard called the anguish of Abraham. You know the story: an angel has ordered Abraham to sacrifice his son; if it really were an angel who has come and said, "You are Abraham, you shall sacrifice your son," everything would be all right. But everyone might first wonder, "Is it really an angel, and am I really Abraham? What proof do I have?"

There was a madwoman who had hallucinations; someone used to speak to her on the telephone and give her orders. Her doctor asked her, "Who is it who talks to you?" She answered, "He says it's God." What proof did she really have that it was God? If an angel comes to me, what proof is there that it's an angel? And if I hear voices, what proof is there that they come from heaven and not from hell, or from the subconscious, or a pathological condition? What proves that they are addressed to me? What proof is there that I have been appointed to impose my choice and my conception of man on humanity? I'll never find any proof or sign to convince me of that. If a voice addresses me, it is always for me to decide that this is the angel's voice; if I consider that such an act is a good one, it is I who will choose to say that it is good rather than bad.

Now, I'm not being singled out as an Abraham, and yet at every moment I'm obliged to perform exemplary acts. For every man, everything happens as if all mankind had its eyes fixed on him and were guiding itself by what he does. And every man ought to say to himself, "Am I really the kind of man who has the right to act in such a way that humanity might guide itself by my actions?" And if he does not say that to himself, he is masking his anguish.

There is no question here of the kind of anguish which would lead to quietism, to inaction. It is a matter of a simple sort of anguish that anybody who has had responsibilities is familiar with. For example, when a military officer takes the responsibility for an attack and sends a certain number of men to death, he chooses to do so, and in the main he alone makes the choice. Doubtless, orders come from above, but they are too broad; he interprets them, and on this interpretation depend the lives of ten or fourteen or twenty men. In making a decision he can not help having a certain anguish. All leaders know this anguish. That doesn't keep them from acting; on the contrary, it is the very condition of their action. For it implies that they envisage a number of possibilities, and when they choose one, they realize that it has value only because it is chosen. We shall see that this kind of anguish, which is the kind that existentialism describes, is explained, in addition, by a direct responsibility to the other men whom it involves. It is not a curtain separating us from action, but is part of action itself.

When we speak of forlornness, a term Heidegger was fond of, we mean only that God does not exist and that we have to face all the consequences of this. The existentialist is strongly opposed to a certain kind of secular ethics which would like to abolish God with the least possible expense. About 1880, some French teachers tried to set up a secular ethics which went something like this: God is a useless and costly hypothesis; we are discarding it; but, meanwhile, in order for there to be an ethics, a society, a civilization, it is essential that certain values be taken seriously and that they be considered as having an *a priori* existence. It must be obligatory, *a priori*, to be honest, not to lie, not to beat your wife, to have children, etc., etc. So we're going to try a little device which will make it possible to show that values exist all the same, inscribed in a heaven of ideas, though otherwise God does not exist. In other words—and this, I believe, is the tendency of everything called reformism in France—nothing will be changed if God does not exist. We shall find ourselves with the same norms of honesty, progress, and humanism, and we shall have made of God an outdated hypothesis which will peacefully die off by itself.

The existentialist, on the contrary, thinks it very distressing that God does not exist, because all possibility of finding values in a heaven of ideas disappears along with Him; there can no longer be an *a priori* Good, since there is no infinite and perfect consciousness to think it. Nowhere is it written that the Good exists, that we must be honest, that we must not lie; because the fact is we are on a plane where there are only men. Dostoievsky said, "If God didn't exist, everything would be possible." That is the very starting point of existentialism. Indeed, everything is permissible if God does not exist, and as a result man is forlorn, because neither within him nor without does he find anything to cling to. He can't start making excuses for himself.

If existence really does precede essence, there is no explaining things away by reference to a fixed and given human nature. In other words, there is no determinism, man is free, man is freedom. On the other hand, if God does not exist, we find no values or commands to turn to which legitimize our conduct.

So, in the bright realm of values, we have no excuse behind us, nor justification before us. We are alone, with no excuses.

That is the idea I shall try to convey when I say that man is condemned to be free. Condemned, because he did not create himself, yet, in other respects is free; because, once thrown into the world, he is responsible for everything he does. The existentialist does not believe in the power of passion. He will never agree that a sweeping passion is a ravaging torrent which fatally leads a man to certain acts and is therefore an excuse. He thinks that man is responsible for his passion.

The existentialist does not think that man is going to help himself by finding in the world some omen by which to orient himself. Because he thinks that man will interpret the omen to suit himself. Therefore, he thinks that man, with no support and no aid, is condemned every moment to invent man. Ponge, in a very fine article, has said, "Man is the future of man." That's exactly it. But if it is taken to mean that this future is recorded in heaven, that God sees it, then it is false, because it would really no longer be a future. If it is taken to mean that, whatever a man may be, there is a future to be forged, a virgin future before him, then this remark is sound. But then we are forlorn.

To give you an example which will enable you to understand forlornness better, I shall cite the case of one of my students who came to see me under the following circumstances: his father was on bad terms with his mother, and, moreover, was inclined to be a collaborationist; his older brother had been killed in the German offensive of 1940, and the young man, with somewhat immature but generous feelings, wanted to avenge him. His mother lived alone with him, very much upset by the half-treason of her husband and the death of her older son; the boy was her only consolation.

The boy was faced with the choice of leaving for England and joining the Free French Forces—that is, leaving his mother behind—or remaining with his mother and helping her to carry on. He was fully aware that the woman lived only for him and that his going-off—and perhaps his death—would plunge her into despair. He was also aware that every act that he did for his mother's sake was a sure thing, in the sense that it was helping her to carry on, whereas every effort he made toward going off and fighting was an uncertain move which might run aground and prove completely useless; for example, on his way to England he might, while passing through Spain, be detained indefinitely in a Spanish camp; he might reach England or Algiers and be stuck in an office at a desk job. As a result, he was faced with two very different kinds of action: one, concrete, immediate, but concerning only one individual; the other concerned an incomparably vaster group, a national collectivity, but for that very reason was dubious, and might be interrupted en route. And, at the same time, he was wavering between two kinds of ethics. On the one hand, an ethics of sympathy, of personal devotion; on the other, a broader ethics, but one whose efficacy was more dubious. He had to choose between the two.

Who could help him choose? Christian doctrine? No. Christian doctrine says, "Be charitable, love your neighbor, take the more rugged path, etc., etc." But which is the more rugged path? Whom should he love as a brother? The fighting man or his mother? Which does the greater good, the vague act of fighting in a group, or the concrete one of helping a particular human being to go on living? Who can decide *a priori*? Nobody. No book of ethics can tell him. The Kantian ethics says, "Never treat any person as a means, but as an end." Very well, if I stay with mother, I'll treat her as an end and not as a means; but by virtue of this very fact, I'm running the risk of treating the people around me who are fighting, as means; and, conversely, if I go to join those who are fighting, I'll be treating them as an end, and, by doing that, I run the risk of treating my mother as a means.

If values are vague, and if they are always too broad for the concrete and specific case that we are considering, the only thing left for us is to trust our instincts. That's what this young man tried to do; and when I saw him, he said, "In the end, feeling is what counts. I ought to choose whichever pushes me in one direction. If I feel that I love my mother enough to sacrifice everything else for her—my desire for vengeance, for action, for adventure—then I'll stay with her. If, on the contrary, I feel that my love for my mother isn't enough, I'll leave."

But how is the value of a feeling determined? What gives his feeling for his mother value? Precisely the fact that he remained with her. I may say that I like so-and-so well enough to sacrifice a certain amount of money for him, but I may say so only if I've done it. I may say "I love my mother well enough to remain with her" if I have remained with her. The only way to determine the value of this affection is, precisely, to perform an act which confirms and defines it. But, since I require this affection to justify my act, I find myself caught in a vicious circle.

On the other hand, Gide has well said that a mock feeling and a true feeling are almost indistinguishable; to decide that I love my mother and will remain with her, or to remain with her by putting on an act, amount somewhat to the same thing. In other words, the feeling is formed by the acts one performs; so, I can not refer to it in order to act upon it. Which means that I can neither seek within myself the true condition which will impel me to act, nor apply to a system of ethics for concepts which will permit me to act. You will say, "At least, he did go to a teacher for advice." But if you seek advice from a priest, for example, you have chosen this priest; you already knew, more or less, just about what advice he was going to give you. In other words, choosing your adviser is involving yourself. The proof of this is that if you are a Christian, you will say, "Consult a priest." But some priests are collaborating, some are just marking time, some are resisting. Which to choose? If the young man chooses a priest who is resisting or collaborating, he has already decided on the kind of advice he's going to get. Therefore, in coming to see me he knew the answer I was going to give him, and I had only one answer to give: "You're free, choose, that is, invent." No general ethics can show you what is to be done; there are no omens in the world. The Catholics will reply, "But there are." Granted—but, in any case, I myself choose the meaning they have.

When I was a prisoner, I knew a rather remarkable young man who was a Jesuit. He had entered the Jesuit order in the following way: he had had a number of very bad breaks; in childhood, his father died, leaving him in poverty, and he was a scholarship student at a religious institution where he was constantly made to feel that he was being kept out of charity; then, he failed to get any of the honors and distinctions that children like; later on, at about eighteen, he bungled a love affair; finally, at twenty-two, he failed in military training, a childish enough matter, but it was the last straw.

This young fellow might well have felt that he had botched everything. It was a sign of something, but of what? He might have taken refuge in bitterness or despair. But he very wisely looked upon all this as a sign that he was not made for secular triumphs, and that only the triumphs of religion, holiness, and faith were open to him. He saw the hand of God in all this, and so he entered the order. Who can help seeing that he alone decided what the sign meant?

Some other interpretation might have been drawn from this series of setbacks; for example, that he might have done better to turn carpenter or revolutionist. Therefore, he is fully responsible for the interpretation. Forlornness implies that we ourselves choose our being. Forlornness and anguish go together.

As for despair, the term has a very simple meaning. It means that we shall confine ourselves to reckoning only with what depends upon our will, or on the ensemble of probabilities which make our action possible. When we want something, we always have to reckon with probabilities. I may be counting on the arrival of a friend. The friend is coming by rail or street-car; this supposes that the train will arrive on schedule, or that the street-car will not jump the track. I am left in the realm of possibility; but possibilities are to be reckoned with only to the point where my action comports with the ensemble of these possibilities, and no further. The moment the possibilities I am considering are not rigorously involved by my action, I ought to disengage myself from them, because no God, no scheme, can adapt the world and its possibilities to my will. When Descartes said, "Conquer yourself rather than the world," he meant essentially the same thing.

The Marxists to whom I have spoken reply, "You can rely on the support of others in your action, which obviously has certain limits because you're not going to live forever. That means: rely on both what others are doing elsewhere to help you, in China, in Russia, and what they will do later on, after your death, to carry on the action and lead it to its fulfillment, which will be the revolution. You even *have* to rely upon that, otherwise you're immoral." I reply at once that I will always rely on fellow-fighters insofar as these comrades are involved with me in a common struggle, in the unity of a party or a group in which I can more or less make my weight felt; that is, one whose ranks I am in as a fighter and whose movements I am aware of at every moment. In such a situation, relying on the unity and will of the party is exactly like counting on the fact that the train will arrive on time or that the car won't jump the track. But, given that man is free and that there is no human nature for me to depend on, I can not count on men whom I do not know by relying on human goodness or man's concern for the good of society. I don't know what will become of the Russian revolution; I may make an example of it to the extent that at the present time it is apparent that the proletariat plays a part in Russia that it plays in no other nation. But I can't swear that this will inevitably lead to a triumph of the proletariat. I've got to limit myself to what I see.

Given that men are free and that tomorrow they will freely decide what man will be, I can not be sure that, after my death, fellow-fighters will carry on my work to bring it to its maximum perfection. Tomorrow, after my death, some men may decide to set up Fascism, and the others may be cowardly and muddled enough to let them do it. Fascism will then be the human reality, so much the worse for us.

Actually, things will be as man will have decided they are to be. Does that mean that I should abandon myself to quietism? No. First, I should involve myself; then, act on the old saw, "Nothing ventured, nothing gained." Nor does it mean that I shouldn't belong to a party, but rather that I shall have no illusions and shall do what I can. For example, suppose I ask myself, "Will socialization, as such, ever come about?" I know nothing about it. All I know is that I'm going to do everything in my power to bring it about. Beyond that, I can't count on anything. Quietism is the attitude of people who say, "Let others do what I can't do." The doctrine I am presenting is the very opposite of quietism, since it declares, "There is no reality except in action." Moreover, it goes further, since it adds, "Man is nothing else than his plan; he exists only to the extent that he fulfills himself; he is therefore nothing else than the ensemble of his acts, nothing else than his life."

According to this, we can understand why our doctrine horrifies certain people. Because often the only way they can bear their wretchedness is to think, "Circumstances have been against me. What I've been and done doesn't show my true worth. To be sure, I've had no great love, no great friendship, but that's because I haven't met a man or woman who was worthy. The books I've written haven't been very good because I haven't had the proper leisure. I haven't had children to devote myself to because I didn't find a man with whom I could have spent my life. So there remains within me, unused and quite viable, a host of propensities, inclinations, possibilities, that one wouldn't guess from the mere series of things I've done."

Now, for the existentialist there is really no love other than one which manifests itself in a person's being in love. There is no genius other than one which is expressed in works of art; the genius of Proust is the sum of Proust's works; the genius of Racine is his series of tragedies. Outside of that, there is nothing. Why say that Racine could have written another tragedy, when he didn't write it? A man is involved in life, leaves his impress on it, and outside of that there is nothing. To be sure, this may seem a harsh thought to someone whose life hasn't been a success. But, on the other hand, it prompts people to understand that reality alone is what counts, that dreams, expectations, and hopes warrant no more than to define a man as a disappointed dream, as miscarried hopes, as vain expectations. In other words, to define him negatively and not positively. However, when we say, "You are nothing else than your life," that does not imply that the artist will be judged solely on the basis of his works of art; a thousand other things will contribute toward summing him up. What we mean is that a man is nothing else than a series of undertakings, that he is the sum, the organization, the ensemble of the relationships which make up these undertakings.

When all is said and done, what we are accused of, at bottom, is not our pessimism, but an optimistic toughness. If people throw up to us our works of fiction in which we write about people who are soft, weak, cowardly, and sometimes even downright bad, it's not because these people are soft, weak, cowardly, or bad; because if we were to say, as Zola did, that they are that way because of heredity, the workings of environment, society, because of biological or psychological determinism, people would be reassured. They would say, "Well, that's what we're like, no one can do anything about it." But when the existentialist writes about a coward, he says that this coward is responsible for his cowardice. He's not like that because he has a cowardly heart or lung or brain; he's not like that on account of his physiological make-up; but he's like that because he has made himself a coward by his acts. There's no such thing as a cowardly constitution; there are nervous constitutions; there is poor blood, as the common people say, or there are strong constitutions. But the man whose blood is poor is not a coward on that account, for what makes cowardice is the act of renouncing or yielding. A constitution is not an act; the coward is defined on the basis of the acts he performs. People feel, in a vague sort of way, that this coward we're talking about is guilty of being a coward, and the thought frightens them. What people would like is that a coward or a hero be born that way.

One of the complaints most frequently made about *The Ways of Freedom*** can be summed up as follows: "After all, these people are so spineless, how are you going to make heroes out of them?" This objection almost makes me laugh, for it assumes that people are born heroes. That's what people really want to think. If you're born cowardly, you may set your mind perfectly at rest; there's nothing you can do about it; you'll be cowardly all your life, whatever you may do. If you're born a hero, you may set your mind just as much at rest; you'll be a hero all your life; you'll drink like a hero and eat like a hero. What the existentialist says is that the coward makes himself cowardly, that the hero makes himself heroic. There's always a possibility for the coward not to be cowardly any more and for the hero to stop being heroic. What counts is total involvement; some one particular action or set of circumstances is not total involvement.

Thus, I think we have answered a number of the charges concerning existentialism. You see that it can not be taken for a philosophy of quietism, since it defines man in terms of action; nor for a pessimistic description of man—there is no doctrine more optimistic, since man's destiny is within himself; nor for an attempt to discourage man from acting, since it tells him that the only hope is in his acting and that action is the only thing that enables a man to live. Consequently, we are dealing here with an ethics of action and involvement.

Nevertheless, on the basis of a few notions like these, we are still charged with immuring man in his private subjectivity. There again we're very much misunderstood. Subjectivity of the individual is indeed our point of departure, and this for strictly philosophic reasons. Not because we are bourgeois,

---

* *Les Chemins de la Liberté*, Sartre's trilogy of novels.—Tr.

but because we want a doctrine based on truth and not a lot of fine theories, full of hope but with no real basis. There can be no other truth to start from than this: *I think; therefore, I exist.* There we have the absolute truth of consciousness becoming aware of itself. Every theory which takes man out of the moment in which he becomes aware of himself is, at its very beginning, a theory which confounds truth, for outside the Cartesian *cogito*, all views are only probable, and a doctrine of probability which is not bound to a truth dissolves into thin air. In order to describe the probable, you must have a firm hold on the true. Therefore, before there can be any truth whatsoever, there must be an absolute truth; and this one is simple and easily arrived at; it's on everyone's doorstep; it's a matter of grasping it directly.

Secondly, this theory is the only one which gives man dignity, the only one which does not reduce him to an object. The effect of all materialism is to treat every man, including the one philosophizing, as an object, that is, as an ensemble of determined reactions in no way distinguished from the ensemble of qualities and phenomena which constitute a table or a chair or a stone. We definitely wish to establish the human realm as an ensemble of values distinct from the material realm. But the subjectivity that we have thus arrived at, and which we have claimed to be truth, is not a strictly individual subjectivity, for we have demonstrated that one discovers in the *cogito* not only himself, but others as well.

The philosophies of Descartes and Kant to the contrary, through the *I think* we reach our own self in the presence of others, and the others are just as real to us as our own self. Thus, the man who becomes aware of himself through the *cogito* also perceives all others, and he perceives them as the condition of his own existence. He realizes that he can not be anything (in the sense that we say that someone is witty or nasty or jealous) unless others recognize it as such. In order to get any truth about myself, I must have contact with another person. The other is indispensable to my own existence, as well as to my knowledge about myself. This being so, in discovering my inner being I discover the other person at the same time, like a freedom placed in front of me which thinks and wills only for or against me. Hence, let us at once announce the discovery of a world which we shall call intersubjectivity; this is the world in which man decides what he is and what others are.

Besides, if it is impossible to find in every man some universal essence which would be human nature, yet there does exist a universal human condition. It's not by chance that today's thinkers speak more readily of man's condition than of his nature. By condition they mean, more or less definitely, the *a priori* limits which outline man's fundamental situation in the universe. Historical situations vary; a man may be born a slave in a pagan society or a feudal lord or a proletarian. What does not vary is the necessity for him to exist in the world, to be at work there, to be there in the midst of other people, and to be mortal there. The limits are neither subjective nor objective, or, rather, they have an objective and a subjective side. Objective because they are to be found everywhere and are recognizable everywhere; subjective because they are *lived* and are nothing if man does not live them, that is, freely determine his existence with reference to them. And though the configurations may differ, at least none of them are completely strange to me, because they all appear as attempts either to pass beyond these limits or recede from them or deny them or adapt to them. Consequently, every configuration, however individual it may be, has a universal value.

Every configuration, even the Chinese, the Indian, or the

Negro, can be understood by a Westerner. "Can be understood" means that by virtue of a situation that he can imagine, a European of 1945 can, in like manner, push himself to his limits and reconstitute within himself the configuration of the Chinese, the Indian, or the African. Every configuration has universality in the sense that every configuration can be understood by every man. This does not at all mean that this configuration defines man forever, but that it can be met with again. There is always a way to understand the idiot, the child, the savage, the foreigner, provided one has the necessary information.

In this sense we may say that there is a universality of man; but it is not given, it is perpetually being made. I build the universal in choosing myself; I build it in understanding the configuration of every other man, whatever age he might have lived in. This absoluteness of choice does not do away with the relativeness of each epoch. At heart, what existentialism shows is the connection between the absolute character of free involvement, by virtue of which every man realizes himself in realizing a type of mankind, an involvement always comprehensible in any age whatsoever and by any person whosoever, and the relativeness of the cultural ensemble which may result from such a choice; it must be stressed that the relativity of Cartesianism and the absolute character of Cartesian involvement go together. In this sense, you may, if you like, say that each of us performs an absolute act in breathing, eating, sleeping, or behaving in any way whatever. There is no difference between being free, like a configuration, like an existence which chooses its essence, and being absolute. There is no difference between being an absolute temporarily localized, that is, localized in history, and being universally comprehensible.

This does not entirely settle the objection to subjectivism. In fact, the objection still takes several forms. First, there is the following: we are told, "So you're able to do anything, no matter what!" This is expressed in various ways. First we are accused of anarchy; then they say, "You're unable to pass judgment on others, because there's no reason to prefer one configuration to another"; finally they tell us, "Everything is arbitrary in this choosing of yours. You take something from one pocket and pretend you're putting it into the other."

These three objections aren't very serious. Take the first objection. "You're able to do anything, no matter what" is not to the point. In one sense choice is possible, but what is not possible is not to choose. I can always choose, but I ought to know that if I do not choose, I am still choosing. Though this may seem purely formal, it is highly important for keeping fantasy and caprice within bounds. If it is true that in facing a situation, for example, one in which, as a person capable of having sexual relations, of having children, I am obliged to choose an attitude, and if I in any way assume responsibility for a choice which, in involving myself, also involves all mankind, this has nothing to do with caprice, even if no *a priori* value determines my choice.

If anybody thinks that he recognizes here Gide's theory of the arbitrary act, he fails to see the enormous difference between this doctrine and Gide's. Gide does not know what a situation is. He acts out of pure caprice. For us, on the contrary, man is in an organized situation in which he himself is involved. Through his choice, he involves all mankind, and he can not avoid making a choice: either he will remain chaste, or he will marry without having children, or he will marry and have children; anyhow, whatever he may do, it is impossible for him not to take full responsibility for the way he handles this problem. Doubtless, he chooses without referring to pre-established values, but it is unfair to accuse him of caprice. Instead, let us say that moral choice is to be compared to the making of a work of art. And before going any further, let it be said at once that we are not dealing here with an aesthetic ethics, because our opponents are so dishonest that they even accuse us of that. The example I've chosen is a comparison only.

Having said that, may I ask whether anyone has ever accused an artist who has painted a picture of not having drawn his inspiration from rules set up *a priori*? Has any one ever asked, "What painting ought he to make?" It is clearly understood that there is no definite painting to be made, that the artist is engaged in the making of his painting, and that the painting to be made is precisely the painting he will have made. It is clearly understood that there are no *a priori* aesthetic values, but that there are values which appear subsequently in the coherence of the painting, in the correspondence between what the artist intended and the result. Nobody can tell what the painting of tomorrow will be like. Painting can be judged only after it has once been made. What connection does that have with ethics? We are in the same creative situation. We never say that a work of art is arbitrary. When we speak of a canvas of Picasso, we never say that it is arbitrary; we understand quite well that he was making himself what he is at the very time he was painting, that the ensemble of his work is embodied in his life.

The same holds on the ethical plane. What art and ethics have in common is that we have creation and invention in both cases. We can not decide *a priori* what there is to be done. I think that I pointed that out quite sufficiently when I mentioned the case of the student who came to see me, and who might have applied to all the ethical systems, Kantian or otherwise, without getting any sort of guidance. He was obliged to devise his law himself. Never let it be said by us that this man—who, taking affection, individual action, and kind-heartedness toward a specific person as his ethical first principle, chooses to remain with his mother, or who, preferring to make a sacrifice, chooses to go to England—has made an arbitrary choice. Man makes himself. He isn't ready made at the start. In choosing his ethics, he makes himself, and force of circumstances is such that he can not abstain from choosing one. We define man only in relationship to involvement. It is therefore absurd to charge us with arbitrariness of choice.

In the second place, it is said that we are unable to pass judgment on others. In a way this is true, and in another way, false. It is true in this sense, that, whenever a man sanely and sincerely involves himself and chooses his configuration, it is impossible for him to prefer another configuration, regardless of what his own may be in other respects. It is true in this sense, that we do not believe in progress. Progress is betterment. Man is always the same. The situation confronting him varies. Choice always remains a choice in a situation. The problem has not changed since the time one could choose between those for and those against slavery, for example, at the time of the Civil War, and the present time, when one can side with the Maquis Resistance Party, or with the Communists.

But, nevertheless, one can still pass judgment, for, as I have said, one makes a choice in relationship to others. First, one can judge (and this is perhaps not a judgment of value, but a logical judgment) that certain choices are based on error and others on truth. If we have defined man's situation as a free choice, with no excuses and no recourse, every man who takes refuge behind the excuse of his passions, every man who sets up a determinism, is a dishonest man.

The objection may be raised, "But why mayn't he choose himself dishonestly?" I reply that I am not obliged to pass moral judgment on him, but that I do define his dishonesty as an error. One can not help considering the truth of the matter. Dishonesty is obviously a falsehood because it belies the complete freedom of involvement. On the same grounds, I maintain that there is also dishonesty if I choose to state that certain values exist prior to me; it is self-contradictory for me to want them and at the same time state that they are imposed on me. Suppose someone says to me, "What if I want to be dishonest?" I'll answer, "There's no reason for you not to be, but I'm saying that that's what you are, and that the strictly coherent attitude is that of honesty."

Besides, I can bring moral judgment to bear. When I declare that freedom in every concrete circumstance can have no other aim than to want itself, if man has once become aware that in his forlornness he imposes values, he can no longer want but one thing, and that is freedom, as the basis of all values. That doesn't mean that he wants it in the abstract. It means simply that the ultimate meaning of the acts of honest men is the quest for freedom as such. A man who belongs to a communist or revolutionary union wants concrete goals; these goals imply an abstract desire for freedom; but this freedom is wanted in something concrete. We want freedom for freedom's sake and in every particular circumstance. And in wanting freedom we discover that it depends entirely on the freedom of others, and that the freedom of others depends on ours. Of course, freedom as the definition of man does not depend on others, but as soon as there is involvement, I am obliged to want others to have freedom at the same time that I want my own freedom. I can take freedom as my goal only if I take that of others as a goal as well. Consequently, when, in all honesty, I've recognized that man is a being in whom existence precedes essence, that he is a free being who, in various circumstances, can want only his freedom, I have at the same time recognized that I can want only the freedom of others.

Therefore, in the name of this will for freedom, which freedom itself implies, I may pass judgment on those who seek to hide from themselves the complete arbitrariness and the complete freedom of their existence. Those who hide their complete freedom from themselves out of a spirit of seriousness or by means of deterministic excuses, I shall call cowards; those who try to show that their existence was necessary, when it is the very contingency of man's appearance on earth, I shall call stinkers. But cowards or stinkers can be judged only from a strictly unbiased point of view.

Therefore though the content of ethics is variable, a certain form of it is universal. Kant says that freedom desires both itself and the freedom of others. Granted. But he believes that the formal and the universal are enough to constitute an ethics. We, on the other hand, think that principles which are too abstract run aground in trying to decide action. Once again, take the case of the student. In the name of what, in the name of what great moral maxim do you think he could have decided, in perfect peace of mind, to abandon his mother or to stay with her? There is no way of judging. The content is always concrete and thereby unforeseeable; there is always the element of invention. The one thing that counts is knowing whether the inventing that has been done, has been done in the name of freedom.

For example, let us look at the following two cases. You will see to what extent they correspond, yet differ. Take *The Mill on the Floss*. We find a certain young girl, Maggie Tulliver, who is an embodiment of the value of passion and who is aware of it. She is in love with a young man, Stephen, who is engaged to an insignificant young girl. This Maggie Tulliver, instead of heedlessly preferring her own happiness, chooses, in the name of human solidarity, to sacrifice herself and give up the man she loves. On the other hand, Sanseverina, in *The Charterhouse of Parma*, believing that passion is man's true value, would say that a great love deserves sacrifices; that it is to be preferred to the banality of the conjugal love that would tie Stephen to the young ninny he had to marry. She would choose to sacrifice the girl and fulfill her happiness; and, as Stendhal shows, she is even ready to sacrifice herself for the sake of passion, if this life demands it. Here we are in the presence of two strictly opposed moralities. I claim that they are much the same thing; in both cases what has been set up as the goal is freedom.

You can imagine two highly similar attitudes: one girl prefers to renounce her love out of resignation; another prefers to disregard the prior attachment of the man she loves out of sexual desire. On the surface these two actions resemble those we've just described. However, they are completely different. Sanseverina's attitude is much nearer that of Maggie Tulliver, one of heedless rapacity.

Thus, you see that the second charge is true and, at the same time, false. One may choose anything if it is on the grounds of free involvement.

The third objection is the following: "You take something from one pocket and put it into the other. That is, fundamentally, values aren't serious, since you choose them." My answer to this is that I'm quite vexed that that's the way it is; but if I've discarded God the Father, there has to be someone to invent values. You've got to take things as they are. Moreover, to say that we invent values means nothing else but this: life has no meaning *a priori*. Before you come alive, life is nothing; it's up to you to give it a meaning, and value is nothing else but the meaning that you choose. In that way, you see, there is a possibility of creating a human community.

I've been reproached for asking whether existentialism is humanistic. It's been said, "But you said in *Nausea* that the humanists were all wrong. You made fun of a certain kind of humanist. Why come back to it now?" Actually, the word humanism has two very different meanings. By humanism one can mean a theory which takes man as an end and as a higher value. Humanism in this sense can be found in Cocteau's tale *Around the World in Eighty Hours* when a character, because he is flying over some mountains in an airplane, declares, "Man is simply amazing." That means that I, who did not build the airplanes, shall personally benefit from these particular inventions, and that I, as man, shall personally consider myself responsible for, and honored by, acts of a few particular men. This would imply that we ascribe a value to man on the basis of the highest deeds of certain men. This humanism is absurd, because only the dog or the horse would be able to make such an over-all judgment about man, which they are careful not to do, at least to my knowledge.

But it can not be granted that a man may make a judgment about man. Existentialism spares him from any such judgment. The existentialist will never consider man as an end because he is always in the making. Nor should we believe that there is a mankind to which we might set up a cult in the manner of Auguste Comte. The cult of mankind ends in the self-enclosed humanism of Comte, and, let it be said, of fascism. This kind of humanism we can do without.

But there is another meaning of humanism. Fundamentally it is this: man is constantly outside of himself; in projecting himself, in losing himself outside of himself, he makes for man's existing; and, on the other hand, it is by pursuing transcendent goals that he is able to exist; man, being this state of passing-beyond, and seizing upon things only as they bear upon this passing-beyond, is at the heart, at the center of this passing-beyond. There is no universe other than a human universe, the universe of human subjectivity. This connection between transcendency, as a constituent element of man—not in the sense that God is transcendent, but in the sense of passing beyond—and subjectivity, in the sense that man is not closed in on himself but is always present in a human universe, is what we call existentialist humanism. Humanism, because we remind man that there is no lawmaker other than himself, and that in his forlornness he will decide by himself; because we point out that man will fulfill himself as man, not in turning toward himself, but in seeking outside of himself a goal which is just this liberation, just this particular fulfillment.

From these few reflections it is evident that nothing is more unjust than the objections that have been raised against us. Existentialism is nothing else than an attempt to draw all the consequences of a coherent atheistic position. It isn't trying to plunge man into despair at all. But if one calls every attitude of unbelief despair, like the Christians, then the word is not being used in its original sense. Existentialism isn't so atheistic that it wears itself out showing that God doesn't exist. Rather, it declares that even if God did exist, that would change nothing. There you've got our point of view. Not that we believe that God exists, but we think that the problem of His existence is not the issue. In this sense existentialism is optimistic, a doctrine of action, and it is plain dishonesty for Christians to make no distinction between their own despair and ours and then to call us despairing.

FREEDOM AND RESPONSIBILITY

Although the considerations which are about to follow are of interest primarily to the ethicist, it may nevertheless be worthwhile after these descriptions and arguments to return to the freedom of the for-itself and to try to understand what the fact of this freedom represents for human destiny.

The essential consequence of our earlier remarks is that man being condemned to be free carries the weight of the whole world on his shoulders; he is responsible for the world and for himself as a way of being. We are taking the word "responsibility" in its ordinary sense as "consciousness (of) being the incontestable author of an event or of an object." In this sense the responsibility of the for-itself is overwhelming since he* is the one by whom it happens that *there* is a world; since he is also the one who makes himself be, then whatever may be the situation in which he finds himself, the for-itself must wholly assume this situation with its peculiar coefficient of adversity, even though it be insupportable. He must assume the situation with the proud consciousness of being the author of it, for the very worst disadvantages or the worst threats which can endanger my person have meaning only in and through my project; and it is on the

---

* I am shifting to the personal pronoun here since Sartre is describing the for-itself in concrete personal terms rather than as a metaphysical entity. Strictly speaking, of course, this is his position throughout, and the French "*il*" is indifferently "he" or "it." Tr.

ground of the engagement which I am that they appear. It is therefore senseless to think of complaining since nothing foreign has decided what we feel, what we live, or what we are.

Furthermore this absolute responsibility is not resignation; it is simply the logical requirement of the consequences of our freedom. What happens to me happens through me, and I can neither affect myself with it nor revolt against it nor resign myself to it. Moreover everything which happens to me is *mine*. By this we must understand first of all that I am always equal to what happens to me *qua* man, for what happens to a man through other men and through himself can be only human. The most terrible situations of war, the worst tortures do not create a non-human state of things; there is no non-human situation. It is only through fear, flight, and recourse to magical types of conduct that I shall decide on the non-human, but this decision is human, and I shall carry the entire responsibility for it. But in addition the situation is *mine* because it is the image of my free choice of myself, and everything which it presents to me is *mine* in that this represents me and symbolizes me. Is it not I who decide the coefficient of adversity in things and even their unpredictability by deciding myself?

Thus there are no *accidents* in a life; a community even which suddenly bursts forth and involves me in it does not come from the outside. If I am mobilized in a war, this war is *my* war; it is in my image and I deserve it. I deserve it first because I could always get out of it by suicide or by desertion; these ultimate possibles are those which must always be present for us when there is a question of envisaging a situation. For lack of getting out of it, I have *chosen* it. This can be due to inertia, to cowardice in the face of public opinion, or because I prefer certain other values to the value of the refusal to join in the war (the good opinion of my relatives, the honor of my family, *etc.*). Any way you look at it, it is a matter of a choice. This choice will be repeated later on again and again without a break until the end of the war. Therefore we must agree with the statement by J. Romains, "In war there are no innocent victims."* If therefore I have preferred war to death or to dishonor, everything takes place as if I bore the entire responsibility for this war. Of course others have declared it, and one might be tempted perhaps to consider me as a simple accomplice. But this notion of complicity has only a juridical sense, and it does not hold here. For it depended on me that for me and by me this war should not exist, and I have decided that it does exist. There was no compulsion there, for the compulsion could have got no hold on a freedom. I did not have any excuse; for as we have said repeatedly, the peculiar character of human reality is that it is without excuse. Therefore it remains for me only to lay claim to this war.

But in addition the war is *mine* because by the sole fact that it arises in a situation which I cause to be and that I can discover it there only by engaging myself for or against it, I can no longer distinguish at present the choice which I make of myself from the choice which I make of the war. To live this war is to choose myself through my choice of myself. There can be no question of considering it as "four years of vacation" or as a "reprieve," as a "recess," the essential part of my responsibilities being elsewhere in my married, family, or professional life. In this war which I have chosen I choose myself from day to day, and I make it mine by making myself. If it is going to be four empty years, then it is I who bear the responsibility for this.

Finally, as we pointed out earlier, each person is an absolute choice of self from the standpoint of a world of knowl-

---

* J. Romains: *Les hommes de bonne volonté;* "Prélude à Verdun."

edges and of techniques which this choice both assumes and illumines; each person is an absolute upsurge at an absolute date and is perfectly unthinkable at another date. It is therefore a waste of time to ask what I should have been if this war had not broken out, for I have chosen myself as one of the possible meanings of the epoch which imperceptibly led to war. I am not distinct from this same epoch; I could not be transported to another epoch without contradiction. Thus *I am* this war which restricts and limits and makes comprehensible the period which preceded it. In this sense we may define more precisely the responsibility of the for-itself if to the earlier quoted statement, "There are no innocent victims," we add the words, "We have the war we deserve." Thus, totally free, undistinguishable from the period for which I have chosen to be the meaning, as profoundly responsible for the war as if I had myself declared it, unable to live without integrating it in *my* situation, engaging myself in it wholly and stamping it with my seal, I must be without remorse or regrets as I am without excuse; for from the instant of my upsurge into being, I carry the weight of the world by myself alone without anything or any person being able to lighten it.

Yet this responsibility is of a very particular type. Someone will say, "I did not ask to be born." This is a naïve way of throwing greater emphasis on our facticity. I am responsible for everything, in fact, except for my very responsibility, for I am not the foundation of my being. Therefore everything takes place as if I were compelled to be responsible. I am *abandoned* in the world, not in the sense that I might remain abandoned and passive in a hostile universe like a board floating on the water, but rather in the sense that I find myself suddenly alone and without help, engaged in a world for which I bear the whole responsibility without being able, whatever I do, to tear myself away from this responsibility for an instant. For I am responsible for my very desire of fleeing responsibilities. To make myself passive in the world, to refuse to act upon things and upon Others is still to choose myself, and suicide is one mode among others of being-in-the-world. Yet I find an absolute responsibility for the fact that my facticity (here the fact of my birth) is directly inapprehensible and even inconceivable, for this fact of my birth never appears as a brute fact but always across a projective reconstruction of my for-itself. I am ashamed of being born or I rejoice over it, or in attempting to get rid of my life I affirm that I live and I assume this life as bad. Thus in a certain sense I *choose* being born. This choice itself is integrally affected with facticity since I am not able not to choose, but this facticity in turn will appear only in so far as I surpass it toward my ends. Thus facticity is everywhere, but inapprehensible; I never encounter anything except my responsibility. That is why I can not ask, "*Why* was I born?" or curse the day of my birth or declare that I did not ask to be born, for these various attitudes toward my birth—*i.e.*, toward the *fact* that I realize a presence in the world—are absolutely nothing else but ways of assuming this birth in full responsibility and of making it *mine*. Here again I encounter only myself and my projects so that finally my abandonment—*i.e.*, my facticity—consists simply in the fact that I am condemned to be wholly responsible for myself. I am the being which *is* in such a way that in its being its being is in question. And this "is" of my being *is* as present and inapprehensible.

Under these conditions since every event in the world can be revealed to me only as an *opportunity* (an opportunity made use of, lacked, neglected, *etc.*), or better yet since everything which happens to us can be considered as a *chance* (*i.e.*, can appear to us only as a way of realizing this being which is in question in our being) and since others as transcendences-transcended are themselves only *opportunities*and *chances*, the responsibility of the for-itself extends to the entire world as a peopled-world. It is precisely thus that the for-itself apprehends itself in anguish; that is, as a being which is neither the foundation of its own being nor of the Other's being nor of the in-itselfs which form the world, but a being which is compelled to decide the meaning of being—within it and everywhere outside of it. The one who realizes in anguish his condition as *being* thrown into a responsibility which extends to his very abandonment has no longer either remorse or regret or excuse; he is no longer anything but a freedom which perfectly reveals itself and whose being resides in this very revelation. But as we pointed out at the beginning of this work, most of the time we flee anguish in bad faith.

THE DESIRE TO BE GOD

The most discerning ethicists have shown how a desire reaches beyond itself. Pascal believed that he could discover in hunting, for example, or tennis, or in a hundred other occupations, the need of being diverted. He revealed that in an activity which would be absurd if reduced to itself, there was a meaning which transcended it; that is, an indication which referred to the reality of man in general and to his condition. Similarly Stendhal in spite of his attachment to ideologists, and Proust in spite of his intellectualistic and analytical tendencies, have shown that love and jealousy can not be reduced to the strict desire of possessing a *particular* woman, but that these emotions aim at laying hold of the world in its entirety through the woman. This is the meaning of Stendhal's crystallization, and it is precisely for this reason that Love as Stendhal describes it appears as a mode of being in the world. Love is a fundamental relation of the for-itself to the world and to itself (selfness) through a particular woman; the woman represents only a conducting body which is placed in the circuit. These analyses may be inexact or only partially true; nevertheless they make us suspect a method other than pure analytical description. In the same way Catholic novelists immediately see in carnal love its surpassing toward God—in Don Juan, "the eternally unsatisfied," in sin, "the place empty of God." There is no question here of finding again an abstract behind the concrete; the impulse toward God is no *less concrete* than the impulse toward a particular woman. On the contrary, it is a matter of rediscovering under the partial and incomplete aspects of the subject the veritable concreteness which can be only the totality of his impulse toward being, his original relation to himself, to the world, and to the Other, in the unity of internal relations and of a fundamental project. This impulse can be only purely individual and unique. Far from estranging us from the person, as Bourget's analysis, for example, does in constituting the individual by means of a summation of general maxims, this impulse will not lead us to find in the need of writing—and of writing particular books—the need of activity in general. On the contrary, rejecting equally the theory of malleable clay and that of the bundle of drives, we will discover the individual person in the initial project which constitutes him. It is for this reason that the irreducibility of the result attained will be revealed as self-evident, not because it is the poorest and the most abstract but because it is the richest. The intuition here will be accompanied by an individual fullness.

The best way to conceive of the fundamental project of human reality is to say that man is the being whose project is to be God. Whatever may be the myths and rites of the religion considered, God is first "sensible to the heart" of man as the one who identifies and defines him in his ultimate and fundamental project. If man possesses a pre-ontological comprehension of the being of God, it is not the great wonders of nature nor the power of society which have conferred it upon him. God, value and supreme end of transcendence, represents the permanent limit in terms of which man makes known to himself what he is. To be man means to reach toward being God. Or if you prefer, man fundamentally is the desire to be God.

It may be asked, if man on coming into the world is borne toward God as toward his limit, if he can choose only to be God, what becomes of freedom? For freedom is nothing other than a choice which creates for itself its own possibilities, but it appears here that the initial project of being God, which "defines" man, comes close to being the same as a human "nature" or an "essence." The answer is that while the *meaning* of the desire is ultimately the project of being God, the desire is never *constituted* by this meaning; on the contrary, it always represents a particular discovery of its ends. These ends in fact are pursued in terms of a particular empirical situation, and it is this very pursuit which constitutes the surroundings *as a situation*. The desire of being is always realized as the desire of a mode of being. And this desire of a mode of being expresses itself in turn as the meaning of the myriads of concrete desires which constitute the web of our conscious life. Thus we find ourselves before very complex symbolic structures which have *at least* three stories. An empirical desire can discern a symbolization of a fundamental concrete desire which is the person himself and which represents the mode in which he has decided that being would be in question in his being. This fundamental desire in turn expresses concretely in the world within the particular situation enveloping the individual, an abstract meaningful structure which is the desire of being in general; it must be considered as human reality in the person, and it brings about his community with others, thus making it possible to state that there is a truth concerning man and not only concerning individuals who cannot be compared. Absolute concreteness, completion, existence as a totality belong then to the free and fundamental desire which is the unique person. Empirical desire is only a symbolization of this; it refers to this and derives its meaning from it while remaining partial and reducible, for the empirical desire can not be conceived in isolation. On the other hand, the desire of being in its abstract purity is the *truth* of the concrete fundamental desire, but it does not exist by virtue of reality. Thus the fundamental project, the person, the free realization of human truth is everywhere in all desires. . . . It is never apprehended except through desires—as we can apprehend space only through bodies which shape it for us, though space is a specific reality and not a concept. Or, if you like, it is like the *object* of Husserl, which reveals itself only by *Abschattungen*, and which nevertheless does not allow itself to be absorbed by any one *Abschattung*. We can understand after these remarks that the abstract, ontological "desire to be" is unable to represent the fundamental, *human* structure of the individual; it cannot be an obstacle to his freedom. Freedom in fact . . . is strictly identified with nihilation. The only being which can be called free is the being which nihilates its being. Moreover we know that nihilation is *lack of being* and can not be otherwise. Freedom is precisely the being which makes itself a lack of being. But since desire, as we have established, is identical with lack of being, freedom can arise only as being which makes itself a desire of being; that is, as the project-for-itself of being in-itself-for-itself. Here we have arrived at an abstract structure which can by no means be considered as the nature or essence of freedom. Freedom is existence, and in it existence precedes essence. The upsurge of freedom is immediate and concrete and is not to be distinguished from its choice; that is, from the person himself. But the structure under consideration can be called the *truth* of freedom; that is, it is the human meaning of freedom.

It should be possible to establish the human truth of the person, as we have attempted to do by an ontological phenomenology. The catalogue of empirical desires ought to be made the object of appropriate psychological investigations, observation and induction and, as needed, experience can serve to draw up this list. They will indicate to the philosopher the comprehensible relations which unite to each other various desires and various patterns of behaviors, and will bring to light certain concrete connections between the subject of experience and "situations" experientially defined (which at bottom originate only from limitations applied in the name of positivity to the fundamental situation of the subject in the world). But in establishing and classifying fundamental desires of *individual persons* neither of these methods is appropriate. Actually there can be no question of determining *a priori* and ontologically what appears in all the unpredictability of a free act. . . . The very fact that we can subject any man whatsoever to such an investigation—this is what belongs to human reality in general. Or, if you prefer, this is what can be established by an ontology. But the inquiry itself and its results are on principle wholly outside the possibilities of an ontology.

Part II

THE PROBLEM OF NOTHINGNESS

THE ORIGIN OF NEGATION

1. THE QUESTION

Descartes found himself faced with a problem when he had to deal with the relation between soul and body. He planned then to look for the solution on that level where the union of thinking substance and extended substance was actually effected—that is, in the imagination. His advice is valuable. To be sure, our concern is not that of Descartes and we do not conceive of imagination as he did. But what we can retain is the reminder that it is not profitable first to separate the two terms of a relation in order to try to join them together again later. The relation is a synthesis. Consequently the results of analysis can not be covered over again by the moments of this synthesis.

Laporte says that an abstraction is made when something not capable of existing in isolation is thought of as in an isolated state. The concrete by contrast is a totality which can exist by itself alone. Husserl is of the same opinion; for him *red* is an abstraction because color can not exist without form. On the other hand, a spatial-temporal *thing*, with all its determinations, is an example of the concrete. From this point of view, consciousness is an abstraction since it conceals within itself an ontological source in the region of the in-itself, and conversely the phenomenon is likewise an abstraction since it must "appear" to consciousness. The concrete can be only the synthetic totality of which consciousness, like the phenomenon, constitutes only moments. The concrete is man within the world in that specific union of man with the world which Heidegger, for example, calls "being-in-the-world." We deliberately begin with the abstract if we question "experience" as Kant does, inquiring into the conditions of its possibility—or if we effect a phenomenological reduction like Husserl, who would reduce the world to the state of the noema-correlate of consciousness. But we will no more succeed in restoring the concrete by the summation or organization of the elements which we have abstracted from it than Spinoza can reach substance by the infinite summation of its modes.

The relation of the regions of being is an original emergence and is a part of the very structure of these beings. But we discovered this in our first observations. It is enough now to open our eyes and question ingenuously this totality which is man-in-the-world. It is by the description of this totality that we shall be able to reply to these two questions: (1) What is the synthetic relation which we call being-in-the-world? (2) What must man and the world be in order for a relation between them to be possible? In truth, the two questions are interdependent, and we can not hope to reply to them separately. But each type of human conduct, being the conduct of man in the world, can release for us simultaneously man, the world, and the relation which unites them, only on condition that we envisage these forms of conduct as realities objectively apprehensible and not as subjective affects which disclose themselves only in the face of reflection.

We shall not limit ourselves to the study of a single pattern of conduct. We shall try on the contrary to describe several and proceeding from one kind of conduct to another, attempt to penetrate into the profound meaning of the relation "man-world." But first of all we should choose a single pattern which can serve us as a guiding thread in our inquiry.

Now this very inquiry furnishes us with the desired conduct; this man that *I am*—if I apprehend him such as he is at this moment in the world, I establish that he stands before being in an attitude of interrogation. At the very moment when I ask, "Is there any conduct which can reveal to me the relation of man with the world?" I pose a question. This question I can consider objectively, for it matters little whether the questioner is myself or the reader who reads my work and who is questioning along with me. But on the other hand, the question is not simply the objective totality of the words printed on this page; it is indifferent to the symbols which express it. In a word, it is a human attitude filled with meaning. What does this attitude reveal to us?

In every question we stand before a being which we are questioning. Every question presupposes a being who questions and a being which is questioned. This is not the original relation of man to being-in-itself, but rather it stands within the limitations of this relation and takes it for granted. On the other hand, this being which we question, we question *about* something. That *about which* I question the being participates in the transcendence of being. I question being about its ways of being or about its being. From this point of view the question is a kind of expectation; I expect a reply from the being questioned. That is, on the basis of a pre-interrogative familiarity with being, I expect from this being a revelation of its being or of its way of being. The reply will be a "yes" or a "no." It is the existence of these two equally objective and contradictory possibilities which on principle distinguishes the question from affirmation or negation. There are questions which on the surface do not permit a negative reply—like, for example, the one which we put earlier, "What does this attitude reveal to us?" But actually we see that it is always possible with questions of this type to reply, "Nothing" or "Nobody" or "Never." Thus at the moment when I ask, "Is there any conduct which can reveal to me the relation of man with the world?" I admit *on principle* that possibility of a negative reply such as, "No, such a conduct does not exist." This means that we admit to being faced with the transcendent fact of the non-existence of such conduct.

One will perhaps be tempted not to believe in the objective existence of a non-being; one will say that in this case the fact simply refers me to my subjectivity; I would learn from the transcendent being that the conduct sought is a pure fiction. But in the first place, to call this conduct a pure fiction is to disguise the negation without removing it. "To be pure fiction" is equivalent here to "to be only a fiction." Consequently to destroy the reality of the negation is to cause the reality of the reply to disappear. This reply, in fact, is the very being which gives it to me; that is, reveals the negation to me. There exists then for the questioner the permanent objective possibility of a negative reply. In relation to this possibility the questioner by the very fact that he is questioning, posits himself as in a state of indetermination; he *does not know* whether the reply will be affirmative or negative. Thus the question is a bridge set up between two non-beings: the non-being of knowing in man, the possibility of non-being of being in transcendent being. Finally the question implies the existence of a truth. By the very question the questioner affirms that he expects an objective reply, such that we can say of it, "It is thus and not otherwise." In a word the truth, as differentiated from being, introduces a third non-being as determining the question— the non-being of limitation. This triple non-being conditions every question and in particular the metaphysical question, which is *our* question.

We set out upon our pursuit of being, and it seemed to us that the series of our questions had led us to the heart of being. But behold, at the moment when we thought we were arriving at the goal, a glance cast on the question itself has revealed to us suddenly that we are encompassed with nothingness. The permanent possibility of non-being, outside us and within, conditions our questions about being. Furthermore it is non-being which is going to limit the reply. What being *will be* must of necessity arise on the basis of what *it is not*. Whatever being is, it will allow this formulation: "Being is *that* and outside of that, *nothing.*"

Thus a new component of the real has just appeared to us—non-being. Our problem is thereby complicated, for we may no longer limit our inquiry to the relations of the human being to being in-itself, but must include also the relations of being with non-being and the relations of human non-being with transcendent-being. But let us consider further.

2. NEGATIONS

Someone will object that being-in-itself can not furnish negative replies. Did not we ourselves say that it was beyond affirmation as beyond negation? Furthermore ordinary experience reduced to itself does not seem to disclose any non-being to us. I think that there are fifteen hundred francs in my wallet, and I find only thirteen hundred; that does not mean, someone will tell us, that experience had discovered for me the non-being of fifteen hundred francs but simply that I have counted thirteen hundred-franc notes. Negation proper (we are told) is unthinkable; it could appear only on the level of an act of judgment by which I should establish a comparison between the result anticipated and the result obtained. Thus negation would be simply a quality of judgment and the expectation of the questioner would be an expectation of the judgment-response. As for Nothingness, this would derive its origin from negative judgments; it would be a concept establishing the transcendent unity of all these judgments, a propositional function of the type, "X is not."

We see where this theory is leading; its proponents would make us conclude that being-in-itself is full positivity and does not contain in itself any negation. This negative judgment, on the other hand, by virtue of being a subjective act, is strictly identified with the affirmative judgment. They can not see that Kant, for example, has distinguished in its internal texture the negative act of judgment from the affirmative act. In each case a synthesis of concepts is operative; that synthesis, which is a concrete and full event of psychic life, is operative here merely in the manner of the copula "is" and there in the manner of the copula "is not." In the same way the manual operation of sorting out (separation) and the manual operation of assembling (union) are two objective conducts which possess the same reality of fact. Thus negation would be "at the end" of the act of judgment without, however, being "in" being. It is like an unreal encompassed by two full realities neither of which claims it; being-in-itself, if questioned about negation, refers to judgment, since being is only what it is—and judgment, a *wholly* psychic positivity, refers to being since judgment formulates a negation which concerns being and which consequently is transcendent. Negation, the result of concrete psychic operations, is supported in existence by these very operations and is incapable of existing by itself; it has the existence of a noema-correlate; its *esse* resides exactly in its *percipi*. Nothingness, the conceptual unity of negative judgments, can not have the slightest trace of reality, save that which the Stoics confer on their "lecton."* Can we accept this concept?

The question can be put in these terms: Is negation as the structure of the judicative proposition at the origin of nothingness? Or on the contrary is nothingness as the structure of the real, the origin and foundation of negation? Thus the problem of being had referred us first to that of the question as a human attitude, and the problem of the question now refers us to that of the being of negation.

It is evident that non-being always appears within the limits of a human expectation. It is because I expect to find fifteen hundred francs that I find *only* thirteen hundred. It is because a physicist *expects* a certain verification of his hypothesis that nature can tell him no. It would be in vain to deny that negation appears on the original basis of a relation of man to the world. The world does not disclose its non-beings to one who has not first posited them as possibilities. But is this to say that these non-beings are to be reduced to pure subjectivity? Does this mean to say that we ought to give them the importance and the type of existence of the Stoic "lecton," of Husserl's noema? We think not.

First it is not true that negation is only a quality of judgment. The question is formulated by an interrogative judgment, but it is not itself a judgment; it is a pre-judicative attitude. I can question by a look, by a gesture. In posing a question I stand

---

* An abstraction or something with purely nominal existence—like space or time. Tr.

facing being in a certain way and this relation to being is a relation of being; the judgment is only one optional expression of it. At the same time it is not necessarily a person whom the questioner questions about being; this conception of the question, by making of it an intersubjective phenomenon, detaches it from the being to which it adheres and leaves it in the air as pure modality of dialogue. On the contrary, we must consider the question in dialogue to be only a particular species of the genus "question"; the being in question is not necessarily a thinking being. If my car breaks down, it is the *carburetor*, the *spark plugs, etc.*, that I question. If my watch stops, I can question the watchmaker about the cause of the stopping, but it is the various mechanisms of the watch that the watchmaker will in turn question. What I expect from the carburetor, what the watchmaker expects from the works of the watch, is not a judgment; it is a disclosure of being on the basis of which we can make a judgment. And if I expect a disclosure of being, I am prepared at the same time for the eventuality of a disclosure of a non-being. If I question the carburetor, it is because I consider it possible that "there is nothing there" in the carburetor. Thus my question by its nature envelops a certain prejudicative comprehension of non-being; it is in itself a relation of being with non-being, on the basis of the original transcendence; that is, in a relation of being with being.

Moreover if the proper nature of the question is obscured by the fact that questions are frequently put by one man to other men, it should be pointed out here that there are numerous non-judicative conducts which present this immediate comprehension of non-being on the basis of being—in its original purity. If, for example, we consider *destruction*, we must recognize that it is an *activity* which doubtless could utilize judgment as an instrument but which can not be defined as uniquely or even primarily judicative. "Destruction" presents the same structure as "the question." In a sense, certainly, man is the only being by whom a destruction can be accomplished. A geological plication, a storm do not destroy—or at least they do not destroy *directly;* they merely modify the distribution of masses of beings. There is no *less* after the storm than before. There is *something else.* Even this expression is improper, for to posit otherness there must be a witness who can retain the past in some manner and compare it to the present in the form of *no longer.* In the absence of this witness, there is being before as after the storm—that is all. If a cyclone can bring about the death of certain living beings, this death will be destruction only if it is experienced as such. In order for destruction to exist, there must be first a relation of man to being—*i.e.,* a transcendence; and within the limits of this relation, it is necessary that man apprehend one being as destructible. This supposes a limiting cutting into being by a being, which, as we saw in connection with truth, is already a process of nihilation. The being under consideration is *that* and outside of that *nothing.* The gunner who has been assigned an objective carefully points his gun in a certain direction *excluding* all others. But even this would still be nothing unless the being of the gunner's objective is revealed as *fragile.* And what is fragility if not a certain probability of non-being for a given being under determined circumstances? A being is fragile if it carries in its being a definite possibility of non-being. But once again it is through man that fragility comes into being, for the individualizing limitation which we mentioned earlier is the condition of fragility; *one* being is fragile and not *all* being, for the latter is beyond all possible destruction. Thus the relation of individualizing limitation which man enters into with *one* being on the original basis of his relation to being causes fragility to enter into this being as the appearance of a permanent possibility of non-being. But this is not all. In order for destructibility to exist, man must determine himself in the face of this possibility of non-being, either positively or negatively; he must either take the necessary measures to realize it (destruction proper) or, by a negation of non-being, to maintain it always on the level of a simple possibility (by preventive measures). Thus it is man who renders cities destructible, precisely because he posits them as fragile and as precious and because he adopts a system of protective measures with regard to them. It is because of this ensemble of measures that an earthquake or a volcanic eruption can *destroy* these cities or these human constructions. The original meaning and aim of war are contained in the smallest building of man. It is necessary then to recognize that destruction is an essentially human thing and that *it is man* who destroys his cities through the agency of earthquakes or directly, who destroys his ships through the agency of cyclones or directly. But at the same time it is necessary to acknowledge that destruction supposes a pre-judicative comprehension of nothingness as such and a conduct *in the face of nothingness*. In addition destruction although coming into being through man, is an *objective fact* and not a thought. Fragility has been impressed upon the very being of this vase, and its destruction would be an irreversible absolute event which I could only verify. There is a transphenomenality of non-being as of being. The examination of "destruction" leads us then to the same results as the examination of "the question."

But if we wish to decide with certainty, we need only to consider an example of a negative judgment and to ask ourselves whether it causes non-being to appear at the heart of being or merely limits itself to determining a prior revelation. I have an appointment with Pierre at four o'clock. I arrive at the café a quarter of an hour late. Pierre is always punctual. Will he have waited for me? I look at the room, the patrons, and I say, "He is not here." Is there an intuition of Pierre's absence, or does negation indeed enter in only with judgment? At first sight it seems absurd to speak here of intuition since to be exact there could not be an intuition of *nothing* and since the absence of Pierre is this nothing. Popular consciousness, however, bears witness to this intuition. Do we not say, for example, "I suddenly saw that he was not there." Is this just a matter of misplacing the negation? Let us look a little closer.

It is certain that the café by itself with its patrons, its tables, its booths, its mirrors, its light, its smoky atmosphere, and the sounds of voices, rattling saucers, and footsteps which fill it— the café is a fullness of being. And all the intuitions of detail which I can have are filled by these odors, these sounds, these colors, all phenomena which have a transphenomenal being. Similarly Pierre's actual presence in a place which I do not know is also a plenitude of being. We seem to have found fullness everywhere. But we must observe that in perception there is always the construction of a figure on a ground. No one object, no group of objects is especially designed to be organized as specifically either ground or figure; all depends on the direction of my attention. When I enter this café to search for Pierre, there is formed a synthetic organization of all the objects in the café, on the ground of which Pierre is given as about to appear. This organization of the café as the ground is an original nihilation. Each element of the setting, a person, a table, a chair, attempts to isolate itself, to lift itself upon the ground constituted by the totality of the other objects, only to fall back once more into the undifferentiation of this ground; it melts into the ground. For the ground is that which is seen only in addition, that which is the object of a purely marginal attention. Thus the original nihilation of all the figures which appear and are swallowed up in the total neutrality of a *ground* is the necessary condition for the appearance of the principal figure, which is here the person of Pierre. This nihilation is given to my intuition; I am witness to the successive disappearance of all the objects which I look at—in particular of the faces, which detain me for an instant (Could this be Pierre?) and which as quickly decompose precisely because they "are not" the face of Pierre. Nevertheless if I should finally discover Pierre, my intuition would be filled by a solid element, I should be suddenly arrested by his face and the whole café would organize itself around him as a discrete presence.

But now Pierre is not here. This does not mean that I discover his absence in some precise spot in the establishment. In fact Pierre is absent from the *whole* café; his absence fixes the café in its evanescence; the café remains *ground*; it persists in offering itself as an undifferentiated totality to my only marginal attention; it slips into the background; it pursues its nihilation. Only it makes itself ground for a determined figure; it carries the figure everywhere in front of it, presents the figure everywhere to me. This figure which slips constantly between my look and the solid, real objects of the café is precisely a perpetual disappearance; it is Pierre raising himself as nothingness on the ground of the nihilation of the café. So that what is offered to intuition is a flickering of nothingness; it is the nothingness of the ground, the nihilation of which summons and demands the appearance of the figure, and it is the figure—the nothingness which slips as a *nothing* to the surface of the ground. It serves as foundation for the judgment—"Pierre is not here." It is in fact the intuitive apprehension of a double nihilation. To be sure, Pierre's absence supposes an original relation between me and this café; there is an infinity of people who are without any relation with this café for want of a real expectation which establishes their absence. But, to be exact, I myself expected to see Pierre, and my expectation has caused the absence of Pierre to *happen* as a real event concerning this café. It is an objective fact at present that I have *discovered* this absence, and it presents itself as a synthetic relation between Pierre and the setting in which I am looking for him. Pierre absent haunts this café and is the condition of its self-nihilating organization as ground. By contrast, judgments which I can make subsequently to amuse myself, such as, "*Wellington* is not in this café, *Paul Valéry* is no longer here, *etc.*"—these have a purely abstract meaning; they are pure applications of the principle of negation without real or efficacious foundation, and they never succeed in establishing a *real* relation between the café and Wellington or Valéry. Here the relation "is not" is merely *thought*. This example is sufficient to show that non-being does not come to things by a negative judgment; it is the negative judgment, on the contrary, which is conditioned and supported by non-being.

How could it be otherwise? How could we even conceive of the negative form of judgment if all is plenitude of being and positivity? We believed for a moment that the negation could arise from the comparison instituted between the result anticipated and the result obtained. But let us look at that comparison. Here is an original judgment, a concrete, positive psychic act which establishes a fact: "There are 1300 francs in my wallet." Then there is another which is something else, no longer it but an establishing of fact and an affirmation: "I expected to find 1500 francs." There we have real and objective facts, psychic, and positive events, affirmative judgments. Where are we to place negation? Are we to believe that it is a pure and simple application of a category? And do we wish to hold that the mind in itself possesses the *not* as a form of sorting out and separation? But in this case we remove even the slightest suspicion of negativity from the negation. If we admit that the category of the "not" which exists *in fact* in the mind and is a positive and concrete process to brace and systematize our knowledge, if we admit first that it is suddenly released by the presence in us of certain affirmative judgments and then that it comes suddenly to mark with its seal certain thoughts which result from these judgments—by these considerations we will have carefully stripped negation of all negative function. For negation is a refusal of existence. By means of it a being (or a way of being) is posited, then thrown back to nothingness. If negation is a category, if it is only a sort of plug set indifferently on certain judgments, then how will we explain the fact that it can nihilate a being, cause it suddenly to arise, and then appoint it to be thrown back to non-being? If prior judgments establish fact, like those which we have taken for examples, negation must be like a free discovery, it must tear us away from this wall of positivity which encircles us. Negation is an abrupt break in continuity which can not in any case *result* from prior affirmations; it is an original and irreducible event. Here we are in the realm of consciousness. Consciousness moreover can not produce a negation except in the form of consciousness of negation. No category can "inhabit" consciousness and reside there in the manner of a thing. The *not*, as an abrupt intuitive discovery, appears as consciousness (of being), consciousness of the *not*. In a word, if being is everywhere, it is not only Nothingness which, as Bergson maintains, is inconceivable; for negation will never be derived from being. The necessary condition for our saying *not* is that non-being be a perpetual presence in us and outside of us, that nothingness haunt being.

But where does nothingness come from? If it is the original condition of the questioning attitude and more generally of all philosophical or scientific inquiry, what is the original relation of the human being to nothingness? What is the original nihilating conduct?

3. THE DIALECTICAL CONCEPT OF NOTHINGNESS

It is still too soon for us to hope to disengage the *meaning* of this nothingness, against which the question has suddenly thrown us. But there are several conclusions which we can formulate even now. In particular it would be worthwhile to determine the relations between being and that non-being which haunts it. We have established a certain parallelism between the types of conduct man adopts in the face of being and those which he maintains in the face of Nothingness, and we are immediately tempted to consider being and non-being as two complementary components of the real—like dark and light. In short we would then be dealing with two strictly contemporary notions which would somehow be united in the production of existents and which it would be useless to consider in isolation. Pure being and pure non-being would be two abstractions which could be reunited only on the basis of concrete realities.

Such is certainly the point of view of Hegel. It is in the *Logic* in fact that he studies the relations of Being and Non-Being, and he calls the *Logic* "The system of the pure determinations of thought." He defines more fully by saying, "Thoughts as they are ordinarily represented, are not pure thoughts, for by a being which is thought, we understand a being of which the content is an empirical content. In logic thoughts are apprehended in such a way that they have no other content than the content of pure thought, which content is engendered by it."* To be sure, these determinations are "what is deepest in things" but at the same time when one considers them "in and for themselves," one deduces them from thought itself and discovers in them their truth. However the effort of Hegelian logic is to "make clear the inadequacy of the notions (which it) considers one by one and the necessity, in order to understand them, of raising each to a more complete notion which surpasses them while integrating them."†

One can apply to Hegel what Le Senne said of the philosophy of Hamelin: "Each of the lower terms depends on the higher term, as the abstract on the concrete which is necessary for it to realize itself." The true concrete for Hegel is the Existent with its essence; it is the Totality produced by the synthetic integration of all the abstract moments which are surpassed in it by requiring their complement. In this sense Being will be the most abstract of abstractions and the poorest, if we consider it in itself—that is, by separating it from its surpassing toward Essence. In fact "Being is related to Essence as the immediate to the mediate. Things in general 'are,' but their being consists in manifesting their essence. Being passes into Essence. One can express this by saying, 'Being presupposes Essence.' Although Essence appears in relation to Being as mediated, Essence is nevertheless the true origin. Being returns to its ground; Being is surpassed in Essence."‡

Thus Being cut from Essence which is its ground becomes

---

* Introduction v. P. c. 2cd. EξxxIv; quoted by Lefebvre: *Morceaux choisis.*

† Laporte: *Le Problème de l'Abstraction*, p. 25 (Presses Universitaires, 1940).

‡ *Treatise on Logic*, written by Hegel between 1808 and 1811, to serve as the basis før his course at the gymnasium at Nuremberg.

"mere empty immediacy." This is how the *Phenomenology of Mind* defines it by presenting pure Being "from the point of view of truth" as the immediate. If the beginning of logic is to be the immediate, we shall then find beginning in *Being*, which is "the indetermination which precedes all determination, the undetermined as the absolute point of departure."

But Being thus undetermined immediately "passes into" its opposite. "This pure Being," writes Hegel in *Logic* (of the *Encyclopaedia*) is "pure abstraction and consequently absolute negation, which taken in its immediate moment is also non-being." Is Nothingness not in fact simple identity with itself, complete emptiness, absence of determinations and of content? Pure being and pure nothingness are then the same thing. Or rather it is true to say that they are different; but "as here the difference is not yet determined difference—for being and non-being constitute the immediate moment such as it is in them—this difference can not be named; it is only a pure opinion."* This means concretely that *"there is nothing in heaven or on earth which does not contain in itself being and nothingness."*†

It is still too soon for us to discuss the Hegelian concept itself; we need all the results of our study in order to take a position regarding this. It is appropriate here to observe only that being is reduced by Hegel to a signification of the existent. Being is enveloped by essence, which is its foundation and origin. Hegel's whole theory is based on the idea that a philosophical procedure is necessary in order at the outset of logic to rediscover the immediate in terms of the mediated, the abstract in terms of the concrete on which it is grounded. But we have already remarked that being does not hold the same relation to

---

* Hegel: P.C.—E.988.

† Hegel: *Greater Logic*, chap. 1.

the phenomenon as the abstract holds to the concrete. Being is not one "structure among others," one moment of the object; it is the very condition of all structures and of all moments. It is the ground on which the characteristics of the phenomenon will manifest themselves. Similarly it is not admissible that the being of things "consists in manifesting their essence." For then a being of that being would be necessary. Furthermore if the being of things "consisted" in manifesting their essence, it would be hard to see how Hegel could determine a pure moment of Being where we could not find at least a trace of that original structure. It is true that the understanding determines pure being, isolates and fixes it in its very determinations. But if surpassing toward essence constitutes the original character of being, and if the understanding is limited to "determining and persevering in the determinations," we can not see precisely how it does not determine being as "consisting in manifesting."

It might be said in defense of Hegel that every determination is negation. But the understanding in this sense is limited to denying that its object is *other* than it is. That is sufficient doubtless to prevent all dialectical process, but not enough to effect its disappearance at the threshold of its surpassing. In so far as being surpasses itself *toward something else*, it is not subject to the determinations of the understanding. But in so far as it surpasses *itself*—that is, in so far as it is in its very depths the origin of its own surpassing—being must on the contrary appear such as it *is* to the understanding which fixes it in its own determinations. To affirm that being is only what it is would be at least to leave being intact so far as it *is* its own surpassing. We see there the ambiguity of the Hegelian notion of "surpassing" which sometimes appears to be an upsurge from the inmost depth of the being considered and at other times an external movement by which this being is involved. It is not enough to affirm that the understanding finds in being only what it is; we must also explain how being, which is what it is, can be *only that*. Such an explanation would derive its legitimacy from the consideration of the phenomenon of being as such and not from the negating processes of the understanding.

But what needs examination here is especially Hegel's statement that being and nothingness constitute two opposites, the difference between which on the level of abstraction under consideration is only a simple "opinion."

To oppose being to nothingness as thesis and antithesis, as Hegel does, is to suppose that they are logically contemporary. Thus simultaneously two opposites arise as the two limiting terms of a logical series. Here we must note carefully that opposites alone can enjoy this simultaneity because they are equally positive (or equally negative). But non-being is not the opposite of being; it is its contradiction. This implies that logically nothingness is subsequent to being since it is being, first posited, then denied. It can not be therefore that being and non-being are concepts with the same content since on the contrary non-being supposes an irreducible mental act. Whatever may be the original undifferentiation of being, non-being is that same undifferentiation *denied*. This permits Hegel to make being pass into nothingness; this is what by implication has introduced negation into his very definition of being. This is self-evident since any definition is negative, since Hegel has told us, making use of a statement of Spinoza's, that *omnis determinatio est negatio*. And does he not write, "It does not matter what the determination or content is which would distinguish being from something else; whatever would give it a content would prevent it from maintaining itself in its purity. It is pure indetermination and emptiness. *Nothing* can be apprehended in it."

Thus anyone who introduces negation into being from outside will discover subsequently that he makes it pass into non-being. But here we have a play on words involving the very idea of negation. For if I refuse to allow being any determination or content, I am nevertheless forced to affirm at least that it *is*. Thus, let anyone deny being whatever he wishes, he can not cause it *not to be*, thanks to the very fact that he denies that it is this or that. Negation can not touch the nucleus of being of Being, which is absolute plenitude and entire positivity. By contrast Non-being is a negation which aims at this nucleus of absolute density. Non-being is denied at the heart of Being. When Hegel writes, "(Being and nothingness) are empty abstractions, and the one is as empty as the other,"* he forgets that emptiness is emptiness *of* something.† Being is empty of all other determination than identity with itself, but non-being is empty *of being*. In a word, we must recall here against Hegel that being *is* and that nothingness *is not*.

Thus even though being can not be the support of any differentiated quality, nothingness is logically subsequent to it since it supposes being in order to deny it, since the irreducible quality of the *not* comes to add itself to that undifferentiated mass of being in order to release it. That does not mean only that we should refuse to put *being* and *non-being* on the same plane, but also that we must be careful never to posit nothingness as an original abyss from which being arose. The use which we make of the notion of nothingness in its familiar form always supposes a preliminary specification of being. It is striking in this connection that language furnishes us with

---

* P.c. 2 ed. E.ξLxxxvii.

† It is so much the more strange in that Hegel is the first to have noted that "every negation is a determined negation;" that is, it depends on a content.

a nothingness of *things* and a nothingness of human beings.*
But the specification is still more obvious in the majority
of instances. We say, pointing to a particular collection of
objects, "Touch *nothing*," which means, very precisely, nothing of that collection. Similarly if we question someone on well
determined events in his private or public life, he may reply,
"I know *nothing*." And this nothing includes the totality of
the facts on which we questioned him. Even Socrates with his
famous statement, "I know that I know nothing," designates by
this *nothing* the totality of being considered as Truth.

If adopting for the moment the point of view of naive cos-
mogonies, we tried to ask ourselves what "was there" before
a world existed, and if we replied "nothing," we would be
forced to recognize that this "before" like this "nothing" is
in effect retroactive. What we deny today, we who are established in being, is what there was of being before this being.
Negation here springs from a consciousness which is turned
back toward the beginning. If we remove from this original
emptiness its characteristic of being empty *of this world* and
of every whole taking the form of a world, as well as its characteristic of *before*, which presupposes an *after*, then the very
negation disappears, giving way to a total indetermination
which it would be impossible to conceive, even and especially
as a nothingness. Thus reversing the statement of Spinoza, we
could say that every negation is determination. This means
that being is prior to nothingness and establishes the ground
for it. By this we must understand not only that being has a
logical precedence over nothingness but also that it is from
being that nothingness derives concretely its efficacy. This is

---

* *Ne ... rien* = "nothing" as opposed to *ne ... personne* = "nobody," which are equally
fundamental negative expressions. Sartre here conveniently has based his ontology on
the exigencies of a purely French syntax. Tr.

what we mean when we say that *nothingness haunts being*. That means that being has no need of nothingness in order to be conceived and that we can examine the idea of it exhaustively without finding there the least trace of nothingness. But on the other hand, nothingness, *which is not*, can have only a borrowed existence, and it gets its being from being. Its nothingness of being is encountered only within the limits of being, and the total disappearance of being would not be the advent of the reign of non-being, but on the contrary the concomitant disappearance of nothingness. *Non-being exists only on the surface of being.*

4. THE PHENOMENOLOGICAL CONCEPT OF NOTHINGNESS

There is another possible way of conceiving being and nothingness as complements. One could view them as two equally necessary components of the real without making being "pass into" nothingness—as Hegel does—and without insisting on the posteriority of nothingness as we attempted to do. We might on the contrary emphasize the reciprocal forces of repulsion which being and non-being exercise on each other, the real in some way being the tension resulting from these antagonistic forces. It is toward this new conception that Heidegger is oriented.*

We need not look far to see the progress which Heidegger's theory of nothingness has made over that of Hegel. First, being and non-being are no longer empty abstractions. Heidegger in his most important work has shown the legitimacy of rais-

---

* Heidegger: *Qu'est-ce que la métaphysique* (Tr. by Corbin, N.R.F. 1938). In English "What is Metaphysics?" Tr. by R.F.C. Hull and Alan Crick. From *Existence and Being*, ed. by Werner Brock, Henry Regnery, 1949.

ing the question concerning being; the latter has no longer the character of a Scholastic universal, which it still retained with Hegel. There is a meaning of being which must be clarified; there is a "pre-ontological comprehension" of being which is involved in every kind of conduct belonging to "human reality"—*i.e.*, in each of its projects. Similarly difficulties which customarily arise as soon as a philosopher touches on the problem of Nothingness are shown to be without foundation; they are important in so far as they limit the function of the understanding, and they show simply that this problem is not *within the province* of the understanding. There exist on the other hand numerous attitudes of "human reality" which imply a "comprehension" of nothingness: hate, prohibitions, regret, *etc.* For "*Dasein*" there is even a permanent possibility of finding oneself "face to face" with nothingness and discovering it as a phenomenon: this possibility is anguish.

Heidegger, while establishing the possibilities of a concrete apprehension of Nothingness, never falls into the error which Hegel made; he does not preserve a being for Non-Being, not even an abstract being. Nothing is not; it nihilates itself.* It is supported and conditioned by transcendence. We know that for Heidegger the being of human reality is defined as "being-in-the-world." The world is a synthetic complex of instrumental realities inasmuch as they point one to another in ever widening circles, and inasmuch as man makes himself known in terms of this complex which he is. This means both that "human reality" springs forth *invested* with being and "finds

---

* Heidegger uses the by now famous expression "*Das Nichts nichtet*" or "Nothing nothings." I think "nihilate" is a closer equivalent to Sartre's *néantise* than "annihilate" because the fundamental meaning of the term is "to make nothing" rather than "to destroy or do away with." *Nichtet*, *néantise*, and *nihilate* are all, of course, equally without foundation in the dictionaries of the respective languages. Tr.

itself" (*sich befinden*) in being—and also that human reality causes being, which surrounds it, to be disposed around human reality in the form of the world.

But human reality can make being appear as organized totality in the world only by surpassing being. All determination for Heidegger is surpassing since it supposes a withdrawal taken from a particular point of view. This passing beyond the world, which is a condition of the very rising up of the world as such, is effected by the *Dasein* which directs the surpassing *toward itself*. The characteristic of selfness (*Selbstheit*), in fact, is that man is always separated from what he is by all the breadth of the being which he is not. He makes himself known to himself from the other side of the world and he looks from the horizon toward himself to recover his inner being. Man is "a being of distances." In the movement of turning inward which traverses all of being, being arises and organizes itself as the world without there being either priority of the movement over the world, or the world over the movement. But this appearance of the self beyond the world—that is, beyond the totality of the real—is an emergence of "human reality" in nothingness. It is in nothingness alone that being can be surpassed. At the same time it is from the point of view of beyond the world that being is organized into the world, which means on the one hand that human reality rises up as an emergence of being in non-being and on the other hand that the world is "suspended" in nothingness. Anguish is the discovery of this double, perpetual nihilation. It is in terms of this surpassing of the world that *Dasein* manages to realize the contingency of the world; that is, to raise the question, "How does it happen that there is something rather than nothing?" Thus the contingency of the world appears to human reality in so far as human reality has established itself in nothingness in order to apprehend the contingency.

Here then is nothingness surrounding being on every side and at the same time expelled from being. Here nothingness is given as that by which the world receives its outlines as the world. Can this solution satisfy us?

Certainly it can not be denied that the apprehension of the world *qua* world, is a nihilation. From the moment the world appears *qua* world it gives itself as *being only that.* The necessary counterpart of this apprehension then is indeed the emergence of "human reality" in nothingness. But where does "human reality" get its power of emerging thus in non-being? Without a doubt Heidegger is right in insisting on the fact that negation derives its foundation from nothingness. But if nothingness provides a ground for negation, it is because nothingness envelops the *not* within itself as its essential structure. In other words, it is not as undifferentiated emptiness or as a disguised otherness* that nothingness provides the ground for negation. Nothingness stands at the origin of the negative judgment because it is itself negation. It founds the negation as an *act* because it is the negation as *being.* Nothingness can be nothingness only by nihilating itself expressly as nothingness of the world; that is, in its nihilation it must direct itself expressly toward this world in order to constitute itself as refusal of the world. Nothingness carries being in its heart. But how does the emergence account for this nihilating refusal? Transcendence, which is "the project of self beyond," is far from being able to establish nothingness; on the contrary, it is nothingness which is at the very heart of transcendence and which conditions it.

---

* What Hegel would call "immediate otherness."

Now the characteristic of Heidegger's philosophy is to describe *Dasein* by using positive terms which hide the implicit negations. *Dasein* is "outside of itself, in the world"; it is "a being of distances"; it is care; it is "its own possibilities," etc. All this amounts to saying that *Dasein* "is not" in itself, that it "is not" in immediate proximity to itself, and that it "surpasses" the world inasmuch as it posits itself as *not being in itself* and as *not being in the world*. In this sense Hegel is right rather than Heidegger when he states that Mind is the negative. Actually we can put to each of them the same question, phrased slightly differently. We should say to Hegel: "It is not sufficient to posit mind as mediation and the negative; it is necessary to demonstrate negativity as the structure of being of mind. What must mind be in order to be able to constitute itself as negative?" And we can ask the same question of Heidegger in these words: "If negation is the original structure of transcendence, what must be the original structure of 'human reality' in order for it to be able to transcend the world?" In both cases we are shown a negating activity and there is no concern to ground this activity upon a negative being. Heidegger in addition makes of Nothingness a sort of intentional correlate of transcendence, without seeing that he has already inserted it into transcendence itself as its original structure.

Furthermore what is the use of affirming that Nothingness provides the ground for negation, if it is merely to enable us to form subsequently a theory of non-being which by definition separates Nothingness from all concrete negation? If I emerge in nothingness *beyond* the world, how can this extra-mundane nothingness furnish a foundation for those little pools of non-being which we encounter each instant in the depth of being? I say, "Pierre is not there," "I have no more money," etc. Is it really necessary to surpass the world toward nothingness and to return subsequently to being in order to provide a ground for these everyday judgments? And how can the operation be affected? To accomplish it we are not required to make the world slip into nothingness; standing within the limits of being, we simply deny an attribute to a subject. Will someone say that each attribute refused, each being denied is taken up by one and the same extra-mundane nothingness, that non-being is like the fullness of what is not, that the world is suspended in non-being as the real is suspended in the heart of possibilities? In this case each negation would necessarily have for origin a particular surpassing: the surpassing of one being toward another. But what is this surpassing, if not simply the Hegelian mediation—and have we not already and in vain sought in Hegel the nihilating ground of the mediation? Furthermore even if the explanation is valid for the simple, radical negations which deny to a determined object any kind of presence in the depth of being (*e.g.*, "Centaurs *do not exist*"—"*There is* no reason for him to be late"—"The ancient Greeks *did not practice* polygamy"), negations which, if need be, can contribute to constituting Nothingness as a sort of geometrical place for unfulfilled projects, all inexact representations, all vanished beings or those of which the idea is only a fiction—even so this interpretation of non-being would no longer be valid for a certain kind of reality which is in truth the most frequent: namely, those negations which include non-being in their being. How can we hold that these are at once partly within the universe and partly outside in extramundane nothingness?

Take for example the notion of distance, which conditions the determination of a location, the localization of a point. It is easy to see that it possesses a negative moment. Two points are distant when they are *separated* by a certain length. The length, a positive attribute of a segment of a straight line, inter-

venes here by virtue of the negation of an absolute, undifferentiated proximity. Someone might perhaps seek to reduce
distance to *being only* the length of the segment of which the
two points considered, A and B, would be the limits. But does
he not see that he has changed the direction of attention in
this case and that he has, under cover of the same word, given
another object to intuition? The organized complex which is
constituted by the segment *with* its two limiting terms can
furnish actually two different objects to knowledge. We can
in fact give the *segment* as immediate object of intuition, in
which case this segment represents a full, concrete tension, of
which the length is a positive attribute and the two points A
and B appear only as a moment of the whole; that is, as they
are implicated by the segment itself as its limits. Then the
negation, expelled from the segment and its length, takes refuge in the two *limits*: to say that point B is a limit of the segment is to say that the segment *does not* extend beyond this
point. Negation is here a secondary structure of the object. If,
on the other hand, we direct our attention to the two points
A and B, they arise as immediate objects of intuition on the
ground of space. The segment disappears as a full, concrete
object; it is apprehended in terms of two points as the emptiness, the negativity which separates them. Negation is not
subject to the points, which cease to be *limits* in order to
impregnate the very length of the segment with distance. Thus
the total form constituted by the segment and its two limits
with its inner structure of negation is capable of letting itself
be apprehended in two ways. Rather there are two forms, and
the condition of the appearance of the one is the disintegration
of the other, exactly as in perception we constitute a particular object as a *figure* by rejecting another so as to make of it
a *ground*, and conversely. In both instances we find the same

quantity of negation which at one time passes into the notion of limits and at another into the notion of distance, but which in each case can not be suppressed. Will someone object that the idea of distance is psychological and that it designates only the extension which must be *cleared* in order to go from point A to point B? We shall reply that the same negation is included in this *to clear* since this notion expresses precisely the passive resistance of the remoteness. We will willingly admit with Heidegger that "human reality" is "remote-from-itself"; that is, that it rises in the world as that which creates distances and at the same time causes them to be removed (*entfernend*). But this remoteness-from-self, even if it is the necessary condition in order that *there may be* remoteness in general, envelops remoteness in itself as the negative structure which must be surmounted. It will be useless to attempt to reduce distance to the simple result of a *measurement*. What has become evident in the course of the preceding discussion is that the two points and the segment which is inclosed between them have the indissoluble unity of what the Germans call a *Gestalt*. Negation is the cement which realizes this unity. It defines precisely the immediate relation which connects these two points and which presents them to intuition as the indissoluble unity of the distance. This negation can be covered over only by claiming to reduce distance to the measurement of a length, for negation is the *raison d'être* of that measurement.

What we have just shown by the examination of *distance*, we could just as well have brought out by describing realities like absence, change, otherness, repulsion, regret, distraction, *etc.* There is an infinite number of realities which are not only objects of judgment, but which are experienced, opposed, feared, *etc.*, by the human being and which in their inner structure are inhabited by negation, as by a necessary condition of their existence. We shall call them *négatités*.* Kant caught a glimpse of their significance when he spoke of regulative concepts (*e.g.* the immortality of the soul), types of syntheses of negative and positive in which negation is the condition of positivity. The function of negation varies according to the nature of the object considered. Between wholly positive realities (which however retain negation as the condition of the sharpness of their outlines, as that which fixes them as what they are) and those in which the positivity is only an appearance concealing a whole of nothingness, all gradations are possible. In any case it is impossible to throw these negations back into an extra-mundane nothingness since they are dispersed in being, are supported by being, and are conditions of reality. Nothingness beyond the world accounts for absolute negation; but we have just discovered a swarm of ultra-mundane beings which possess as much reality and efficacy as other beings, but which inclose within themselves non-being. They require an explanation which remains within the limits of the real. Nothingness if it is supported by being, vanishes *qua nothingness*, and we fall back upon being. Nothingness can be nihilated only on the foundation of being; if nothingness can be given, it is neither before nor after being, nor in a general way outside of being. Nothingness lies coiled in the heart of being—like a worm.

5. THE ORIGIN OF NOTHINGNESS

It would be well at this point to cast a glance backward and to measure the road already covered. We raised first the question

---

* A word coined by Sartre with no equivalent term in English. Tr.

of being. Then examining this very question conceived as a type of human conduct, we questioned this in turn. We next had to recognize that no question could be asked, in particular not that of being, if negation did not exist. But this negation itself when inspected more closely referred us back to Nothingness as its origin and foundation. In order for negation to exist in the world and in order that we may consequently raise questions concerning Being, it is necessary that in some way Nothingness be given. We perceived then that Nothingness can be conceived neither *outside of* being, nor as a complementary, abstract notion, nor as an infinite milieu where being is suspended. Nothingness must be given at the heart of Being, in order for us to be able to apprehend that particular type of realities which we have called *négatités*. But this intramundane Nothingness cannot be produced by Being-in-itself; the notion of Being as full positivity does not contain Nothingness as one of its structures. We can not even say that Being excludes it. Being lacks all relation with it. Hence the question which is put to us now with a particular urgency: if Nothingness can be conceived neither outside of Being, nor in terms of Being, and if on the other hand, since it is non-being, it can not derive from itself the necessary force to "nihilate itself," *where does Nothingness come from?*

If we wish to pursue the problem further, we must first recognize that we can not grant to nothingness the property of "nihilating itself." For although the expression "to nihilate itself" is thought of as removing from nothingness the last semblance of being, we must recognize that only *Being* can nihilate itself; however it comes about, in order to nihilate itself, it must *be*. But Nothingness *is not*. If we can speak of it, it is only because it possesses an appearance of being, a borrowed being, as we have noted above. Nothingness is not, Nothingness "is made-to-be,"* Nothingness does not nihilate itself; Nothingness "is nihilated." It follows therefore that there must exist a Being (this can not be the In-itself) of which the property is to nihilate Nothingness, to support it in its being, to sustain it perpetually in its very existence, a *being by which nothingness comes to things.* But how can this Being be related to Nothingness so that through it Nothingness comes to things? We must observe first that the being postulated can not be passive in relation to Nothingness, can not receive it; Nothingness could not *come* to this being except through another Being—which would be an infinite regress. But on the other hand, the Being by which Nothingness comes to the world can not *produce* Nothingness while remaining indifferent to that production—like the Stoic cause which produces its effect without being itself changed. It would be inconceivable that a Being which is full positivity should maintain and create outside itself a Nothingness or transcendent being, for there would be nothing in Being by which Being could surpass itself toward Non-Being. The Being by which Nothingness arrives in the world must nihilate Nothingness in its Being, and even so it still runs the risk of establishing Nothingness as a transcendent in the very heart of immanence unless it nihilates Nothingness in its being *in connection with its own being.* The Being by which Nothingness arrives in the world is a being such that in its Being, the Nothingness of its Being is

---

* The French is *est été*, which literally means "is been," an expression as meaningless in ordinary French as in English. Maurice Natanson suggests "is-was." (*A Critique of Jean-Paul Sartre's Ontology*, University of Nebraska Studies, March 1951, p. 59.) I prefer "is made-to-be" because Sartre seems to be using *être* as a transitive verb, here in the passive voice, thus suggesting that nothingness has been subjected to an act involving being. Other passages containing this expression will, I believe, bear out this interpretation. Tr.

in question. *The being by which Nothingness comes to the world must be its own Nothingness.* By this we must understand not a nihilating act, which would require in turn a foundation in Being, but an ontological characteristic of the Being required. It remains to learn in what delicate, exquisite region of Being we shall encounter that Being which is its own Nothingness.

We shall be helped in our inquiry by a more complete examination of the conduct which served us as a point of departure. We must return to the question. We have seen, it may be recalled, that every question in essence posits the possibility of a negative reply. In a question we question a being about its being or its way of being. This way of being or this being is veiled; there always remains the possibility that it may unveil itself as a Nothingness. But from the very fact that we presume that an Existent can always be revealed as *nothing*, every question supposes that we realize a nihilating withdrawal in relation to the given, which becomes a simple *presentation*, fluctuating between being and Nothingness.

It is essential therefore that the questioner have the permanent possibility of dissociating himself from the causal series which constitutes being and which can produce only being. If we admitted that the question is determined in the questioner by universal determinism, the question would thereby become unintelligible and even inconceivable. A real cause, in fact, produces a real effect and the caused being is wholly engaged by the cause in positivity; to the extent that its being depends on the cause, it can not have within itself the tiniest germ of nothingness. Thus in so far as the questioner must be able to effect in relation to the questioned a kind of nihilating withdrawal, he is not subject to the causal order of the world; he detaches himself from Being. This means that by a double movement of nihilation, he nihilates the thing questioned in relation to himself by placing it in a *neutral* state, between being and non-being—and that he nihilates himself in relation to the thing questioned by wrenching himself from being in order to be able to bring out of himself the possibility of a non-being. Thus in posing a question, a certain negative element is introduced into the world. We see nothingness making the world iridescent, casting a shimmer over things. But at the same time the question emanates from a questioner who in order to motivate himself in his being as one who questions, disengages himself from being. This disengagement is then by definition a human process. Man presents himself at least in this instance as a being who causes Nothingness to arise in the world, inasmuch as he himself is affected with non-being to this end.

These remarks may serve as guiding thread as we examine the *négatités* of which we spoke earlier. There is no doubt at all that these are transcendent realities; distance, for example, is imposed on us as something which we have to take into account, which must be cleared with effort. However these realities are of a very peculiar nature; they all indicate immediately an essential relation of human reality to the world. They derive their origin from an act, an expectation, or a project of the human being; they all indicate an aspect of being as it appears to the human being who is engaged in the world. The relations of man in the world, which the *négatités* indicate, have nothing in common with the relations a *posteriori* which are brought out by empirical activity. We are no longer dealing with those relations *of instrumentality* by which, according to Heidegger, objects in the world disclose themselves to "human reality." Every *négatité* appears rather as one of the essential conditions of this relation of instrumentality. In order for the totality of being to order itself around us as instruments, in order for it to parcel itself into differentiated complexes which refer one to another and which can *be used*, it is necessary that negation rise up not as a thing among other things but as the rubric of a category which presides over the arrangement and the redistribution of great masses of being in things. Thus the rise of man in the midst of the being which "invests" him causes a world to be discovered. But the essential and primordial moment of this rise is the negation. Thus we have reached the first goal of this study. Man is the being through whom nothingness comes to the world. But this question immediately provokes another: What must man be in his being in order that through him nothingness may come to being?

Being can generate only being and if man is inclosed in this process of generation, only being will come out of him. If we are to assume that man is able to question this process—*i.e.*, to make it the object of interrogation—he must be able to hold it up to view as a totality. He must be able to put himself *outside of* being and by the same stroke weaken the structure of the being of being. Yet it is not given to "human reality" to annihilate even provisionally the mass of being which it posits before itself. Man's *relation* with being is that he can modify it. For man to put a particular existent out of circuit is to put himself out of circuit in relation to that existent. In this case he is not subject to it; he is out of reach; it can not act on him, for he has retired *beyond a nothingness*. Descartes following the Stoics has given a name to this possibility which human reality has to secrete a nothingness which isolates it—it is *freedom*. But freedom here is only a name. If we wish to penetrate further into the question, we must not be content with this reply and we ought to ask now: What is human freedom if through it nothingness comes into the world?

It is not yet possible to deal with the problem of freedom

in all its fullness. In fact the steps which we have completed up to now show clearly that freedom is not a faculty of the human soul to be envisaged and described in isolation. What we have been trying to define is the being of man in so far as he conditions the appearance of nothingness, and this being has appeared to us as freedom. Thus freedom as the requisite condition for the nihilation of nothingness is not a *property* which belongs among others to the essence of the human being. We have already noticed furthermore that with man the relation of existence to essence is not comparable to what it is for the things of the world. Human freedom precedes essence in man and makes it possible; the essence of the human being is suspended in his freedom. What we call freedom is impossible to distinguish from the *being* of "human reality." Man does not exist *first* in order to be free *subsequently;* there is no difference between the being of man and his *being-free.* This is not the time to make a frontal attack on a question which can be treated exhaustively only in the light of a rigorous elucidation of the human being. Here we are dealing with freedom in connection with the problem of nothingness and only to the extent that it conditions the appearance of nothingness.

What first appears evident is that human reality can detach itself from the world—in questioning, in systematic doubt, in sceptical doubt, in the ἐποχή, *etc.—only* if by nature it has the possibility of self-detachment. This was seen by Descartes, who is establishing doubt on freedom when he claims for us the possibility of suspending our judgments. Alain's position is similar. It is also in this sense that Hegel asserts the freedom of the mind to the degree that mind is mediation—*i.e.,* the Negative. Furthermore it is one of the trends of contemporary philosophy to see in human consciousness a sort of escape from the self; such is the meaning of the transcendence of

Heidegger. The intentionality of Husserl and of Brentano has also to a large extent the characteristic of a detachment from self. But we are not yet in a position to consider freedom as an inner structure of consciousness. We lack for the moment both instruments and techniques to permit us to succeed in that enterprise. What interests us at present is a temporal operation since questioning is, like doubt, a kind of behavior; it assumes that the human being reposes first in the depths of being and then detaches himself from it by a nihilating withdrawal. Thus we are envisaging the condition of the nihilation as a relation to the self in the heart of a temporal process. We wish simply to show that by identifying consciousness with a causal sequence indefinitely continued, one transmutes it into a plenitude of being and thereby causes it to return into the unlimited totality of being—as is well illustrated by the futility of the efforts to dissociate psychological determinism from universal determinism and to constitute it as a separate series.

The room of someone absent, the books of which he turned the pages, the objects which he touched are in themselves only *books, objects; i.e.,* full actualities. The very traces which he has left can be deciphered as traces of him only within a situation where he has been already posited as absent. The dog-eared book with the well-read pages is not by itself a book of which Pierre has turned the pages, of which he no longer turns the pages. If we consider it as the present, transcendent motivation of my perception or even as the synthetic flux, regulated by my sensible impressions, then it is merely a volume with turned-down, worn pages; it can refer only to itself or to present objects, to the lamp which illuminates it, to the table which holds it. It would be useless to invoke an association by contiguity as Plato does in the *Phaedo*, where he makes the image of the absent one appear on the margin of the perception of the lyre or of the cithara which he has touched. This image, if we consider it in itself and in the spirit of classical theories, is a definite plenitude; it is a concrete and positive psychic fact. Consequently we must of necessity pass on it a doubly negative judgment: subjectively, to signify that the image *is not* a perception; objectively, to deny that the Pierre of whom I form the image *is here* at this moment.

This is the famous problem of the characteristics of the true image, which has concerned so many psychologists from Taine to Spaier. Association, we see, does not solve the problem; it pushes it back to the level of reflection. But in every way it demands a negation; that is, at the very least, a nihilating withdrawal of consciousness in relation to the image apprehended as subjective phenomenon, in order to posit it precisely as being only a subjective phenomenon.

Now I have attempted to show elsewhere* that if we posit the image *first* as a renascent perception, it is radically impossible to distinguish it *subsequently* from actual perceptions. The image must enclose in its very structure a nihilating thesis. It constitutes itself *qua* image while positing its object as existing *elsewhere* or *not existing*. It carries within it a double negation; first it is the nihilation of the world (since the world is not offering the imagined object as an actual object of perception), secondly the nihilation of the object of the image (it is posited as not actual), and finally by the same stroke it is the nihilation of itself (since it is not a concrete, full psychic process). In explaining how I apprehend the absence of Pierre in the room, it would be useless to invoke those famous "empty intentions" of Husserl, which are in great part constitutive of perception. Among the various perceptive intentions,

---

* *L'imagination.* Alcanate and determine existe, 1936.

indeed, there are relations of *motivation* (but motivation is not causation), and among these intentions, some are full (*i.e.*, filled with what they aim at) and others empty. But precisely because the matter which should fill the empty intentions *does not exist*, it can not be this which motivates them in their structure. And since the other intentions are full, neither can they motivate the empty intentions inasmuch as the latter are empty. Moreover these intentions are of psychic nature and it would be an error to envisage them in the mode of things; that is, as recipients which would first be given, which according to circumstances could be emptied or filled, and which would be by nature indifferent to their state of being empty or filled. It seems that Husserl has not always escaped the materialist illusion. To be empty an intention must be conscious of itself as empty and precisely as empty *of* the exact matter at which it aims. An empty intention constitutes itself as empty to the exact extent that it posits its matter as non-existing or absent. In short an empty intention is a consciousness of negation which transcends itself toward an object which it posits as absent or non-existent.

Thus whatever may be the explanation which we give of it, Pierre's absence, in order to be established or realized, requires a negative moment by which consciousness in the absence of all prior determination, constitutes itself as negation. If in terms of my perceptions of the room, I conceive of the former inhabitant who is no longer in the room, I am of necessity forced to produce an act of thought which no prior state can determine nor motivate, in short to effect in myself a break with being. And in so far as I continually use *négatités* to isolate and determine existents—*i.e.*, to think them—the succession of my "states of consciousness" is a perpetual separation of effect from cause, since every nihilating process must derive its source only from itself. Inasmuch as my present state would be a prolongation of my prior state, every opening by which negation could slip through would be completely blocked. Every psychic process of nihilation implies then a cleavage between the immediate psychic past and the present. This cleavage is precisely nothingness. At least, someone will say, there remains the possibility of successive implication between the nihilating processes. My establishment of Pierre's absence could still be determinant for my regret at not seeing him; you have not excluded the possibility of a determinism of nihilations. But aside from the fact that the original nihilation of the series must necessarily be disconnected from the prior positive processes, what can be the meaning of a motivation of nothingness by nothingness? A being indeed can *nihilate itself* perpetually, but to the extent that it nihilates itself, it foregoes being the origin of another phenomenon, even of a second nihilation.

It remains to explain what this separation is, this disengaging of consciousness which conditions every negation. If we consider the prior consciousness envisaged as motivation, we see suddenly and evidently that *nothing* has just slipped in between that state and the present state. There has been no break in continuity within the flux of the temporal development, for that would force us to return to the inadmissible concept of the infinite divisibility of time and of the temporal point or instant as the limit of the division. Neither has there been an abrupt interpolation of an opaque element to separate prior from subsequent in the way that a knife blade cuts a piece of fruit in two. Nor is there a *weakening* of the motivating force of the prior consciousness; it remains what it is, it does not lose anything of its urgency. What separates prior from subsequent is exactly *nothing*. This nothing is absolutely impassable, just because it is nothing; for in every obstacle to be cleared there is something positive which gives itself as about to be cleared. The prior consciousness is always *there* (though with the modification of "pastness"). It constantly maintains a relation of interpretation with the present consciousness, but on the basis of this existential relation it is put out of the game, out of the circuit, between parentheses—exactly as in the eyes of one practicing the phenomenological ἐποχή, the world both is within him and outside of him.

Thus the condition on which human reality can deny all or part of the world is that human reality carry nothingness within itself as the *nothing* which separates its present from all its past. But this is still not all, for the *nothing* envisaged would not yet have the sense of nothingness; a suspension of being which would remain unnamed, which would not be consciousness of suspending being would come from outside consciousness and by reintroducing opacity into the heart of this absolute lucidity, would have the effect of cutting it in two. Furthermore this nothing would by no means be negative. Nothingness, as we have seen above, is the ground of the negation because it conceals the negation within itself, because it is the negation as being. It is necessary then that conscious being constitute itself in relation to its past as separated from this past by a nothingness. It must necessarily be conscious of this cleavage in being, but not as a phenomenon which it experiences, rather as a structure of consciousness which it is. Freedom is the human being putting his past out of play by secreting his own nothingness. Let us understand indeed that this original necessity of being its own nothingness does not belong to consciousness intermittently and on the occasion of particular negations. This does not happen just at a particular moment in psychic life when negative or interrogative attitudes appear; consciousness continually experiences itself as the nihilation of its past being.

But someone doubtless will believe that he can use against us here an objection which we have frequently raised ourselves: if the nihilating consciousness exists only as consciousness of nihilation, we ought to be able to define and describe a constant mode of consciousness, present *qua* consciousness, which would be consciousness of nihilation. Does this consciousness exist? Behold a new question has been raised here: if freedom is the being of consciousness, consciousness ought to exist as consciousness of freedom. What form does this consciousness of freedom assume? In freedom the human being *is*his own past (as also his own future) in the form of nihilation. If our analysis has not led us astray there ought to exist for the human being, in so far as he is conscious of being, a certain mode of standing opposite his past and his future, as being both this past and this future and as not being them. We shall be able to furnish an immediate reply to this question; it is in anguish that man gets the consciousness of his freedom, or if you prefer, anguish is the mode of being of freedom as consciousness of being; it is in anguish that freedom is, in its being, in question for itself.

Kierkegaard describing anguish in the face of what one lacks characterizes it as anguish in the face of freedom. But Heidegger, whom we know to have been greatly influenced by Kierkegaard,* considers anguish instead as the apprehension of nothingness. These two descriptions of anguish do not appear to us contradictory; on the contrary the one implies the other.

First we must acknowledge that Kierkegaard is right;

---

* J. Wahl: *Etudes Kierkegaardiennes*, Kierkegaard et Heidegger.

anguish is distinguished from fear in that fear is fear of beings in the world whereas anguish is anguish before myself Vertigo is anguish to the extent that I am afraid not of falling over the precipice, but of throwing myself over. A situation provokes fear if there is a possibility of my life being changed from without; my being provokes anguish to the extent that I distrust myself and my own reactions in that situation. The artillery preparation which precedes the attack can provoke fear in the soldier who undergoes the bombardment, but anguish is born in him when he tries to foresee the conduct with which he will face the bombardment, when he asks himself if he is going to be able to "hold up." Similarly the recruit who reports for active duty at the beginning of the war can in some instances be afraid of death, but more often he is "afraid of being afraid"; that is, he is filled with anguish before himself. Most of the time dangerous or threatening situations present themselves in facets; they will be apprehended through a feeling of fear or of anguish according to whether we envisage the situation as acting on the man or the man as acting on the situation. The man who has just received a hard blow—for example, losing a great part of his wealth in a crash—can have the fear of threatening poverty. He will experience anguish a moment later when nervously wringing his hands (a symbolic reaction to the action which is imposed but which remains still wholly undetermined), he exclaims to himself: "What am I going to do? But what am I going to do?" In this sense fear and anguish are exclusive of one another since fear is unreflective apprehension of the transcendent and anguish is reflective apprehension of the self; the one is born in the destruction of the other. The normal process in the case which I have just cited is a constant transition from the one to the other. But there exist also situations where anguish appears pure; that is, without ever being preceded or followed by fear. If, for example, I have been raised to a new dignity and charged with a delicate and flattering mission, I can feel anguish at the thought that I will not be capable perhaps of fulfilling it, and yet I will not have the least fear in the world of the consequences of my possible failure.

What is the meaning of anguish in the various examples which I have just given? Let us take up again the example of vertigo. Vertigo announces itself through fear; I am on a narrow path—without a guard-rail—which goes along a precipice. The precipice presents itself to me as *to be avoided*; it represents a danger of death. At the same time I conceive of a certain number of causes, originating in universal determinism, which can transform that threat of death into reality; I can slip on a stone and fall into the abyss; the crumbling earth of the path can give way under my steps. Through these various anticipations, I am given to myself as a thing; I am passive in relation to these possibilities; they come to me from without; in so far as I am also an object in the world, subject to gravitation, they are my possibilities. At this moment *fear* appears, which in terms of the situation is the apprehension of myself as a destructible transcendent in the midst of transcendents, as an object which does not contain in itself the origin of its future disappearance. My reaction will be of the reflective order; I will pay attention to the stones in the road; I will keep myself as far as possible from the edge of the path. I realize myself as pushing away the threatening situation with all my strength, and I project before myself a certain number of future conducts destined to keep the threats of the world at a distance from me. These conducts are my possibilities. I escape fear by the very fact that I am placing myself on a plane where my *own* possibilities are substituted for the transcendent probabilities where human action had no place.

But these conducts, precisely because they are *my* possibilities, do not appear to me as determined by foreign causes. Not only is it not strictly certain that they will be effective; in particular it is not strictly certain that they will be adopted, for they do not have existence sufficient in itself. We could say, varying the expression of Berkeley, that their "being is a sustained-being" and that their "possibility of being is only an ought-to-be-sustained." Due to this fact their possibility has as a necessary condition the possibility of negative conduct (*not* to pay attention to the stones in the road, to run, to think of something else) and the possibility of the opposite conduct (to throw myself over the precipice). The possibility which I make *my* concrete possibility can appear as *my* possibility only by raising itself on the basis of the totality of the logical possibilities which the situation allows. But these rejected possibles in turn have no other being than their "sustained-being;" it is I who sustains them in being, and inversely, their present non-being is an "ought-not-to-be-sustained." No external cause will remove them. I alone am the permanent source of their non-being, I engage myself in them; in order to cause *my* possibility to appear, I posit the other possibilities so as to nihilate them. This would not produce anguish if I could apprehend myself in my relations with these possibles as a cause producing its effects. In this case the effect defined as my possibility *would be strictly* determined. But then it would cease to be *possible;* it would become simply "about-to-happen." If then I wished to avoid anguish and vertigo, it would be enough if I were to consider the motives (instinct of self-preservation, prior fear, *etc.*), which make me reject the situation envisaged, as *determining* my prior activity in the same way that the presence at a determined point of one given mass determines the courses followed by other masses; it would be necessary, in other words, that I apprehend in myself a strict psychological determinism. But I am in anguish precisely because any conduct on my part is only *possible*, and this means that while constituting a totality of motives *for* pushing away that situation, I at the same moment apprehend these motives as not sufficiently effective. At the very moment when I apprehend my being as *horror* of the precipice, I am conscious of that horror as *not determinant* in relation to my possible conduct. In one sense that horror calls for prudent conduct, and it is in itself a pre-outline of that conduct; in another sense, it posits the final developments of that conduct only as possible, precisely because I do not apprehend it as the *cause* of these final developments but as need, appeal, *etc.*

Now as we have seen, consciousness of being is the being of consciousness. There is no question here of a contemplation which I could make after the event, of a horror already constituted; it is the very being of horror to appear to itself as "not being the cause" of the conduct it calls for. In short, to avoid fear, which reveals to me a transcendent future strictly determined, I take refuge in reflection, but the latter has only an undetermined future to offer. This means that in establishing a certain conduct as a possibility and precisely because it is *my* possibility, I am aware that *nothing* can compel me to adopt that conduct. Yet I am indeed already there in the future; it is for the sake of that being which I will be there at the turning of the path that I now exert all my strength, and in this sense there is already a relation between my future being and my present being. But a nothingness has slipped into the heart of this relation; I *am* not the self which I will be. First I am not that self because time separates me from it. Secondly, I am not that self because what I am is not the foundation of what I will be. Finally I am not that self because no actual existent can determine strictly what I am going to be. Yet as I am already what I will be (otherwise I would not be interested in any one being more than another), *I am the self which I will be, in the mode of not being it.* It is through my horror that I am carried toward the future, and the horror nihilates itself in that it constitutes the future as possible. Anguish is precisely my consciousness of being my own future, in the mode of not-being. To be exact, the nihilation of horror as a *motive*, which has the effect of reinforcing horror as a *state*, has as its positive counterpart the appearance of other forms of conduct (in particular that which consists in throwing myself over the precipice) as *my* possible *possibilities*. If *nothing* compels me to save my life, *nothing* prevents me from precipitating myself into the abyss. The decisive conduct will emanate from a self which I am not yet. Thus the self which I am depends on the self which I am not yet to the exact extent that the self which I am not yet does not depend on the self which I am. Vertigo appears as the apprehension of this dependence. I approach the precipice, and my scrutiny is searching for myself in my very depths. In terms of this moment, I play with my possibilities. My eyes, running over the abyss from top to bottom, imitate the possible fall and realize it symbolically; at the same time suicide, from the fact that it becomes a *possibility* possible for *me*, now causes to appear possible motives for adopting it (suicide would cause anguish to cease). Fortunately these motives in their turn, from the sole fact that they are motives of a possibility, present themselves as ineffective, as non-determinant; they can no more *produce* the suicide than my horror of the fall can *determine* me to avoid it. It is this counter-anguish which generally puts an end to anguish by transmuting it into indecision. Indecision in its turn, calls for decision. I abruptly put myself at a distance from the edge of the precipice and resume my way.

The example which we have just analyzed has shown us what we could call "anguish in the face of the future." There exists another: anguish in the face of the past. It is that of the gambler who has freely and sincerely decided not to gamble any more and who when he approaches the gaming table, suddenly sees all his resolutions melt away. This phenomenon has often been described as if the sight of the gaming table reawakened in us a tendency which entered into conflict with our former resolution and ended by drawing us in spite of this. Aside from the fact that such a description is done in materialistic terms and peoples the mind with opposing forces (there is, for example, the moralists' famous "struggle of reason with the passions"), it does not account for the facts. In reality—the letters of Dostoevsky bear witness to this—there is nothing in us which resembles an inner *debate* as if we had to weigh motives and incentives before deciding. The earlier resolution of "not playing anymore" is always *there*, and in the majority of cases the gambler when in the presence of the gaming table turns toward it as if to ask it for help; for he does not wish to play, or rather having taken his resolution the day before, he thinks of himself still as not wishing to play anymore; he believes in the effectiveness of this resolution. But what he apprehends then in anguish is precisely the total inefficacy of the past resolution. It is there doubtless but fixed, ineffectual, surpassed by the very fact that I am conscious *of* it. The resolution is still *me* to the extent that I realize constantly my identity with myself across the temporal flux, but it is no longer *me*—due to the fact that it has become an object *for* my consciousness. I am not subject to it, it fails in the mission which I have given it. The resolution is there still, I *am* it in the mode of not-being. What the gambler apprehends at this instant is again the permanent rupture in determinism; it is nothingness which separates him from himself; I should have liked so much not to gamble anymore; yesterday I even had a synthetic apprehension of the situation (threatening ruin, disappointment of my relatives) as *forbidding me* to play. It seemed to me that I had established a *real barrier* between gambling and myself, and now I suddenly perceive that my former understanding of the situation is no more than a memory of an idea, a memory of a feeling. In order for it to come to my aid once more, I must remake it *ex nihilo* and freely. The not-gambling is only one of my possibilities, as the fact of gambling is another of them, neither more nor less. I *must rediscover* the fear of financial ruin or of disappointing my family, *etc.*, I must re-create it as experienced fear. It stands behind me like a boneless phantom. It depends on me alone to lend it flesh. I am alone and naked before temptation as I was the day before. After having patiently built up barriers and walls after enclosing myself in the magic circle of a resolution, I perceive with anguish that *nothing* prevents me from gambling. The anguish *is me* since by the very fact of taking my position in existence as consciousness of being, I make myself *not to be* the past of good resolutions *which I am.*

It would be in vain to object that the sole condition of this anguish is ignorance of the underlying psychological determinism. According to such a view my anxiety would come from lack of knowing the real and effective incentives which in the darkness of the unconscious determine my action. In reply we shall point out first that anguish has not appeared to us as a *proof* of human freedom; the latter was given to us as the necessary condition for the question. We wished only to show that there exists a specific consciousness of freedom, and we wished to show that this consciousness is anguish. This means that we wished to establish anguish in its essential structure as consciousness of freedom. Now from this point of view the existence of a psychological determinism could not invalidate the results of our description. Either indeed anguish is actually an unrealized ignorance of this determinism—and then anguish apprehends itself in fact as freedom—or else one may claim that anguish is consciousness of being ignorant of the real causes of our acts. In the latter case anguish would come from that of which we have a presentiment, a screen deep within ourselves for monstrous motives which would suddenly release guilty acts. But in this case we should suddenly appear to ourselves as *things in the world*; we should be to ourselves our own transcendent situation. Then anguish would disappear to give away to *fear*, for fear is a synthetic apprehension of the transcendent as dreadful.

This freedom which reveals itself to us in anguish can be characterized by the existence of that *nothing* which insinuates itself between motives and act. It is not *because* I am free that my act is not subject to the determination of motives; on the contrary, the structure of motives as ineffective is the condition of my freedom. If someone asks what this *nothing* is which provides a foundation for freedom, we shall reply that we can not describe it since it *is* not, but we can at least hint at its meaning by saying that this nothing is made-to-be by the human being in his relation with himself. The nothing here corresponds to the necessity for the motive to appear as motive only as a correlate of a consciousness of motive. In short, as soon as we abandon the hypothesis of the contents of consciousness, we must recognize that there is never a motive *in* consciousness; motives are only *for* consciousness. And due to the very fact that the motive can arise only as appearance, it constitutes itself as ineffective. Of course it does not have the externality of a temporal-spatial thing; it always belongs to subjectivity and it is apprehended as *mine*. But it is by nature transcendence in immanence, and consciousness is not subject to it because of the very fact that consciousness posits it; for consciousness has now the task of conferring on the motive its meaning and its importance. Thus the *nothing* which separates the motive from consciousness characterizes itself as transcendence in immanence. It is by arising as immanence that consciousness nihilates the nothing which makes consciousness exist for itself as transcendence. But we see that the nothingness which is the condition of all transcendent negation can be elucidated only in terms of two other original nihilations: (1) Consciousness *is not* its own motive inasmuch as it is *empty* of all content. This refers us to a nihilating structure of the pre-reflective *cogito*. (2) Consciousness confronts its past and its future as facing a self which it is in the mode of not-being. This refers us to a nihilating structure of temporality.

There can be for us as yet no question of elucidating these two types of nihilation; we do not at the moment have the necessary techniques at our disposal. It is sufficient to observe here that the definitive explanation of negation can not be given without a description of self-consciousness and of temporality.

What we should note at present is that freedom, which manifests itself through anguish, is characterized by a constantly renewed obligation to remake the *Self* which designates the free being. As a matter of fact when we showed earlier that my possibilities were filled with anguish because it depended on *me* alone to sustain them in their existence, that did not mean that they derived from a *Me* which to itself at least, would first be given and would then pass in the temporal flux from one consciousness to another consciousness. The gambler who must realize anew the synthetic apperception of a *situation* which would forbid him to play, must rediscover at the same time the *self* which can appreciate that situation, which "is in situation." This *self* with its *a priori* and historical content is the *essence* of man. Anguish as the manifestation of freedom in the face of self means that man is always separated by a nothingness from his essence. We should refer here to Hegel's statement: "*Wesen ist was gewesen ist.*" Essence is what has been. Essence is everything in the human being which we can indicate by the words—that *is*. Due to this fact it is the totality of characteristics which *explain* the act. But the act is always beyond that essence; it is a human act only in so far as it surpasses every explanation which we can give of it, precisely because the very application of the formula "that is" to man causes all that is designated, *to have-been*. Man continually carries with him a pre-judicative comprehension of his essence, but due to this very fact he is separated from it by a nothingness. Essence is all that human reality apprehends in itself as *having been*. It is here that anguish appears as an apprehension of self inasmuch as it exists in the perpetual mode of detachment from what is; better yet, in so far as it makes itself exist as such. For we can never apprehend an *Erlebnis* as a living consequence of that *nature* which is ours. The overflow of our consciousness progressively constitutes that nature, but it remains always behind us and it dwells in us as the permanent object of our retrospective comprehension. It is in so far as this nature is a demand without being a recourse that it is apprehended in anguish.

In anguish freedom is anguished before itself inasmuch

as it is instigated and bound by nothing. Someone will say, freedom has just been defined as a permanent structure of the human being; if anguish manifests it, then anguish ought to be a permanent state of my affectivity. But, on the contrary, it is completely exceptional. How can we explain the rarity of the phenomenon of anguish?

We must note first of all that the most common situations of our life, those in which we apprehend our possibilities as such by means of actively realizing them, do not manifest themselves to us through anguish because their very structure excludes anguished apprehension. Anguish in fact is the recognition of a possibility as *my* possibility; that is, it is constituted when consciousness sees itself cut from its essence by nothingness or separated from the future by its very freedom. This means that a nihilating nothing removes from me all excuse and that at the same time what I project as my future being is always nihilated and reduced to the rank of simple possibility because the future which I am remains out of my reach. But we ought to remark that in these various instances we have to do with a temporal form where I await myself in the future, where I "make an appointment with myself on the other side of that hour, of that day, or of that month." Anguish is the fear of not finding myself at that appointment, of no longer even wishing to bring myself there. But I can also find myself engaged in acts which reveal my possibilities to me at the very instant when they are realized. In lighting this cigarette I learn my concrete possibility, or if you prefer, my desire of smoking. It is by the very act of drawing toward me this paper and this pen that I give to myself as my most immediate possibility the act of working at this book; there I am engaged, and I discover it at the very moment when I am already throwing myself into it. At that instant, to be sure, it remains my possibility, since I can at each instant turn myself away from my work, push away the notebook, put the cap on my fountain pen. But this possibility of interrupting the action is rejected on a second level by the fact that the action which discovers itself to me through my act tends to crystallize as a transcendent, relatively independent form. The consciousness of man *in action* is non-reflective consciousness. It is consciousness *of* something, and the transcendent which discloses itself to this consciousness is of a particular nature; it is a *structure of exigency* in the world, and the world correlatively discloses in it complex relations of instrumentality. In the act of tracing the letters which I am writing, the whole sentence, still unachieved, is revealed as a passive exigency to be written. It is the very meaning of the letters which I form, and its appeal is not put into question, precisely because I can not write the words without transcending them toward the sentence and because I discover it as the necessary condition for the meaning of the words which I am writing. At the same time in the very framework of the act an indicative complex of instruments reveals itself and organizes itself (pen-ink-paper-lines-margin, *etc.*), a complex which can not be apprehended for itself but which rises in the heart of the transcendence which discloses to me as a passive exigency the sentence to be written. Thus in the quasi-generality of everyday acts, I am engaged, I have ventured, and I discover my possibilities by realizing them and in the very act of realizing them as exigencies, urgencies, instrumentalities.

Of course in every act of this kind, there remains the possibility of putting this act into question—in so far as it refers to more distant, more essential ends—as to its ultimate meanings and my essential possibilities. For example, the sentence which I write is the meaning of the letters which I trace, but the whole work which I wish to produce is the meaning of the sentence. And this work is a possibility in connection with which I can feel anguish; it is truly my possibility, and I do not know whether I will continue it tomorrow; tomorrow in relation to it my freedom can exercise its nihilating power. But that anguish implies the apprehension of the work as such as *my* possibility. I must place myself directly opposite it and realize my relation to it. This means that I ought not only to raise with reference to it objective questions such as, "Is it necessary to write this work?" for these questions refer me simply to wider objective significations, such as, "Is it opportune to write it *at this moment? Isn't* this just a repetition of another such book? Is its material of sufficient interest? Has it been sufficiently thought through?" *etc.*—all significations which remain transcendent and give themselves as a multitude of exigencies in the world.

In order for my freedom to be anguished in connection with the book which I am writing, this book must appear in its relation with me. On the one hand, I must discover my essence as *what I have been*—I have been "wanting to write this book," I have conceived it, I have believed that it would be interesting to write it, and I have constituted myself in such a way that it is not possible to *understand me* without taking into account the fact that this book *has been* my essential possibility. On the other hand, I must discover the nothingness which separates my freedom from this essence: *I have been* "wanting to write," but *nothing*, not even what I have been, can compel me to write it. Finally, I must discover the nothingness which separates me from what I shall be: I discover that the permanent possibility of abandoning the book is the very condition of the possibility of writing it and the very meaning of my freedom. It is necessary that in the very constitution of the book as my possibility,

I apprehend my freedom as being the possible destroyer in the present and in the future of what I am. That is, I must place myself on the plane of reflection. So long as I remain on the plane of action, the book to be written is only the distant and presupposed meaning of the act which reveals my possibilities to me. The book is only the implication of the action; it is not made an object and posited for itself; it does not "raise the question"; it is conceived neither as necessary nor contingent. It is only the permanent, remote meaning in terms of which I can understand what I am writing in the present, and hence, it is conceived as *being;* that is, only by positing the book as *the existing basis* on which my present, existing sentence emerges, can I confer a determined meaning upon my sentence.

Now at each instant we are thrust into the world and engaged there. This means that we act before positing our possibilities and that these possibilities which are disclosed as realized or in process of being realized refer to meanings which necessitate special acts in order to be put into question. The alarm which rings in the morning refers to the possibility of my going to work, which is *my* possibility. But to apprehend the summons of the alarm as a summons is to get up. Therefore the very act of getting up is reassuring, for it eludes the question, Is work my possibility? Consequently it does not put me in a position to apprehend the possibility of quietism, of refusing to work, and finally the possibility of refusing the world and the possibility of death. In short, to the extent that I apprehend the meaning of the ringing, I am already up at its summons; this apprehension guarantees me against the anguished intuition that it is I who confer on the alarm clock its exigency—I and I alone.

In the same way, what we might call everyday morality is exclusive of ethical anguish. There is ethical anguish when I consider myself in my original relation to values. Values in actuality are demands which lay claim to a foundation. But this foundation can in no way be *being*, for every value which would base its ideal nature on its being would thereby cease even to be a value and would realize the heteronomy of my will. Value derives its being from its exigency and not its exigency from its being. It does not deliver itself to a contemplative intuition which would apprehend it as *being* value and thereby would remove from it its right over my freedom. On the contrary, it can be revealed only to an active freedom which makes it exist as value by the sole fact of recognizing it as such. It follows that my freedom is the unique foundation of values and that *nothing*, absolutely nothing, justifies me in adopting this or that particular value, this or that particular scale of values. As a being by whom values exist, I am unjustifiable. My freedom is anguished at being the foundation of values while itself without foundation. It is anguished in addition because values, due to the fact that they are essentially revealed to a freedom, can not disclose themselves without being at the same time "put into question," for the possibility of overturning the scale of values appears complementarily as *my* possibility. It is anguish before values which is the recognition of the ideality of values.

Ordinarily, however, my attitude with respect to values is eminently reassuring. In fact I am engaged in a world of values. The anguished apperception of values as sustained in being by my freedom is a secondary and mediated phenomenon. The immediate is the world with its urgency; and in this world where I engage myself, my acts cause values to spring up like partridges. My indignation has given to me the negative value "baseness," my admiration has given the positive value "grandeur." Above all my obedience to a multitude of tabus, which is real, reveals these tabus to me as existing in fact. The bourgeois who call themselves "respectable citizens" do not become respectable as the result of contemplating moral values. Rather from the moment of their arising in the world they are thrown into a pattern of behavior the meaning of which is respectability. Thus respectability acquires a being; it is not put into question. Values are sown on my path as thousands of little real demands, like the signs which order us to keep off the grass.

Thus in what we shall call the world of the immediate, which delivers itself to our unreflective consciousness, we do not first appear to ourselves to be thrown subsequently into enterprises. Our being is immediately "in situation"; that is, it arises in enterprises and knows itself first in so far as it is reflected in those enterprises. We discover ourselves then in a world peopled with demands, in the heart of projects "in the course of realization." I write. I am going to smoke. I have an appointment this evening with Pierre. I must not forget to reply to Simon. I do not have the right to conceal the truth any longer from Claude. All these trivial passive expectations of the real, all these commonplace, everyday values, derive their meaning from an original projection of myself which stands as my choice of myself in the world. But to be exact, this projection of myself toward an original possibility, which causes the existence of values, appeals, expectations, and in general a world, appears to me only beyond the world as the meaning and the abstract, logical signification of my enterprises. For the rest, there exist concretely alarm clocks, signboards, tax forms, policemen, so many guard rails against anguish. But as soon as the enterprise is held at a distance from me, as soon as I am referred to myself because I must await myself in the future, then I discover myself suddenly as the one who gives its meaning to the alarm clock, the one who by a signboard forbids himself to walk on a flower bed or on the lawn, the one from whom the boss's order borrows its urgency, the one who decides the interest of the book which he is writing, the one finally who makes the values exist in order to determine his action by their demands. I emerge alone and in anguish confronting the unique and original project which constitutes my being; all the barriers, all the guard rails collapse, nihilated by the consciousness of my freedom. I do not have nor can I have recourse to any value against the fact that it is I who sustain values in being. Nothing can ensure me against myself, cut off from the world and from my essence by this nothingness which I *am*. I have to realize the meaning of the world and of my essence; I make my decision concerning them—without justification and without excuse.

Anguish then is the reflective apprehension of freedom by itself. In this sense it is mediation, for although it is immediate consciousness of itself, it arises from the negation of the appeals of the world. It appears at the moment that I disengage myself from the world where I had been engaged—in order to apprehend myself as a consciousness which possesses a pre-ontological comprehension of its essence and a pre-judicative sense of its possibilities. Anguish is opposed to the mind of the serious man who apprehends values in terms of the world and who resides in the reassuring, materialistic substantiation of values. In the serious mood I define myself in terms of the object by pushing aside *a priori* as impossible all enterprises in which I am not engaged at the moment; the meaning which my freedom has given to the world, I apprehend as coming from the world and constituting my obligations. In anguish I apprehend myself at once as totally free and as not being able to derive the meaning of the world except as coming from myself.

We should not however conclude that being brought on to the reflective plane and envisaging one's distant or immediate possibilities suffice to apprehend oneself in *pure* anguish. In each instance of reflection anguish is born as a structure of the reflective consciousness in so far as the latter considers consciousness as an object of reflection; but it still remains possible for me to maintain various types of conduct with respect to my own anguish—in particular, patterns of flight. Everything takes place, in fact, as if our essential and immediate behavior with respect to anguish is flight. Psychological determinism, before being a theoretical conception, is first an attitude of excuse, or if you prefer, the basis of all attitudes of excuse. It is reflective conduct with respect to anguish; it asserts that there are within us antagonistic forces whose type of existence is comparable to that of things. It attempts to fill the void which encircles us, to re-establish the links between past and present, between present and future. It provides us with a *nature* productive of our acts, and these very acts it makes transcendent; it assigns to them a foundation in something other than themselves by endowing them with an inertia and externality eminently reassuring because they constitute a permanent game of *excuses*. Psychological determinism denies that transcendence of human reality which makes it emerge in anguish beyond its own essence. At the same time by reducing us to *never being anything but what we are*, it reintroduces in us the absolute positivity of being-in-itself and thereby reinstates us at the heart of being.

But this determinism, a reflective defense against anguish, is not given as a reflective *intuition*. It avails nothing against the *evidence* of freedom; hence it is given as a faith to take refuge in, as the ideal end toward which we can flee to escape anguish. That is made evident on the philosophical plane by the fact that deterministic psychologists do not claim to found their thesis on the pure givens of introspection. They present it as a satisfying hypothesis, the value of which comes from the fact that it accounts for the facts—or as a necessary postulate for establishing all psychology. They admit the existence of an immediate consciousness of freedom, which their opponents hold up against them under the name of "proof by intuition of the inner sense." They merely focus the debate on the *value* of this inner revelation. Thus the intuition which causes us to apprehend ourselves as the original cause of our states and our acts has been discussed by nobody. It is within the reach of each of us to try to mediate anguish by rising above it and by *judging* it as an illusion due to the mistaken belief that we are the real causes of our acts. The problem which presents itself then is that of the degree of faith in this mediation. Is an anguish placed under judgment a disarmed anguish? Evidently not. However here a new phenomenon is born, a process of "distraction" in relation to anguish which, once again, supposes within it a nihilating power.

By itself determinism would not suffice to establish distraction since determinism is only a postulate or an hypothesis. This process of detachment is a more complete activity of flight which operates on the very level of reflection. It is first an attempt at distraction in relation to the possibles opposed to *my* possible. When I constitute myself as the comprehension of a possible as *my* possible, I must recognize its existence at the end of my project and apprehend it as myself, awaiting me down there in the future and separated from me by a nothingness. In this sense I apprehend myself as the original source of my possibility, and it is this which ordinarily we call the consciousness of freedom. It is this structure of consciousness and this alone that the proponents of free-will have in mind when they speak of the intuition of the inner sense. But it happens that I force myself at the same time to *be distracted* from the constitution of other possibilities which contradict my possibility. In truth I can not avoid positing their existence by the same movement which generates the chosen possibility as mine. I cannot help constituting them as *living* possibilities; that is, *as having the possibility of becoming my possibilities*. But I force myself to see them as endowed with a transcendent, purely logical being, in short, as things. If on the reflective plane I envisage the possibility of writing this book as *my* possibility, then between this possibility and my consciousness I cause a nothingness of being to arise which constitutes the writing of the book as a possibility and which I apprehend precisely in the permanent possibility that the possibility of not writing the book is *my* possibility. But I attempt to place myself on the other side of the possibility of not writing it as I might do with respect to an observable object, and I let myself be penetrated with what I wish to see there; I try to apprehend the possibility of not writing as needing to be mentioned merely as a reminder, as not concerning me. It must be an external possibility in relation to me, like movement in relation to the motionless billiard ball. If I could succeed in this, the possibilities hostile to *my* possibility would be constituted as logical entities and would lose their effectiveness. They would no longer be threatening since they would be "outsiders," since they would surround my possible as purely *conceivable* eventualities; that is, fundamentally, conceivable *by* another or as *possibles of another who might find himself in the same situation*. They would belong to the objective situation as a transcendent structure, or if you prefer (to utilize Heidegger's terminology)—*I* shall write this book but *someone* could also not write it. Thus I should hide from myself the fact that the possibles are *myself* and that they are immanent conditions of the possibility of my possible. They would preserve just enough being to preserve for my possible its character as gratuitous, as a free possibility for a free being, but they would be disarmed of their threatening character. They would not *interest* me; the chosen possible would appear—due to its selection—as my only concrete possible, and consequently the nothingness which separates me from it and which actually confers on it its possibility would collapse.

But flight before anguish is not only an effort at distraction before the future; it attempts also to disarm the past of its threat. What I attempt to flee here is my very transcendence in so far as it sustains and surpasses my essence. I assert that I *am* my essence in the mode of being of the in-itself. At the same time I always refuse to consider that essence as being historically constituted and as implying my action as a circle implies its properties. I apprehend it, or at least I try to apprehend it as the original beginning of my possible, and I do not admit at all that it has in itself a beginning. I assert then that an act is free when it exactly reflects my essence. However this freedom which would disturb me if it were freedom before myself, I attempt to bring back to the heart of my essence—*i.e.*, of my self. It is a matter of envisaging the self as a little God which inhabits me and which possesses my freedom as a metaphysical virtue. It would be no longer my being which would be free *qua* being but my Self which would be free in the heart of my consciousness. It is a fiction eminently reassuring since freedom has been driven down into the heart of an opaque being; to the extent that my essence is not translucency, that it is transcendent in immanence, freedom would become one of its properties. In short, it is a matter of apprehending my freedom in my self as the freedom of another. We see the principal themes of this fiction: My self becomes the origin of its acts as the other of his, by virtue of a personality already constituted. To be sure, he (the self) lives and transforms himself; we will admit even that each of his acts can contribute to transforming him. But these harmonious, continued transformations are conceived on a biological order. They resemble those which I can establish in my friend Pierre when I see him after a separation. Bergson expressly satisfied these demands for reassurance when he conceived his theory of the profound self which endures and organizes itself, which is constantly contemporary with the consciousness which I have of it and which can not be surpassed by consciousness, which is found at the origin of my acts not as a cataclysmic power but as a father begets his children, in such a way that the act without following from the essence as a strict consequence, without even being foreseeable, enters into a reassuring relation with it, a family resemblance. The act goes farther than the self but along the same road; it preserves, to be sure, a certain irreducibility, but we recognize ourselves in it, and we find ourselves in it as a father can recognize himself and find himself in the son who continues his work. Thus by a projection of freedom—which we apprehend in ourselves—into a psychic object which is the self, Bergson has contributed to disguise our anguish, but it is at the expense of consciousness itself. What he has established and described in this manner is not our freedom as it appears to itself; *it is the freedom of the Other.*

Such then is the totality of processes by which we try to hide anguish from ourselves; we apprehend our particular possible by avoiding considering all other possibles, which we make the possibles of an undifferentiated Other. The chosen possible we do not wish to see as sustained in being by a pure nihilating freedom, and so we attempt to apprehend it as engendered by an object already constituted, which is no other than our self, envisaged and described as if it were another person. We should like to preserve from the original intuition what it reveals to us as our independence and our responsibility but we tone down all the original nihilation in it; moreover we are always ready to take refuge in a belief in determinism if this freedom weighs upon us or if we need an excuse. Thus we flee from anguish by attempting to apprehend ourselves from without as an Other or as *a thing*. What we are accustomed to call a revelation of the inner sense or an original intuition of our freedom contains nothing original; it is an already constructed process, expressly designed to hide from ourselves anguish, the veritable "immediate given" of our freedom.

Do these various constructions succeed in stifling or hiding our anguish? It is certain that we can not overcome anguish, for we *are* anguish. As for veiling it, aside from the fact that the very nature of consciousness and its translucency forbid us to take the expression literally, we must note the particular type of behavior which it indicates. We can hide an external object because it exists independently of us. For the same reason we can turn our look or our attention away from it—that is, very simply, fix our eyes on some other object; henceforth each reality—mine and that of the object—resumes its own life, and the accidental relation which united consciousness to the thing disappears without thereby altering either existence. But if I *am* what I wish to veil, the question takes on quite another aspect. I can in fact wish "not to see" a certain aspect of my being only if I am acquainted with the aspect which I do not wish to see. This means that in my being I must indicate this aspect in order to be able to turn myself away from it; better yet, I must think of it constantly in order to take care not to think of it. In this connection it must be understood not only that I must of necessity perpetually carry within me what I wish to flee but also that I must aim at the object of my flight in order to flee it. This means that anguish, the intentional aim of anguish, and a flight from anguish toward reassuring myths must all be given in the unity of the same consciousness. In a word, I flee in order not to know, but I can not avoid knowing that I am fleeing; and the flight from anguish is only a mode of becoming conscious of anguish. Thus anguish, properly speaking, can be neither hidden nor avoided.

Yet to flee anguish and to be anguish can not be exactly the same thing. If I am my anguish in order to flee it, that presupposes that I can decenter myself in relation to what I am, that I can be anguish in the form of "not-being it," that I can dispose of a nihilating power at the heart of anguish itself. This nihilating power nihilates anguish in so far as I flee it and nihilates itself in so far as *I am anguish in order to flee it.* This attitude is what we call *bad faith.* There is then no question of expelling anguish from consciousness nor of constituting it in an unconscious psychic phenomenon; very simply I can make myself guilty of bad faith while apprehending the anguish which I am, and this bad faith, intended to fill up the nothingness which I *am* in my relation to myself, precisely implies the nothingness which it suppresses.

We are now at the end of our first description. The examination of the negation can not lead us farther. It has revealed to us the existence of a particular type of conduct: conduct in the face of non-being, which supposes a special transcendence needing separate study. We find ourselves then in the presence of two human ekstases: the ekstasis which throws us into being-in-itself and the ekstasis which engages us in non-being. It seems that our original problem, which concerned only the relations of man to being, is now considerably complicated. But in pushing our analysis of transcendence toward non-being to its conclusion, it is possible for us to get valuable information for the understanding of *all* transcendence. Furthermore the problem of nothingness can not be excluded from our inquiry. If man adopts any particular behavior in the face of being-in-itself—and our philosophical question is a type of such behavior—it is because he *is not* this being. We rediscover non-being as a condition of the transcendence toward being. We must then catch hold of the problem of nothingness and not let it go before its complete elucidation.

However the examination of the question and of the negation has given us all that it can. We have been referred by it to empirical freedom as the nihilation of man in the heart of temporality and as the necessary condition for the transcending apprehension of *négatités*. It remains to found this empirical freedom. It can not be both the original nihilation and the ground of all nihilation. Actually it contributes to constituting transcendences in immanence which condition all negative transcendences. But the very fact that the transcendences of empirical freedom are constituted in immanence as *transcendences* shows us that we are dealing with secondary nihilations which suppose the existence of an original nothingness. They are only a stage in the analytical regression which leads us from the examples of transcendence called "négatités" to the being which is its own nothingness. Evidently it is necessary to find the foundation of all negation in a nihilation which is exercised in *the very heart of immanence*; in absolute immanence, in the pure subjectivity of the instantaneous *cogito* we must discover the original act by which man is to himself his own nothingness. What must be the nature of consciousness in order that man in consciousness and in terms of consciousness should arise in the world as the being who is his own nothingness and by whom nothingness comes into the world?

We seem to lack here the instrument to permit us to resolve this new problem; negation directly engages only freedom. We must find in freedom itself the conduct which will permit us to push further. Now this conduct, which will lead us to the threshold of immanence and which remains still sufficiently objective so that we can objectively disengage its conditions of possibility—this we have already encountered. Have we not remarked earlier that in bad faith, we are-anguish-in-order-to-flee-anguish within the unity of a single consciousness? If bad faith is to be possible, we should be able within the same consciousness to meet with the unity of being and non-being—the being-in-order-not-to-be. Bad faith is going to be the next object of our investigation. For man to be able to question, he must be capable of being his own nothingness; that is, he can be at the origin of non-being in being only if his being—in himself and by himself—is paralyzed with nothingness. Thus the transcendences of past and future appear in the temporal being of human reality. But bad faith is instantaneous. What then are we to say that consciousness must be in the instantaneity of the pre-reflective *cogito*—if the human being is to be capable of bad faith?

BAD FAITH

1. BAD FAITH AND FALSEHOOD

The human being is not only the being by whom *négatités* are disclosed in the world; he is also the one who can take negative attitudes with respect to himself. In our Introduction we defined consciousness as "a being such that in its being, its being is in question in so far as this being implies a being other than itself." But now that we have examined the meaning of "the question," we can at present also write the formula thus: "Consciousness is a being, the nature of which is to be conscious of the nothingness of its being." In a prohibition or a veto, for example, the human being denies a future transcendence. But this negation is not explicative. My consciousness is not restricted to *envisioning* a *négatité*. It constitutes itself in its own flesh as the nihilation of a possibility which another human reality projects as *its* possibility. For that reason it must arise in the world as a *Not*; it is as a Not that the slave first apprehends the master, or that the prisoner who is trying to escape sees the guard who is watching him. There are even men (*e.g.*, caretakers, overseers, gaolers,) whose social reality is uniquely that of the Not, who will live and die, having forever been only a Not upon the earth. Others so as to make the Not a part of their very subjectivity, establish their human personality as a perpetual negation. This is the meaning and function of what Scheler calls "the man of resentment"—in reality, the Not. But there exist more subtle behaviors, the description of which will lead us further into the inwardness of consciousness. Irony is one of these. In irony a man annihilates what he posits within one and the same act; he leads us to believe in order not to be believed; he affirms to deny and denies to affirm; he creates a positive object but it has no being other than its nothingness. Thus attitudes of negation toward the self permit us to raise a new question: What are we to say is the being of man who has the possibility of denying himself? But it is out of the question to discuss the attitude of "self-negation" in its universality. The kinds of behavior which can be ranked under this heading are too diverse; we risk retaining only the abstract form of them. It is best to choose and to examine one determined attitude which is essential to human reality and which is such that consciousness instead of directing its negation outward turns it toward itself. This attitude, it seems to me, is *bad faith (mauvaise foi).*

Frequently this is identified with falsehood. We say indifferently of a person that he shows signs of bad faith or that he lies to himself. We shall willingly grant that bad faith is a lie to oneself, on condition that we distinguish the lie to oneself from lying in general. Lying is a negative attitude, we will agree to that. But this negation does not bear on consciousness itself; it aims only at the transcendent. The essence of the lie implies in fact that the liar actually is in complete possession of the truth which he is hiding. A man does not lie about what he is ignorant of; he does not lie when he spreads an error of which he himself is the dupe; he does not lie when he is mistaken. The ideal description of the liar would be a cynical conscious-ness, affirming truth within himself, denying it in his words, and denying that negation as such. Now this doubly nega-tive attitude rests on the transcendent; the fact expressed is transcendent since it does not exist, and the original negation rests on a *truth;* that is, on a particular type of transcendence. As for the inner negation which I effect correlatively with the affirmation for myself of the truth, this rests on *words;* that is, on an event in the world. Furthermore the inner disposition of the liar is positive; it could be the object of an affirmative judgment. The liar intends to deceive and he does not seek to hide this intention from himself nor to disguise the trans-lucency of consciousness; on the contrary, he has recourse to it when there is a question of deciding secondary behavior. It explicitly exercises a regulatory control over all attitudes. As for his flaunted intention of telling the truth ("I'd never want to deceive you! This is true! I swear it!")—all this, of course, is the object of an inner negation, but also it is not recognized by the liar as *his* intention. It is played, imitated, it is the intention of the character which he plays in the eyes of his questioner, but this character, precisely because he *does not exist,* is a transcen-dent. Thus the lie does not put into the play the inner structure of present consciousness; all the negations which constitute it bear on objects which by this fact are removed from con-sciousness. The lie then does not require special ontological foundation, and the explanations which the existence of nega-tion in general requires are valid without change in the case of deceit. Of course we have described the ideal lie; doubtless it happens often enough that the liar is more or less the victim of his lie, that he half persuades himself of it. But these common, popular forms of the lie are also degenerate aspects of it; they represent intermediaries between falsehood and bad faith. The lie is a behavior of transcendence.

The lie is also a normal phenomenon of what Heidegger calls the "*Mit-sein.*"* It presupposes my existence, the existence of the *Other*, my existence *for* the Other, and the existence of the Other *for* me. Thus there is no difficulty in holding that the liar must make the project of the lie in entire clarity and that he must possess a complete comprehension of the lie and of the truth which he is altering. It is sufficient that an over-all opacity hide his intentions from the *Other*; it is sufficient that the Other can take the lie for truth. By the lie consciousness affirms that it exists by nature as *hidden from the Other*; it utilizes for its own profit the ontological duality of myself and myself in the eyes of the Other.

The situation can not be the same for bad faith if this, as we have said, is indeed a lie to oneself. To be sure, the one who practices bad faith is hiding a displeasing truth or presenting as truth a pleasing untruth. Bad faith then has in appearance the structure of falsehood. Only what changes everything is the fact that in bad faith it is from myself that I am hiding the truth. Thus the duality of the deceiver and the deceived does not exist here. Bad faith on the contrary implies in essence the unity of a *single* consciousness. This does not mean that it can not be conditioned by the *Mit-sein* like all other phenomena of human reality, but the *Mit-sein* can call forth bad faith only by presenting itself as *a situation* which bad faith permits surpassing; bad faith does not come from outside to human reality. One does not undergo his bad faith; one is not infected

---

* A "being-with" others in the world. Tr.

with it; it is not a *state*. But consciousness affects itself with bad faith. There must be an original intention and a project of bad faith; this project implies a comprehension of bad faith as such and a pre-reflective apprehension (of) consciousness as affecting itself with bad faith. It follows first that the one to whom the lie is told and the one who lies are one and the same person, which means that I must know in my capacity as deceiver the truth which is hidden from me in my capacity as the one deceived. Better yet I must know the truth very exactly *in order* to conceal it more carefully—and this not at two different moments, which at a pinch would allow us to reestablish a semblance of duality—but in the unitary structure of a single project. How then can the lie subsist if the duality which conditions it is suppressed?

To this difficulty is added another which is derived from the total translucency of consciousness. That which affects itself with bad faith must be conscious (of) its bad faith since the being of consciousness is consciousness of being. It appears then that I must be in good faith, at least to the extent that I am conscious of my bad faith. But then this whole psychic system is annihilated. We must agree in fact that if I deliberately and cynically attempt to lie to myself, I fail completely in this undertaking; the lie falls back and collapses beneath my look; it is ruined *from behind* by the very consciousness of lying to myself which pitilessly constitutes itself well within my project as its very condition. We have here an *evanescent* phenomenon which exists only in and through its own differentiation. To be sure, these phenomena are frequent and we shall see that there is in fact an "evanescence" of bad faith, which, it is evident, vacillates continually between good faith and cynicism: Even though the existence of bad faith is very precarious, and though it belongs to the kind of psychic structures which we might call "metastable,"* it presents nonetheless an autonomous and durable form. It can even be the normal aspect of life for a very great number of people. A person can *live* in bad faith, which does not mean that he does not have abrupt awakenings to cynicism or to good faith, but which implies a constant and particular style of life. Our embarrassment then appears extreme since we can neither reject nor comprehend bad faith.

To escape from these difficulties people gladly have recourse to the unconscious. In the psychoanalytic interpretation, for example, they use the hypothesis of a censor, conceived as a line of demarcation with customs, passport division, currency control, *etc.*, to reestablish the duality of the deceiver and the deceived. Here instinct or, if you prefer, original drives and complexes of drives constituted by our individual history, make up *reality*. It is neither *true* nor *false* since it does not *exist for itself*. It simply *is*, exactly like this table, which is neither true nor false *in itself* but simply *real*. As for the conscious symbols of the instinct, this interpretation takes them not for appearances but for real psychic facts. Fear, forgetting, dreams exist really in the capacity of concrete facts of consciousness in the same way as the words and the attitudes of the liar are concrete, really existing patterns of behavior. The subject has the same relation to these phenomena as the deceived to the behavior of the deceiver. He establishes them in their reality and must interpret them. There is a *truth* in the activities of the deceiver; if the deceived could reattach them to the situation where the deceiver establishes himself and to his project of the lie, they would become integral parts of truth, by

---

* Sartre's own word, meaning subject to sudden changes or transitions. Tr.

virtue of being lying conduct. Similarly there is a truth in the symbolic acts; it is what the psychoanalyst discovers when he reattaches them to the historical situation of the patient, to the unconscious complexes which they express, to the blocking of the censor. Thus the subject deceives himself about the *meaning* of his conduct, he apprehends it in its concrete existence but not in its *truth*, simply because he cannot derive it from an original situation and from a psychic constitution which remain alien to him.

By the distinction between the "id" and the "ego," Freud has cut the psychic whole into two. I am the ego but I *am not* the id. I hold no privileged position in relation to my unconscious psyche. I *am* my own psychic phenomena in so far as I establish them in their conscious reality. For example I am the impulse to steal this or that book from this bookstall. I am an integral part of the impulse; I bring it to light and I determine myself hand-in-hand with it to commit the theft. But I *am* not those psychic facts, in so far as I receive them passively and am obliged to resort to hypotheses about their origin and their true meaning, just as the scholar makes conjectures about the nature and essence of an external phenomenon. This theft, for example, which I interpret as an immediate impulse determined by the rarity, the interest, or the price of the volume which I am going to steal—it is in truth a process derived from self-punishment, which is attached more or less directly to an Oedipus complex. The impulse toward the theft contains a truth which can be reached only by more or less probable hypotheses. The criterion of this truth will be the number of conscious psychic facts which it explains; from a more pragmatic point of view it will be also the success of the psychiatric cure which it allows. Finally the discovery of this truth will necessitate the cooperation of the psychoanalyst, who appears as the *mediator* between my unconscious drives and my conscious life. The Other appears as being able to effect the synthesis between the unconscious thesis and the conscious antithesis. I can know myself only through the mediation of the other, which means that I stand in relation to my "id," in the position of the *Other*. If I have a little knowledge of psychoanalysis, I can, under circumstances particularly favorable, try to psychoanalyze myself. But this attempt can succeed only if I distrust every kind of intuition, only if I apply to my case *from the outside*, abstract schemes and rules already learned. As for the results, whether they are obtained by my efforts alone or with the cooperation of a technician, they will never have the certainty which intuition confers; they will possess simply the always increasing probability of scientific hypotheses. The hypothesis of the Oedipus complex, like the atomic theory, is nothing but an "experimental idea"; as Pierce said, it is not to be distinguished from the totality of experiences which it allows to be realized and the results which it enables us to foresee. Thus psychoanalysis substitutes for the notion of bad faith, the idea of a lie without a liar; it allows me to understand how it is possible for me to be lied to without lying to myself since it places me in the same relation to myself that the Other is in respect to me; it replaces the duality of the deceiver and the deceived, the essential condition of the lie, by that of the "id" and the "ego." It introduces into my subjectivity the deepest inter-subjective structure of the *Mit-sein*. Can this explanation satisfy us?

Considered more closely the psychoanalytic theory is not as simple as it first appears. It is not accurate to hold that the "id" is presented as a thing in relation to the hypothesis of the psychoanalyst, for a thing is indifferent to the conjectures which we make concerning it, while the "id" on the contrary is sensitive to them when we approach the truth. Freud in fact reports resistance when at the end of the first period the doctor is approaching the truth. This resistance is objective behavior apprehended from without: the patient shows defiance, refuses to speak, gives fantastic accounts of his dreams, sometimes even removes himself completely from the psychoanalytic treatment. It is a fair question to ask what part of himself can thus resist. It can not be the "Ego," envisaged as a psychic totality of the facts of consciousness; this could not suspect that the psychiatrist is approaching the end since the ego's relation to the *meaning* of its own reactions is exactly like that of the psychiatrist himself. At the very most it is possible for the ego to appreciate objectively the degree of probability in the hypotheses set forth, as a witness of the psychoanalysis might be able to do, according to the number of subjective facts which they explain. Furthermore, this probability would appear to the ego to border on certainty, which he could not take offense at since most of the time it is he who by a *conscious* decision is in pursuit of the psychoanalytic therapy. Are we to say that the patient is disturbed by the daily revelations which the psychoanalyst makes to him and that he seeks to remove himself, at the same time pretending in his own eyes to wish to continue the treatment? In this case it is no longer possible to resort to the unconscious to explain bad faith; it is there in full consciousness, with all its contradictions. But this is not the way that the psychoanalyst means to explain this resistance; for him it is secret and deep, it comes from afar; it has its roots in the very thing which the psychoanalyst is trying to make clear.

Furthermore it is equally impossible to explain the resistance as emanating from the complex which the psychoanalyst wishes to bring to light. The complex as such is rather the collaborator of the psychoanalyst since it aims at expressing itself in clear consciousness, since it plays tricks on the censor and seeks to elude it. The only level on which we can locate the refusal of the subject is that of the censor. It alone can comprehend the questions or the revelations of the psychoanalyst as approaching more or less near to the real drives which it strives to repress—it alone because it alone *knows* what it is repressing.

If we reject the language and the materialistic mythology of psychoanalysis, we perceive that the censor in order to apply its activity with discernment must know what it is repressing. In fact if we abandon all the metaphors representing the repression as the impact of blind forces, we are compelled to admit that the censor must choose and in order to choose must be aware of so doing. How could it happen otherwise that the censor allows lawful sexual impulses to pass through, that it permits needs (hunger, thirst, sleep) to be expressed in clear consciousness? And how are we to explain that it can relax its surveillance, that it can even be deceived by the disguises of the instinct? But it is not sufficient that it discern the condemned drives; it must also apprehend them *as to be repressed*, which implies in it at the very least an awareness of its activity. In a word, how could the censor discern the impulses needing to be repressed without being conscious of discerning them? How can we conceive of a knowledge which is ignorant of itself? To know is to know that one knows, said Alain. Let us say rather: All knowing is consciousness of knowing. Thus the resistance of the patient implies on the level of the censor an awareness of the thing repressed as such, a comprehension of the end toward which the questions of the psychoanalyst are leading, and an act of synthetic connection by which it compares the *truth* of the repressed complex to the psychoanalytic hypothesis which aims at it. These various operations in their turn imply that the censor is conscious (of) itself. But what type of self-consciousness can the censor have? It must be the consciousness (of) being conscious of the drive to be repressed, but precisely *in order not be conscious of it*. What does this mean if not that the censor is in bad faith?

Psychoanalysis has not gained anything for us since in order to overcome bad faith, it has established between the unconscious and consciousness an autonomous consciousness in bad faith. The effort to establish a veritable duality and even a trinity (*Es, Ich, Ueberich* expressing themselves through the censor) has resulted in a mere verbal terminology. The very essence of the reflexive idea of hiding something from oneself implies the unity of one and the same psychic mechanism and consequently a double activity in the heart of unity, tending on the one hand to maintain and locate the thing to be concealed and on the other hand to repress and disguise it. Each of the two aspects of this activity is complementary to the other; that is, it implies the other in its being. By separating consciousness from the unconscious by means of the censor, psychoanalysis has not succeeded in dissociating the two phases of the act, since the libido is a blind conatus toward conscious expression and since the conscious phenomenon is a passive, faked result. Psychoanalysis has merely localized this double activity of repulsion and attraction on the level of the censor.

Furthermore the problem still remains of accounting for the unity of the total phenomenon (repression of the drive which disguises itself and "passes" in symbolic form), to establish comprehensible connections among its different phases. How can the repressed drive "disguise itself" if it does not include (1) the consciousness of being repressed, (2) the consciousness of having been pushed back becauseit is what it is, (3) a project of disguise? No mechanistic theory of condensation or of transference can explain these modifications by which the drive itself is affected, for the description of the process of disguise implies a veiled appeal to finality. And similarly how are we to account for the pleasure or the anguish which accompanies the symbolic and conscious satisfaction of the drive if consciousness does not include—beyond the censor—an obscure comprehension of the end to be attained as simultaneously desired and forbidden. By rejecting the conscious unity of the psyche, Freud is obliged to imply everywhere a magic unity linking distant phenomena across obstacles, just as sympathetic magic unites the spellbound person and the wax image fashioned in his likeness. The unconscious drive (*Trieb*) through magic is endowed with the character "repressed" or "condemned," which completely pervades it, colors it, and magically provokes its symbolism. Similarly the conscious phenomenon is entirely colored by its symbolic meaning although it can not apprehend this meaning by itself in clear consciousness.

Aside from its inferiority in principle, the explanation by magic does not avoid the coexistence—on the level of the unconscious, on that of the censor, and on that of consciousness—of two contradictory, complementary structures which reciprocally imply and destroy each other. Proponents of the theory have hypostasized and "reified" bad faith; they have not escaped it. This is what has inspired a Viennese psychiatrist, Stekel, to depart from the psychoanalytical tradition and to write in *La femme frigide*:* "Every time that I have been able to carry my investigations far enough, I have established that the crux of the psychosis was conscious." In addition the cases which he reports in his work bear witness to a pathological

---

* N.R.F

bad faith which the Freudian doctrine can not account for. There is the question, for example, of women whom marital infidelity has made frigid; that is, they succeed in hiding from themselves not complexes deeply sunk in half psychological darkness, but acts of conduct which are objectively discoverable, which they can not fail to record at the moment when they perform them. Frequently in fact the husband reveals to Stekel that his wife has given objective signs of pleasure, but the woman when questioned will fiercely deny them. Here we find a pattern of *distraction*. Admissions which Stekel was able to draw out inform us that these pathologically frigid women apply themselves to becoming distracted in advance from the pleasure which they dread; many for example at the time of the sexual act, turn their thoughts away toward their daily occupations, make up their household accounts. Will anyone speak of an unconscious here? Yet if the frigid woman thus distracts her consciousness from the pleasure which she experiences, it is by no means cynically and in full agreement with herself; *it is in order to prove to herself* that she is frigid. We have in fact to deal with a phenomenon of bad faith since the efforts taken in order not to be present to the experienced pleasure imply the recognition that the pleasure is experienced; they imply it *in order to deny it*. But we are no longer on the ground of psychoanalysis. Thus on the one hand the explanation by means of the unconscious, due to the fact that it breaks the psychic unity, can not account for the facts which at first sight it appeared to explain. And on the other hand, there exists an infinity of types of behavior in bad faith which explicitly reject this kind of explanation because their essence implies that they can appear only in the translucency of consciousness. We find that the problem which we had attempted to resolve is still untouched.

2. PATTERNS OF BAD FAITH

If we wish to get out of this difficulty, we should examine more closely the patterns of bad faith and attempt a description of them. This description will permit us perhaps to fix more exactly the conditions for the possibility of bad faith; that is, to reply to the question we raised at the outset: "What must be the being of man if he is to be capable of bad faith?"

Take the example of a woman who has consented to go out with a particular man for the first time. She knows very well the intentions which the man who is speaking to her cherishes regarding her. She knows also that it will be necessary sooner or later for her to make a decision. But she does not want to realize the urgency; she concerns herself only with what is respectful and discreet in the attitude of her companion. She does not apprehend this conduct as an attempt to achieve what we call "the first approach"; that is, she does not want to see possibilities of temporal development which his conduct presents. She restricts this behavior to what is in the present; she does not wish to read in the phrases which he addresses to her anything other than their explicit meaning. If he says to her, "I find you so attractive"! she disarms this phrase of its sexual background; she attaches to the conversation and to the behavior of the speaker, the immediate meanings, which she imagines as objective qualities. The man who is speaking to her appears to her sincere and respectful as the table is round or square, as the wall coloring is blue or gray. The qualities thus attached to the person she is listening to are in this way fixed in a permanence like that of things, which is no other than the projection of the strict present of the qualities into the temporal flux. This is because she does not quite know what she wants. She is profoundly aware of the desire which she inspires, but the desire cruel and naked would humiliate and horrify her. Yet she would find no charm in a respect which would be only respect. In order to satisfy her, there must be a feeling which is addressed wholly to her *personality—i.e.*, to her full freedom—and which would be a recognition of her freedom. But at the same time this feeling must be wholly desire; that is, it must address itself to her body as object. This time then she refuses to apprehend the desire for what it is; she does not even give it a name; she recognizes it only to the extent that it transcends itself toward admiration, esteem, respect and that it is wholly absorbed in the more refined forms which it produces, to the extent of no longer figuring anymore as a sort of warmth and density. But then suppose he takes her hand. This act of her companion risks changing the situation by calling for an immediate decision. To leave the hand there is to consent in herself to flirt, to engage herself. To withdraw it is to break the troubled and unstable harmony which gives the hour its charm. The aim is to postpone the moment of decision as long as possible. We know what happens next; the young woman leaves her hand there, but she *does not notice* that she is leaving it. She does not notice because it happens by chance that she is at this moment all intellect. She draws her companion up to the most lofty regions of sentimental speculation; she speaks of Life, of her life, she shows herself in her essential aspect—a personality, a consciousness. And during this time the divorce of the body from the soul is accomplished; the hand rests inert between the warm hands of her companion—neither consenting nor resisting—a thing.

We shall say that this woman is in bad faith. But we see immediately that she uses various procedures in order to maintain herself in this bad faith. She has disarmed the actions of her companion by reducing them to being only what they are; that is, to existing in the mode of the in-itself. But she permits herself to enjoy his desire, to the extent that she will apprehend it as not being what it is, will recognize its transcendence. Finally while sensing profoundly the presence of her own body—to the degree of being disturbed perhaps—she realizes herself as *not being* her own body, and she contemplates it as though from above as a passive object to which events can *happen* but which can neither provoke them nor avoid them because all its possibilities are outside of it. What unity do we find in these various aspects of bad faith? It is a certain art of forming contradictory concepts which unite in themselves both an idea and the negation of that idea. The basic concept which is thus engendered, utilizes the double property of the human being, who is at once a *facticity* and a *transcendence*. These two aspects of human reality are and ought to be capable of a valid coordination. But bad faith does not wish either to coordinate them nor to surmount them in a synthesis. Bad faith seeks to affirm their identity while preserving their differences. It must affirm facticity as *being* transcendence and transcendence as *being* facticity, in such a way that at the instant when a person apprehends the one, he can find himself abruptly faced with the other.

We can find the prototype of formulae of bad faith in certain famous expressions which have been rightly conceived to produce their whole effect in a spirit of bad faith. Take for example the title of a work by Jacques Chardonne, *Love Is Much More than Love*.* We see here how unity is established between *present* love in its facticity—"the contact of two skins," sensuality, egoism, Proust's mechanism of jealousy, Adler's battle of the *sexes, etc.*—and love as transcendence—Mauriac's "river of

---

* *L'amour, c'est beaucoup plus que l'amour.*

fire," the longing for the infinite, Plato's *eros*, Lawrence's deep cosmic intuition, *etc.* Here we leave facticity to find ourselves suddenly beyond the present and the factual condition of man, beyond the psychological, in the heart of metaphysics. On the other hand, the title of a play by Sarment, *I Am Too Great for Myself,** which also presents characters in bad faith, throws us first into full transcendence in order suddenly to imprison us within the narrow limits of our factual essence. We will discover this structure again in the famous sentence: "He has become what he was" or in its no less famous opposite: "Eternity at last changes each man into himself."† It is well understood that these various formulae have only the appearance of bad faith; they have been conceived in this paradoxical form explicitly to shock the mind and discountenance it by an enigma. But it is precisely this appearance which is of concern to us. What counts here is that the formulae do not constitute new, solidly structured ideas; on the contrary, they are formed so as to remain in perpetual disintegration and so that we may slide at any time from naturalistic present to transcendence and *vice versa*.

We can see the use which bad faith can make of these judgments which all aim at establishing that I am not what I am. If I were only what I *am*, I could, for example, seriously consider an adverse criticism which someone makes of me, question myself scrupulously, and perhaps be compelled to recognize the truth in it. But thanks to transcendence, I am not subject to all that I am. I do not even have to discuss the justice of the reproach. As Suzanne says to Figaro, "To prove that I am right would be to recognize that I can be wrong." I am on a

---

* *Je suis trop grand pour moi.*

† *Il est devenu ce qu'il était. Tel qu'en lui-même enfin l'éternité le change.*

plane where no reproach can touch me since what I really am is my transcendence. I flee from myself, I escape myself, I leave my tattered garment in the hands of the fault-finder. But the ambiguity necessary for bad faith comes from the fact that I affirm here that I *am* my transcendence in the mode of being of a thing. It is only thus, in fact, that I can feel that I escape all reproaches. It is in the sense that our young woman purifies the desire of anything humiliating by being willing to consider it only as pure transcendence, which she avoids even naming. But inversely "I Am Too Great for Myself," while showing our transcendence changed into facticity, is the source of an infinity of excuses for our failures or our weaknesses. Similarly the young coquette maintains transcendence to the extent that the respect, the esteem manifested by the actions of her admirer are already on the plane of the transcendent. But she arrests this transcendence, she glues it down with all the facticity of the present; respect is nothing other than respect, it is an arrested surpassing which no longer surpasses itself toward anything.

But although this *metastable* concept of "transcendence-facticity" is one of the most basic instruments of bad faith, it is not the only one of its kind. We can equally well use another kind of duplicity derived from human reality which we will express roughly by saying that its being-for-itself implies complementarily a being-for-others. Upon any one of my conducts it is always possible to converge two looks, mine and that of the Other. The conduct will not present exactly the same structure in each case. But as we shall see later, as each look perceives it, there is between these two aspects of my being, no difference between appearance and being—as if I were to my self the truth of myself and as if the Other possessed only a deformed image of me. The equal dignity of being, possessed by my being-for-others and by my being-for-myself permits a perpetually disintegrating synthesis and a perpetual game of escape from the for-itself to the for-others and from the for-others to the for-itself. We have seen also the use which our young lady made of our being-in-the-midst-of-the-world—*i.e.*, of our inert presence as a passive object among other objects—in order to relieve herself suddenly from the functions of her being-in-the-world—that is, from the being which causes there to be a world by projecting itself beyond the world toward its own possibilities. Let us note finally the confusing syntheses which play on the nihilating ambiguity of these temporal ekstases, affirming at once that I am what I have been (the man who deliberately *arrests himself* at one period in his life and refuses to take into consideration the later changes) and that I am not what I have been (the man who in the face of reproaches or rancor dissociates himself from his past by insisting on his freedom and on his perpetual re-creation). In all these concepts, which have only a transitive role in the reasoning and which are eliminated from the conclusion (like hypochondriacs in the calculations of physicians), we find again the same structure. We have to deal with human reality as a being which is what it is not and which is not what it is.

But what exactly is necessary in order for these concepts of disintegration to be able to receive even a pretense of existence, in order for them to be able to appear for an instant to consciousness, even in a process of evanescence? A quick examination of the idea of sincerity, the antithesis of bad faith, will be very instructive in this connection. Actually sincerity presents itself as a demand and consequently is not a *state*. Now what is the ideal to be attained in this case? It is necessary that a man be *for himself* only what he *is*. But is this not precisely the definition of the in-itself—or if you prefer—the principle of identity? To posit as an ideal the being of things; is this not to assert by the same stroke that this being does not belong to human reality and that the principle of identity, far from being a universal axiom universally applied, is only a synthetic principle enjoying a merely regional universality? Thus in order that the concepts of bad faith can put us under illusion at least for an instant, in order that the candor of "pure hearts" (*cf.* Gide, Kessel) can have validity for human reality as an ideal, the principle of identity must not represent a constitutive principle of human reality and human reality must not be necessarily what it is but must be able to be what it is not. What does this mean?

If man is what he is, bad faith is for ever impossible and candor ceases to be his idea and becomes instead his being. But is man what he is? And more generally, how can he *be* what he is when he exists as consciousness of being? If candor or sincerity is a universal value, it is evident that the maxim "one must be what one is" does not serve solely as a regulating principle for judgments and concepts by which I express what I am. It posits not merely an ideal of knowing but an idea of *being*; it proposes for us an absolute equivalence of being with itself as a prototype of being. In this sense it is necessary that we *make ourselves* what we are. But what *are we* then if we have the constant obligation to make ourselves what we are, if our mode of being is having the obligation to be what we are?

Let us consider this waiter in the café. His movement is quick and forward, a little too precise, a little too rapid. He comes toward the patrons with a step a little too quick. He bends forward a little too eagerly; his voice, his eyes express an interest a little too solicitous for the order of the customer. Finally there he returns, trying to imitate in his walk the inflexible stiffness of some kind of automaton while carrying his tray with the recklessness of a tight-rope-walker by putting it in a perpetually unstable, perpetually broken equilibrium which he perpetually reestablishes by a light movement of the arm and hand. All his behavior seems to us a game. He applies himself to chaining his movements as if they were mechanisms, the one regulating the other; his gestures and even his voice seem to be mechanisms; he gives himself the quickness and pitiless rapidity of things. He is playing, he is amusing himself. But what is he playing? We need not watch long before we can explain it: he is playing *at being* a waiter in a café. There is nothing there to surprise us. The game is a kind of marking out and investigation. The child plays with his body in order to explore it, to take inventory of it; the waiter in the café plays with his condition in order to *realize* it. This obligation is not different from that which is imposed on all tradesmen. Their condition is wholly one of ceremony. The public demands of them that they realize it as a ceremony; there is the dance of the grocer, of the tailor, of the auctioneer, by which they endeavor to persuade their clientele that they are nothing but a grocer, an auctioneer, a tailor. A grocer who dreams is offensive to the buyer, because such a grocer is not wholly a grocer. Society demands that he limit himself to his function as a grocer, just as the soldier at attention makes himself into a soldier-thing with a direct regard which does not see at all, which is no longer meant to see, since it is the rule and not the interest of the moment which determines the point he must fix his eyes on (the sight "fixed at ten paces"). There are indeed many precautions to imprison a man in what he is, as if we lived in perpetual fear that he might escape from it, that he might break away and suddenly elude his condition.

In a parallel situation, from within, the waiter in the café can not be immediately a café waiter in the sense that this ink-well *is* an inkwell, or the glass is a glass. It is by no means that he can not form reflective judgments or concepts concerning his condition. He knows well what it "means:" the obligation of getting up at five o'clock, of sweeping the floor of the shop before the restaurant opens, of starting the coffee pot going, *etc.* He knows the rights which it allows: the right to the tips, the right to belong to a union, etc. But all these concepts, all these judgments refer to the transcendent. It is a matter of abstract possibilities, of rights and duties conferred on a "person possessing rights." And it is precisely this person *who I have to be* (if I am the waiter in question) and who I am not. It is not that I do not wish to be this person or that I want this person to be different. But rather there is no common measure between his being and mine. It is a "representation" for others and for myself, which means that I can be he only in *representation*. But if I represent myself as him, I am not he; I am separated from him as the object from the subject, separated *by nothing*, but this nothing isolates me from him. I can not be he, I can only play *at being* him; that is, imagine to myself that I am he. And thereby I affect him with nothingness. In vain do I fulfill the functions of a café waiter. I can be he only in the neutralized mode, as the actor is Hamlet, by mechanically making the *typical gestures* of my state and by aiming at myself as an imaginary café waiter through those gestures taken as an "analogue."* What I attempt to realize is a being-in-itself of the café waiter, as if it were not just in my power to confer their value and their urgency upon my duties and the rights of my position, as if it were not my free choice to get up each morning at five o'clock or to remain in bed, even though it

---

* Cf. *L'Imaginaire*. Conclusion.

meant getting fired. As if from the very fact that I sustain this role in existence I did not transcend it on every side, as if I did not constitute myself as one *beyond* my condition. Yet there is no doubt that I *am* in a sense a café waiter—otherwise could I not just as well call myself a diplomat or a reporter? But if I am one, this can not be in the mode of being in-itself. I am a waiter in the mode of *being what I am not.*

Furthermore we are dealing with more than mere social positions; I am never any one of my attitudes, any one of my actions. The good speaker is the one who *plays* at speaking, because he can not *be speaking.* The attentive pupil who wishes to *be* attentive, his eyes riveted on the teacher, his ears open wide, so exhausts himself in playing the attentive role that he ends up by no longer hearing anything. Perpetually absent to my body, to my acts, I am despite myself that "divine absence" of which Valéry speaks. I can not say either that I *am* here or that I *am* not here, in the sense that we say "that box of matches *is* on the table"; this would be to confuse my "being-in-the-world" with a "being-in-the-midst-of-the-world." Nor that I *am* standing, nor that I *am* seated; this would be to confuse my body with the idiosyncratic totality of which it is only one of the structures. On all sides I escape being and yet—I am.

But take a mode of being which concerns only myself: I am sad. One might think that surely I am the sadness in the mode of being what I am. What is the sadness, however, if not the intentional unity which comes to reassemble and animate the totality of my conduct? It is the meaning of this dull look with which I view the world, of my bowed shoulders, of my lowered head, of the listlessness in my whole body. But at the very moment when I adopt each of these attitudes, do I not know that I shall not be able to hold on to it? Let a stranger suddenly appear and I will lift up my head, I will assume a lively cheerfulness. What will remain of my sadness except that I oblig-ingly promise it an appointment for later after the departure of the visitor? Moreover is not this sadness itself a *conduct*? Is it not consciousness which affects itself with sadness as a magi-cal recourse against a situation too urgent?'* And in this case even, should we not say that being sad means first to make oneself sad? That may be, someone will say, but after all doesn't giving oneself the being of sadness mean to *receive* this being? It makes no difference from where I receive it. The fact is that a consciousness which affects itself with sadness *is* sad precisely for this reason. But it is difficult to comprehend the nature of consciousness; the being-sad is not a ready-made being which I give to myself as I can give this book to my friend. I do not possess the property of *affecting myself with being*. If I make myself sad, I must continue to make myself sad from begin-ning to end. I can not treat my sadness as an impulse finally achieved and put it on file without recreating it, nor can I carry it in the manner of an inert body which continues its move-ment after the initial shock. There is no inertia in conscious-ness. If I make myself sad, it is because I *am* not sad—the being of the sadness escapes me by and in the very act by which I affect myself with it. The being-in-itself of sadness perpetually haunts my consciousness (of) being sad, but it is as a value which I can not realize; it stands as a regulative meaning of my sadness, not as its constitutive modality.

Someone may say that my consciousness at least *is*, what-ever may be the object or the state of which it makes itself consciousness. But how do we distinguish my consciousness (of) being sad from sadness? Is it not all one? It is true in a

---

* *Esquisse d'une théorie des émotions.* Hermann Paul. In English. *The Emotions. Out-line of a Theory.* Philosophical Library. 1948.

way that my consciousness *is*, if one means by this that for another it is a part of the totality of being on which judgments can be brought to bear. But it should be noted, as Husserl clearly understood, that my consciousness appears originally to the Other as an absence. It is the object always present as the *meaning* of all my attitudes and all my conduct—and always absent, for it gives itself to the intuition of another as a perpetual question—still better, as a perpetual freedom. When Pierre looks at me, I know of course that he is looking at me. His eyes, things in the world, are fixed on my body, a thing in the world—that is the objective fact of which I can say: it *is*. But it is also a fact *in the world*. The meaning of this look is not a fact in the world, and this is what makes me uncomfortable. Although I make smiles, promises, threats, nothing can get hold of the approbation, the free judgment which I seek; I know that it is always beyond. I sense it in my very attitude, which is no longer like that of the worker toward the things he uses as instruments. My reactions, to the extent that I project myself toward the Other, are no longer for myself but are rather mere *presentations;* they await being constituted as graceful or uncouth, sincere or insincere, *etc.*, by an apprehension which is always beyond my efforts to provoke, an apprehension which will be provoked by my efforts only if of itself it lends them force (that is, only in so far as it causes itself to be provoked from the outside), *which is its own mediator with the transcendent.* Thus the objective fact of the being-in-itself of the consciousness of the Other is posited in order to disappear in negativity and in freedom: consciousness of the Other is as not-being; its being-in-itself "here and now" is not-to-be.

Consciousness of the Other is what it is not.

Furthermore the being of my own consciousness does not appear to me as the consciousness of the Other. It *is* because it makes itself, since its being is consciousness of being. But this means that making sustains being; consciousness has to be its own being, it is never sustained by being; it sustains being in the heart of subjectivity, which means once again that it is inhabited by being but that it is not being: *consciousness is not what it is.*

Under these conditions what can be the significance of the ideal of sincerity except as a task impossible to achieve, of which the very meaning is in contradiction with the structure of my consciousness. To be sincere, we said, is to be what one is. That supposes that I am not originally what I am. But here naturally Kant's "You ought, therefore you can" is implicitly understood. I can *become* sincere; this is what my duty and my effort to achieve sincerity imply. But we definitely establish that the original structure of "not being what one is" renders impossible in advance all movement toward being in itself or "being what one is." And this impossibility is not hidden from consciousness; on the contrary, it is the very stuff of consciousness; it is the embarrassing constraint which we constantly experience; it is our very incapacity to recognize ourselves, to constitute ourselves as being what we are. It is this necessity which means that, as soon as we posit ourselves as a certain being, by a legitimate judgment, based on inner experience or correctly deduced from *a priori* or empirical premises, then by that very positing we surpass this being—and that not toward another being but toward emptiness, toward *nothing*.

How then can we blame another for not being sincere or rejoice in our own sincerity since this sincerity appears to us at the same time to be impossible? How can we in conversation, in confession, in introspection, even attempt sincerity since the effort will by its very nature be doomed to failure and since at the very time when we announce it we have a prejudicative comprehension of its futility? In introspection I try to determine exactly what I am, to make up my mind to be my true self without delay—even though it means consequently to set about searching for ways to change myself. But what does this mean if not that I am constituting myself as a thing? Shall I determine the ensemble of purposes and motivations which have pushed me to do this or that action? But this is already to postulate a causal determinism which constitutes the flow of my states of consciousness as a succession of physical states. Shall I uncover in myself "drives," even though it be to affirm them in shame? But is this not deliberately to forget that these drives are realized with my consent, that they are not forces of nature but that I lend them their efficacy by a perpetually renewed decision concerning their value? Shall I pass judgment on my character, on my nature? Is this not to veil from myself at that moment what I know only too well, that I thus judge a past to which by definition my present is not subject? The proof of this is that the same man who in sincerity posits that he is what in actuality he was, is indignant at the reproach of another and tries to disarm it by asserting that he can no longer be what he was. We are readily astonished and upset when the penalties of the court affect a man who in his new freedom *is no longer* the guilty person he was. But at the same time we require of this man that he recognize himself as *being*this guilty one. What then is sincerity except precisely a phenomenon of bad faith? Have we not shown indeed that in bad faith human reality is constituted as a being which is what it is not and which is not what it is?

Let us take an example: A homosexual frequently has an intolerable feeling of guilt, and his whole existence is determined in relation to this feeling. One will readily foresee that he is in bad faith. In fact it frequently happens that this man, while recognizing his homosexual inclination, while avowing each and every particular misdeed which he has committed, refuses with all his strength to consider himself "*a paederast.*" His case is always "different," peculiar; there enters into it something of a game, of chance, of bad luck; the mistakes are all in the past; they are explained by a certain conception of the beautiful which women can not satisfy; we should see in them the results of a restless search, rather than the manifestations of a deeply rooted tendency, *etc., etc.* Here is assuredly a man in bad faith who borders on the comic since, acknowledging all the facts which are imputed to him, he refuses to draw from them the conclusion which they impose. His friend, who is the most severe critic, becomes irritated with this duplicity. The critic asks only one thing—and perhaps then he will show himself indulgent: that the guilty one recognize himself as guilty, that the homosexual declare frankly—whether humbly or boastfully matters little—"I am a paederast." We ask here: Who is in bad faith? The homosexual or the champion of sincerity?

The homosexual recognizes his faults, but he struggles with all his strength against the crushing view that his mistakes constitute for him a *destiny*. He does not wish to let himself be considered as a thing. He has an obscure but strong feeling that a homosexual is not a homosexual as this table is a table or as this red-haired man is red-haired. It seems to him that he has escaped from each mistake as soon as he has posited it and recognized it; he even feels that the psychic duration by itself cleanses him from each misdeed, constitutes for him an undetermined future, causes him to be born anew. Is he wrong? Does he not recognize in himself the peculiar, irreducible character of human reality? His attitude includes then an undeniable comprehension of truth. But at the same time he needs this perpetual rebirth, this constant escape in order to live; he must constantly put himself beyond reach in order to avoid the terrible judgment of collectivity. Thus he plays on the word *being*. He would be right actually if he understood the phrase, "I am not a paederast" in the sense of "I am not what I am." That is, if he declared to himself, "To the extent that a pattern of conduct is defined as the conduct of a paederast and to the extent that I have adopted this conduct, I am a paederast. But to the extent that human reality can not be finally defined by patterns of conduct, I am not one." But instead he slides surreptitiously towards a different connotation of the word "being." He understands "not being" in the sense of "not-being-in-itself." He lays claim to "not being a paederast" in the sense in which this table *is not* an inkwell. He is in bad faith.

But the champion of sincerity is not ignorant of the transcendence of human reality, and he knows how at need to appeal to it for his own advantage. He makes use of it even and brings it up in the present argument. Does he not wish, first in the name of sincerity, then of freedom, that the homosexual reflect on himself and acknowledge himself as a homosexual? Does he not let the other understand that such a confession will win indulgence for him? What does this mean if not that the man who will acknowledge himself as a homosexual will no longer be *the same* as the homosexual whom he acknowledges being and that he will escape into the region of freedom and of good will? The critic asks the man then to be what he is in order no longer to be what he is. It is the profound meaning of the saying, "A sin confessed is half pardoned." The critic demands of the guilty one that he constitute himself as a thing, precisely in order no longer to treat him as a thing. And this contradiction is constitutive of the demand of sincerity. Who can not see how offensive to the Other and how reassuring for me is a statement such as, "He's just a paederast," which removes a disturbing freedom from a trait and which aims at henceforth constituting all the acts of the Other as consequences following strictly from his essence. That is actually what the critic is demanding of his victim—that he constitute himself as a thing, that he should entrust his freedom to his friend as a fief, in order that the friend should return it to him subsequently—like a suzerain to his vassal. The champion of sincerity is in bad faith to the degree that in order to reassure himself, he pretends to judge, to the extent that he demands that freedom as freedom constitute itself as a thing. We have here only one episode in that battle to the death of consciousnesses which Hegel calls "the relation of the master and the slave." A person appeals to another and demands that in the name of his nature as consciousness he should radically destroy himself as consciousness, but while making this appeal he leads the other to hope for a rebirth beyond this destruction.

Very well, someone will say, but our man is abusing sincerity, playing one side against the other. We should not look for sincerity in the relation of the *Mit-sein* but rather where it is pure—in the relations of a person with himself. But who can not see that objective sincerity is constituted in the same way? Who can not see that the sincere man constitutes himself as a thing in order to escape the condition of a thing by the same act of sincerity? The man who confesses that he is evil has exchanged his disturbing "freedom-for-evil" for an inanimate character of evil; he *is* evil, he clings to himself, he is what he is. But by the same stroke, he escapes from that *thing*, since it is he who contemplates it, since it depends on him to maintain it under his glance or to let it collapse in an infinity of particular acts. He derives a *merit* from his sincerity, and the deserving man is not the evil man as he is evil but as he is beyond his evilness. At the same time the evil is disarmed since it is nothing, save on the plane of determinism, and since in confessing it, I posit my freedom in respect to it; my future is virgin; everything is allowed to me.

Thus the essential structure of sincerity does not differ from that of bad faith since the sincere man constitutes himself as what he is *in order not to be it*. This explains the truth recognized by all that one can fall into bad faith through being sincere. As Valéry pointed out, this is the case with Stendhal. Total, constant sincerity as a constant effort to adhere to oneself is by nature a constant effort to dissociate oneself from oneself. A person frees himself from himself by the very act by which he makes himself an object for himself. To draw up a perpetual inventory of what one is means constantly to redeny oneself and to take refuge in a sphere where one is no longer anything but a pure, free regard. The goal of bad faith, as we said, is to put oneself out of reach; it is an escape. Now we see that we must use the same terms to define sincerity. What does this mean?

In the final analysis the goal of sincerity and the goal of bad faith are not so different. To be sure, there is a sincerity which bears on the past and which does not concern us here; I am sincere if I confess *having had* this pleasure or that intention. We shall see that if this sincerity is possible, it is because in his fall into the past, the being of man is constituted as a being-in-itself. But here our concern is only with the sincerity which aims at itself in present immanence. What is its goal? To bring me to confess to myself what I am in order that I may finally coincide with my being; in a word, to cause myself to be, in the mode of the in-itself, what I am in the mode of "not being what I am." Its assumption is that fundamentally I am already, in the mode of the in-itself, what I have to be. Thus we find at the base of sincerity a continual game of mirror and reflection, a perpetual passage from the being which is what it is to the being which is not what it is and inversely from the being which is not what it is to the being which is what it is. And what is the goal of bad faith? To cause me to be what I am, in the mode of "not being what one is," or not to be what I am in the mode of "being what one is." We find the same game of mirrors. In fact in order for me to have an intention of sincerity, I must at the outset simultaneously be and not be what I am. Sincerity does not assign to me a mode of being or a particular quality, but in relation to that quality it aims at making me pass from one mode of being to another mode of being. This second mode of being, the ideal of sincerity, I am prevented by nature from attaining; and at the very moment when I struggle to attain it, I have a vague prejudicative comprehension that I shall not attain it. But all the same, in order for me to be able to conceive an intention in bad faith, I must have such a nature that within my being I escape from my being. If I were sad or cowardly in the way in which this inkwell is an inkwell, the possibility of bad faith could not even be conceived. Not only should I be unable to escape from my being; I could not even imagine that I could escape from it. But if bad faith is possible by virtue of a simple project, it is because so far as my being is concerned, there is no difference between being and non-being if I am cut off from my project.

Bad faith is possible only because sincerity is conscious of missing its goal inevitably, due to its very nature. I can try to apprehend myself as "*not being cowardly*," when I *am* so, only on condition that the "being cowardly" is itself "in question" at the very moment when it exists, on condition that it is itself *one* question, that at the very moment when I wish to apprehend it, it escapes me on all sides and annihilates itself. The condition under which I can attempt an effort in bad faith is that in one sense, I *am not* this coward which I do not wish to be. But if I were not cowardly in the simple mode of not-being-what-one-is-not, I would be "in good faith" by declaring that I am not cowardly. Thus this inapprehensible coward is evanescent; in order for me not to be cowardly, I must in some way also be cowardly. That does not mean that I must be "a little" cowardly, in the sense that "a little" signifies "to a certain degree cowardly—and not cowardly to a certain degree." No. I must at once both be and not be totally and in all respects a coward. Thus in this case bad faith requires that I should not be what I am; that is, that there be an imponderable difference separating being from non-being in the mode of being of human reality.

But bad faith is not restricted to denying the qualities which I possess, to not seeing the being which I am. It attempts also to constitute myself as being what I am not. It apprehends me positively as courageous when I am not so. And that is possible, once again, only if I am what I am not; that is, if non-being in me does not have being even as non-being. Of course necessarily I *am not* courageous; otherwise bad faith would not be *bad* faith. But in addition my effort in bad faith must include the ontological comprehension that even in my usual being what I *am*, I am not it really and that there is no such difference between the being of "being-sad," for example—which I *am* in the mode of not being what I am—and the "non-being" of not-being-courageous which I wish to hide from myself. Moreover it is particularly requisite that the very negation of being should be itself the object of a perpetual nihilation, that the very meaning of "non-being" be perpetually in question in human reality. If I *were not* courageous in the way in which this inkwell is not a table; that is, if I were isolated in my cowardice, propped firmly against it, incapable of putting it in relation to its opposite, if I were not capable of *determining* myself as cowardly—that is, to deny courage to myself and thereby to escape my cowardice in the very moment that I posit it—if it were not on principle *impossible* for me to coincide with my *not-being-courageous* as well as with my being-courageous-then any project of bad faith would be prohibited me. Thus in order for bad faith to be possible, sincerity itself must be in bad faith. The condition of the possibility for bad faith is that human reality, in its most immediate being, in the intrastructure of the pre-reflective *cogito*, must be what it is not and not be what it is.

3. THE "FAITH" OF BAD FAITH

We have indicated for the moment only those conditions which render bad faith conceivable, the structures of being which permit us to form concepts of bad faith. We can not limit ourselves to these considerations; we have not yet distinguished bad faith from falsehood. The two-faced concepts which we have described would without a doubt be utilized by a liar to discountenance his questioner, although their two-faced quality being established on the being of man and not on some empirical circumstance, can and ought to be evident to all. The true problem of bad faith stems evidently from the fact that bad faith is *faith*. It can not be either a cynical lie or certainty—if certainty is the intuitive possession of the object. But if we take belief as meaning the adherence of being to its object when the object is not given or is given indistinctly, then bad faith is belief; and the essential problem of bad faith is a problem of belief.

How can we believe by bad faith in the concepts which we forge expressly to persuade ourselves? We must note in fact that the project of bad faith must be itself in bad faith. I am not only in bad faith at the end of my effort when I have constructed my two-faced concepts and when I have persuaded myself. In truth, I have not persuaded myself; to the extent that I could be so persuaded, I have always been so. And at the very moment when I was disposed to put myself in bad faith, I of necessity was in bad faith with respect to this same disposition. For me to have represented it to myself as bad faith would have been cynicism; to believe it sincerely innocent would have been in good faith. The decision to be in bad faith does not dare to speak its name; it believes itself and does not believe itself in bad faith; it believes itself and does not believe itself in good faith. It is this which from the upsurge of bad faith, determines the later attitude and, as it were, the *Weltanschauung* of bad faith.

Bad faith does not hold the norms and criteria of truth as they are accepted by the critical thought of good faith. What it decides first, in fact, is the nature of truth. With bad faith appears a method of thinking, a type of being which is like that of objects; the ontological characteristic of the world of bad faith with which the subject suddenly surrounds himself is this: that here being is what it is not, and is not what it is. Consequently a peculiar type of evidence appears; *nonpersuasive* evidence. Bad faith apprehends evidence but it is resigned in advance to not being fulfilled by this evidence, to not being persuaded and transformed into good faith. It makes itself humble and modest; it is not ignorant, it says, that faith is decision and that after each intuition, it must decide and *will what it is*. Thus bad faith in its primitive project and in its coming into the world decides on the exact nature of its requirements. It stands forth in the firm resolution *not to demand too much*, to count itself satisfied when it is barely persuaded, to force itself in decisions to adhere to uncertain truths. This original project of bad faith is a decision in bad faith on the nature of faith. Let us understand clearly that there is no question of a reflective, voluntary decision, but of a spontaneous determination of our being. One *puts oneself* in bad faith as one goes to sleep and one is in bad faith as one dreams. Once this mode of being has been realized, it is as difficult to get out of it as to wake oneself up; bad faith is a type of being in the world, like waking or dreaming, which by itself tends to perpetuate itself, although its structure is of the *metastable* type. But bad faith is conscious of its structure, and it has taken precautions by deciding that the metastable structure is the structure of being and that non-persuasion is the structure of all convictions. It follows that if bad faith is faith and if it includes in its original project its own negation (it determines itself to be not quite convinced in order to convince itself that I am what I am not), then to start with, a faith which wishes itself to be not quite convinced must be possible. What are the conditions for the possibility of such a faith?

I believe that my friend Pierre feels friendship for me. I believe it *in good faith*. I believe it but I do not have for it any self-evident intuition, for the nature of the object does not lend itself to intuition. I *believe it*; that is, I allow myself to give in to all impulses to trust it; I decide to believe in it, and to maintain myself in this decision; I conduct myself, finally, as if I were certain of it—and all this in the synthetic unity of one and the same attitude. This which I define as good faith is what Hegel would call the *immediate*. It is simple faith. Hegel would demonstrate at once that the immediate calls for mediation and that belief by becoming *belief for itself,* passes to the state of non-belief. If I *believe* that my friend Pierre likes me, this means that his friendship appears to me as the meaning of all his acts. Belief is a particular consciousness of *the meaning* of Pierre's acts. But if I know that I believe, the belief appears to me as pure subjective determination without external correlative. This is what makes the very word "to believe" a term utilized indifferently to indicate the unwavering firmness of belief ("My God, I believe in you") and its character as disarmed and strictly subjective. ("Is Pierre my friend? I do not know; I believe so.") But the nature of consciousness is such that in it the mediate and the immediate are one and the same being. To believe is to know that one believes, and to know that one believes is no longer to believe. Thus to believe is not to believe any longer because that is only to believe—this in the unity of one and the same non-thetic self-consciousness. To be sure, we have here forced the description of the phenomenon by designating it with the word *to know;* non-thetic consciousness is not to *know.* But it is in its very translucency at the origin of all knowing. Thus the non-thetic consciousness (of) believing is destructive of belief. But at the same time the very law of the pre-reflective *cogito* implies that the being of believing ought to be the consciousness of believing.

Thus belief is a being which questions its own being, which can realize itself only in its destruction, which can manifest itself to itself only by denying itself. It is a being for which to be is to appear and to appear is to deny itself. To believe is not-to-believe. We see the reason for it; the being of consciousness is to exist by itself, then to make itself be and thereby to pass beyond itself. In this sense consciousness is perpetually escaping itself, belief becomes non-belief, the immediate becomes mediation, the absolute becomes relative, and the relative becomes absolute. The ideal of good faith (to believe what one believes) is, like that of sincerity (to be what one is), an ideal of being-initself. Every belief is a belief that falls short; one never wholly believes what one believes. Consequently the primitive project of bad faith is only the utilization of this self-destruction of the fact of consciousness. If every belief in good faith is an impossible belief, then there is a place for every impossible belief. My inability to *believe* that I am courageous will not discourage me since every belief involves not quite believing. I shall define this impossible belief as *my* belief. To be sure, I shall not be able to hide from myself that I believe in order not to believe and that I do believe *in order to* believe. But the subtle, total annihilation of bad faith by itself can not surprise me; it exists at the basis of all faith. What is it then? At the moment when I wish to believe myself courageous I *know* that I am a coward. And this certainly would come to destroy my belief. But *first*, I *am* not any more courageous than cowardly, if we are to understand this in the mode of being of the-in-itself. In the second place, I do not *know* that I am courageous; such a view of myself can be accompanied only by *belief*, for it surpasses pure reflective certitude. In the third place, it is very true that bad faith does not succeed in believing what it wishes to believe. But it is precisely as the acceptance of not believing what it believes that it is bad faith. Good faith wishes to flee the "not-believing-what-one-believes" by finding refuge in being. Bad faith flees being by taking refuge in "not-believing-what-one-believes." It has disarmed all beliefs in advance—those which it would like to take hold of and, by the same stroke, the others, those which it wishes to flee. In *willing* this self-destruction of belief, from which science escapes by searching for evidence, it ruins the beliefs which are opposed to it, which reveal themselves as *being only* belief. Thus we can better understand the original phenomenon of bad faith.

In bad faith there is no cynical lie nor knowing preparation for deceitful concepts. But the first act of bad faith is to flee what it can not flee, to flee what it is. The very project of flight reveals to bad faith an inner disintegration in the heart of being, and it is this disintegration which bad faith wishes to be. In truth, the two immediate attitudes which we can take in the face of our being are conditioned by the very nature of this being and its immediate relation with the in-itself. Good faith seeks to flee the inner disintegration of my being in the direction of the in-itself which it should be and is not. Bad faith seeks to flee the in-itself by means of the inner disintegration of my being. But it denies this very disintegration as it denies that it is itself bad faith. Bad faith seeks by means of "not-being-what-one-is" to escape from the in-itself which I am not in the mode of being what one is not. It denies itself as bad faith and aims at the in-itself which I am not in the mode of "not-being-what-one-is-not."* If bad faith is possible, it is because it is an immediate, permanent threat to every project of the human being; it is because consciousness conceals in its being a permanent risk of bad faith. The origin of this risk is the fact that the nature of consciousness simultaneously is to be what it is not and not to be what it is. In the light of these remarks we can approach the ontological study of consciousness, not as the totality of the human being, but as the instantaneous nucleus of this being.

---

* If it is indifferent whether one is in good or in bad faith, because bad faith reapprehends good faith and slides to the very origin of the project of good faith; that does not mean that we can not radically escape bad faith. But this supposes a self-recovery of being which was previously corrupted. This self-recovery we shall call authenticity, the description of which has no place here.

Part III

THE EMOTIONS: OUTLINE OF A THEORY

INTRODUCTION

PSYCHOLOGY, PHENOMENOLOGY, AND PHENOMENOLOGICAL PSYCHOLOGY

Psychology is a discipline which aspires to be positive; that is, it tries to draw its resources exclusively from experience. The age of associationists is certainly gone, and contemporary psychologists are no longer prohibited from *asking* and *interpreting*. But like the doctor they want to face their object. When one speaks of contemporary psychology it is still necessary to limit the concept of experience, for, in effect, there can be a host of diverse experiences; for example, one may have to decide whether or not there is an experience of essence or values or a religious experience. The psychologist intends to use only two types of well defined experiences, that which gives us the spatial-temporal perception of organized bodies, and the intuitive knowledge of ourselves that is called reflexive experience. If there are any disputes among the psychologists as to method, they can bear almost solely on the following problem: are these two types of information complementary, should one be subordinated to the other, or should one of them be boldly discarded? But they are in agreement on one essential principle: the inquiry should start, before everything else, with *facts*.

If we ask ourselves what a fact is, we see that it is defined by that which one should *meet* in the course of an investigation and that it always presents itself as an unexpected enrichment and a novelty in relation to anterior facts. It is therefore not necessary to count on the facts to organize themselves in a synthetic totality which by itself might yield its meaning. In other words, if one calls anthropology a discipline which claims to define the essence of man and the human condition, psychology—even the psychology of man—is not and never will be anthropology. It does not intend to define and limit *a priori* the object of its inquiry. The idea of man which it accepts is quite empirical: throughout the world are a number of creatures who present analogous natures to experience. Moreover, other sciences, sociology and psychology, proceed to inform us that there are certain objective connections between these creatures.

No more is needed for the psychologist, in the name of a working hypothesis, to accept prudently to limit his investigations provisionally to this group of creatures. The available sources about them are indeed more easily accessible since they live in society, speak a language, and leave traces of their activity. But the psychologist does not commit himself; he does not know whether the notion of man may not be arbitrary. It may be *too vast;* we do not have to put the Australian primitive into the same psychological class as the American workman of 1939. It may be *too narrow;* nothing says that an abyss separates the higher apes from the human being. In any case, the psychologist rigorously guards against considering the men about him as *his fellow-creatures.* This notion of similitude, on the basis of which one might be able to build an anthropology, seems to him ridiculous and dangerous. He will readily admit, with the reservations made above, that he is a man, that is, that he is a part of the class which has been isolated provisionally. But he will take into consideration that this human character should be conferred upon him *a posteriori* and that he can not, insofar as he is a member of that class, be a privileged object of study, except for the sake of experiments. He will therefore learn *from others* that he is man and his nature as a man will not be revealed to him in a particular way by the pretext that he *is himself* what he studies. Like "objective" experimentation, introspection will furnish only facts.

If it is necessary that there be later a rigorous concept of *man*—and even that is doubtful—this concept can be envisaged only as the crown of a finished science, that is, one which is done with forever. It would be still only a unifying hypothesis, invented to co-ordinate and grade the infinite collection of facts which have been brought to light. This is to say that the idea of man, if ever it takes on a positive meaning, will be only a conjecture aiming to establish connections between disparate materials and will attain verisimilitude only by its success. Pierce defined hypothesis as the sum of the experimental results which it allows us to foresee. Thus, the idea of man can be only the sum of the established facts which it allows us to unite. However, if some psychologists were to use a certain conception of man *before* this ultimate synthesis were possible, it would be a strictly personal act, a conducting wire as it were or, better, like an idea in the Kantian sense, and their first duty would be never to lose sight of the fact that it was a regulating concept.

It follows from so many precautions that psychology, insofar as it claims to be a science, can furnish only a sum of miscellaneous facts, most of which have no connection with the others. What can be more different, for example, than the study of the stroboscopic illusion and the inferiority complex? This confusion is not due to chance but to the very principles of the science of psychology. To expect the *fact* is, by definition, to expect the isolated, to prefer, because of positivism, the accidental to the essential, the contingent to the necessary, disorder to order; it is, on principle, to cast what is essential into the future: "That will do for later, when we shall have assembled enough facts." In short, psychologists do not realize that it is just as impossible to get to essence by accumulating accidents as to reach 1 by adding figures to the right of 0.99.

If their only aim is to accumulate details of knowledge there is nothing to be said; one simply does not see what interest there is in these labors of a collector. But if they are animated, in their modesty, by the hope, in itself praiseworthy, that later on, on the basis of their monographs, an anthropological synthesis will be realized, they are in full contradiction with themselves. It will be said that this is precisely the method and ambition of the natural sciences. The answer to that is that the natural sciences do not aim at knowing *the world*, but the possible conditions of certain general phenomena. This notion of *world* has long since vanished beneath the criticism of methodologists, and precisely because one could not both apply the methods of the positive sciences and hope that they would one day lead to discovering the meaning of the synthetic totality which one calls *world*. But *man* is a being of the same type as *the world*. It is even possible, as Heidegger believes, that the notions of world and of "human reality" (*Dasein*) are inseparable. Psychology should resign itself to doing without human reality for precisely that reason, supposing at least that this human reality does exist.

Applied to a particular example, the study of the emotions,

for example, what will the principles and the methods of the psychologist give us? First of all, our knowledge of the emotion will be added *from without* to other knowledge about the physical being. The emotion will present itself as an irreducible novelty in relation to the phenomena of attention, memory, perception, etc. You can, indeed, inspect these phenomena and the empirical notion of them we build following the psychologist; you can turn them about again and again as you please and you will not discover the slightest essential connection with emotion. All the same the psychologist grants that man has emotions because experience teaches him so.

Thus, emotion is first of all and in principle an *accident*. In textbooks of psychology it is a chapter which follows other chapters, as calcium follows hydrogen or sulphur in textbooks of chemistry. As for studying the possible conditions of an emotion, that is, wondering whether the very structure of human reality makes emotions possible and *how* it makes them possible, that would appear useless and absurd to a psychologist: what good is it to ask whether emotion is possible precisely because it is?

The psychologist will likewise turn to experience to establish the limits and definition of emotive phenomena. In fact, he would be able to observe there that he already has an *idea* of emotion, since, after inspecting the facts, he will draw a line of demarcation between the facts of emotion and those which are not such; indeed, how could experience furnish him with a principle of demarcation if he did not already have it? But the psychologist prefers to hold to the belief that the facts group themselves before his eyes by themselves. At present it is a matter of *studying* emotions one has just isolated. To do that we shall agree to realize affecting situations or to turn to those particularly emotive subjects which pathology offers us.

We shall then apply ourselves to determining the factors of this complex state; we shall isolate the *bodily reactions* (which, moreover, we shall be able to establish with the greatest precision), the *behavior*, and the *state of consciousness*, properly so called. Following this we shall be able to formulate our laws and offer our explanations; that is, we shall try to unite these three types of factors in an irreversible order. If I am a partisan of the intellectual theory, for example, I shall set up a constant and irreversible succession between the inner state considered as antecedent and the physiological disturbances considered as consequents.

If, on the contrary, I think with the partisans of the peripheric theory that "a mother is sad because she weeps," I shall, at bottom, limit myself to reversing the order of the factors. In any case, what is certain is that I shall not seek the explanation or the laws of emotion in the general and essential structures of human reality, but *in the processes of the emotion itself*, with the result that even when it has been duly described and explained it will never be anything but one fact among others, a fact closed in on itself which will never permit either of understanding a thing other than itself or of grasping by means of it the essential reality of man.

It was in reaction against the inadequacies of psychology and psychologism that about thirty years ago a new discipline was constituted called phenomenology. Its founder, Husserl, was struck by this truth: essences and facts are incommensurable, and one who begins his inquiry with facts will never arrive at essences. If I seek the psychic facts which are at the basis of the arithmetic attitude of the man who counts and calculates, I shall never arrive at the reconstitution of the arithmetic essences of unity, number, and operation. However, without giving up the idea of experience (the principle of phenomenology is to go to "things themselves" and the basis of these methods is eidetic intuition), it must be made flexible and must take into account the experience of essences and values; it must even recognize that essences alone permit us to classify and inspect the facts.

If we did not have implicit recourse to the essence of emotion, it would be impossible for us to distinguish the particular group of facts of emotivity among the mass of psychic facts. Since one has had implicit recourse to the essence of emotion as well, phenomenology will therefore prescribe that we have explicit recourse to it and, by concepts, that we set up the content of this essence once and for all. One understands well enough that the idea of man can no longer be an empirical concept, the product of historical generalizations, but that, on the contrary, we have to use, without mentioning it, the "*a priori*" essence of *human being* in order to give a somewhat solid basis to the generalizations of the psychologist. But besides, psychology, considered as a science of certain human facts,could not be a beginning because the psychic facts we meet are never the first ones. They are, in their essential structure, man's reactions against the world. Therefore, they assume man and the world and can only take on their true meaning if one has first elucidated these two notions. If we wish to found a psychology, we shall have to go beyond the psychic, beyond man's situation in the world, to the very source of man, the world, and the psychic: the transcendental and the consecutive consciousness which we attain by "phenomenological reduction" or "putting the world in parentheses."

It is this consciousness which must be interrogated, and what gives value to its responses is precisely that it is *mine*. Thus Husserl knows how to take advantage of this absolute proximity of consciousness in relation to itself from which the psychologist had not wished to profit. He takes advantage knowingly and with full security, since every consciousness exists to the exact extent to which it is conscious of existing. But there, as above, he refuses to interrogate consciousness about *facts;* on the transcendental level we should again find the confusion of psychology. What he is going to try to describe and fix by concepts is precisely the essences which preside as the transcendental field unrolls. Therefore, there will be, for example, a phenomenology of emotion which, after having "put the world in parentheses" will study emotion as a pure transcendental phenomenon—and will do so not by turning to particular emotions but by seeking to attain and elucidate the transcendental essence of emotion as an organized type of consciousness.

Heidegger, another phenomenologist, likewise took as his point of departure this absolute proximity of the investigator and the thing investigated. The thing which differentiates every inquiry about man from other types of rigorous questions is precisely the privileged fact that human reality is *ourselves.* "The existant which we must analyze," writes Heidegger, "is our self. The being of this existant is *mine.*"* Now it is not a matter of indifference that this human reality is *I* precisely because, for human reality, to exist is always to *assume* its being, that is, to be responsible for it instead of receiving it from the outside like a stone. "And as 'human reality' is essentially its own possibility, this existant can 'choose' itself in its being; it can win itself and can lose itself."† This "assumption" of self which characterizes human reality implies an understanding of human reality itself, however obscure this under-

---

* *Sein und Zeit*, p. 41.

† *Ibid.*, p. 41.

standing may be. "In the being of this existant, the latter relates itself to its being."* In effect, understanding is not a quality coming to human reality from the outside; it is its characteristic way of existing. Thus, the human reality which is *I* assumes its own being by understanding it. This understanding is mine. I am, therefore, first, a being who more or less obscurely understands his reality as man, which signifies that I make myself man in understanding myself as such. I may therefore interrogate myself and on the basis of this interrogation lead an analysis of the "human reality" to a successful conclusion which can be used as a foundation for an anthropology. Here, of course, it is no longer a question of introspection, first because introspection meets only the fact, then because my understanding of human reality is obscure and not authentic. It must be cleared up and explained.

In any case, the hermeneutic of existence will be able to found an anthropology, and that anthropology will serve as a basis for any psychology. We are, therefore, in a situation which is the reverse of that of the psychologists, since we *start* from the synthetic totality that is man and establish the essence of man *before* making a start in psychology.

At any rate, phenomenology is the study of phenomena— not facts. And by phenomenon must be understood "that which manifests itself," that whose reality is precisely appearance. "And this 'self-manifestation' is not any sort of manifestation . . . the being of the existent is not something 'behind which' there is still something 'which does not appear.'"† In effect, for human reality to *exist* is, according to Heidegger, to assume its own being in an existential mode of understanding;

---

* *Ibid.*, p. 43.

† *Sein und Zeit*, pp. 35-36.

for consciousness, to *exist* is to *appear*, in Husserl's sense of the word. Since appearance is here the absolute, it is appearance which must be described and interrogated. From this point of view, Heidegger thinks that in every human attitude—for example in emotion, since we were speaking of it a little while ago—we shall find the whole of human reality, since emotion is the human reality which assumes itself and which, "aroused," "directs" itself toward the world. As for Husserl, he thinks that a phenomenological description of emotion will bring to light the essential structure of consciousness, since an emotion is precisely a consciousness. And conversely, a problem arises which the psychologist does not even suspect; can types of consciousness be conceived which would not include emotion among their possibilities, or must we see in it an indispensable structure of consciousness? Therefore, the phenomenologist will interrogate emotion *about consciousness* or *about man*. He will ask it not only what it is but what it has to teach us about a being, one of whose characteristics is exactly that he is capable of being moved. And inversely he will interrogate consciousness, human reality, about emotion: what must a consciousness be for emotion to be possible, perhaps even to be necessary?

We can understand, at the present time, the reasons for the psychologist's mistrust of phenomenology. The psychologist's first precaution consists, in effect, of considering the psychic state in such a way that it removes from it all *signification*. The psychic state is for him always a *fact* and, as such, always accidental. And this accidental character is just what the psychologist holds to most. If one should ask a scientist, "Why do bodies attract each other in accordance with Newton's Law?" he will reply, "I know nothing about that; because it happens to be so." And if one should ask him, "What does this attraction *signify?*" he will reply, "It signifies nothing. It is." In like manner, the psychologist, when questioned about emotion, is quite proud of answering, "It is. Why? I know nothing about that. I simply state it. I know nothing about its signification." For the phenomenologist, on the contrary, every human fact is, in essence, significative. If you remove its signification, you remove its nature as human fact. The task of a phenomenologist, therefore, will be to study the signification of emotion. What are we to understand by that?

To signify is to indicate another thing; and to indicate it in such a way that in developing the signification one will find precisely the thing signified. For the psychologist emotion signifies nothing because he studies it as a fact, that is, by cutting it away from everything else. Therefore, it will be non-significative from its beginning; but if every human fact is really significative, the emotion studied by the psychologist is, by its nature, dead, non-psychic, inhuman. If, in the matter of the phenomenologist, we wish to make of emotion a true phenomenon of consciousness, it will, on the contrary, be necessary to consider it as significative from the first. That is, we shall affirm that it *is* strictly to the extent that it signifies. We shall not first lose ourselves in the study of physiological facts, precisely because, taken by themselves and in isolation, they signify *almost* nothing. They are—that's all. But on the contrary, we shall try, by developing the signification of behavior and of the affected consciousness, to make explicit the thing which is signified. We know what the thing signified is from its origin: the emotion signifies, *in its own way*, the whole of consciousness or, if we put ourselves on the existential level, of human reality. It is not an accident because human reality is not an accumulation of facts. It expresses from a definite point of view the human synthetic totality in its entirety. And we need not understand by that that it is the *effect* of human reality. It is the human reality itself in the form of "emotion." That being so, it is impossible to consider emotion as a psychophysiological disorder. It has its essence, its particular structures, its law of appearing, and its signification. It cannot come to human reality *from the outside*. On the contrary, it is man who *assumes* his emotion, and consequently emotion is an organized form of human existence.

We have no intention of entering here upon a phenomenological study of emotion. Such a study, if one had to sum it up very briefly, would deal with affectivity as an existential mode of human reality. But our ambitions are more limited. We should like to see a study of emotion in a precise and concrete case, if pure psychology can reasonably extract a method and some lessons from phenomenology. We agree that psychology does not put man into question or the world in parentheses. It takes man in the world as he presents himself through a multitude of situations, in the café, with his family, at war. Generally speaking, what interests it is *man in situations*. As such, it is, as we have seen, subordinate to phenomenology, since a really positive study of man in situations should first have elucidated the notions of man, world, being-in-the-world, and situation. But, after all, phenomenology has scarcely been born and all these notions are quite far from their definite elucidation. Should psychology wait until phenomenology reaches maturity? We do not think so. But if it does not wait for the definitive establishment of an anthropology, it ought not lose sight of the fact that this anthropology is realizable, and that if one day it is realized, the psychological disciplines will have to have their source there. For the time being, it should not aim so much at gathering facts as at interrogating *phenomena*, that is, to put it exactly, psychic events, insofar as they are significations and not insofar as they are pure facts. For example, it will recognize that emotion *does not exist* as a corporeal phenomenon, since a body cannot be affected, for want of power to confer a meaning on its own manifestations. It will immediately seek something beyond vascular or respiratory disturbances, this something being the *feeling* of joy or sadness. But as this feeling is not exactly a quality imposed on joy or sadness from the outside, as it exists only to the extent to which it appears, that is, to which it is "assumed" by the human reality, it is consciousness itself which it will interrogate, since joy is joy only insofar as it appears as such.

And precisely because it seeks not facts but significations, it will abandon the methods of inductive introspection or external empirical observation to seek only to grasp and fix the essence of phenomena. It will, therefore, also proclaim itself an eidetic science. However, through the psychic phenomenon it will not aim at the *thing signified* as such, that is, the human totality. It does not have sufficient means at its disposal to attempt this study. What will interest it solely is the phenomenon *insofar as it is significative.* In the same way I can try to grasp the essence of the "proletariat" through the word "proletariat." In that case, I will be practicing sociology. But the linguist studies the word proletariat *insofar as it signifies proletariat* and he will be uneasy about the vicissitudes of the world as a carrier of signification. Such a science is perfectly possible.

What does it lack to be real? To have shown proofs. We have shown that if human reality appears to the psychologist as a collection of miscellaneous data, it is because the psychologist has readily taken a point of view from which its reality had to appear to him as such. But that does not necessarily imply that human reality is anything other than a collection. What we have proved is only that it *cannot* appear otherwise to the psychologist. It remains to know whether it can bear a phenomenological investigation at its roots, that is, whether emotion, for example, is truly a significative phenomenon. The following pages should be regarded as an *experiment* in phenomenological psychology. We shall try to place ourselves on the grounds of signification and to treat emotion as a *phenomenon*.

1. THE CLASSICAL THEORIES

We know all the criticisms which have been raised against the peripheric theory of the emotions. How are we to explain the subtle emotions? Passive joy? How can we grant that commonplace organic reactions can account for qualified psychic states? How can modifications which are qualitative (and, thereby, as if uninterrupted in their vegetative functions) correspond to a qualitative series of states which are irreducible among them? For example, the physiological modifications which correspond to anger differ only in intensity from those which correspond to joy (slightly accelerated respiratory rhythm, slight increase in muscular tonicity, extension of biochemical changes, arterial tension, etc.), yet anger is not more intense joy; it is something else, at least insofar as it presents itself to consciousness. It would serve no purpose to show that in joy there is an excitation which predisposes one to anger, to cite idiots who pass continually (for example, while rocking on a bench and accelerating their rocking) from joy to anger. The idiot who is angry is not "ultra joyful." Even if he has *passed* from joy to anger (and nothing allows us to assert that a host of psychic events has not intervened), anger is not reducible to joy.

It seems to me what is common to all these objections could be summed up thus: William James distinguishes two groups of phenomena in emotion, a group of physiological phenomena and a group of psychological phenomena which we shall hereafter call the *state* of consciousness. The essence of his thesis is that the state of consciousness called "joy, anger, etc." is nothing other than the consciousness of physiological manifestations—their projection in consciousness if you like. But all the critics of James, examining "emotion," a "state" of consciousness, and the concomitant physiological manifestations, do not *recognize* projection in the former which is the shadow cast by the latter. They find *more*, and—whether or not they are clearly conscious of it—*something else. More:* one can, in imagination, push bodily disorders to the limit, but in vain; it could not be understood why the corresponding consciousness would be a *rized* consciousness. Terror is an extremely painful, even unbearable, state, and it is inconceivable that a bodily state perceived for and in itself should appear to consciousness with this frightful character. *Something else:* in effect, even if emotion perceived objectively presents itself as a physiological disorder, insofar as it is a fact it is not at all a disorder or an utter chaos. It has a meaning; it signifies something. And by that we do not mean only that it presents itself as a pure quality; it sets itself up as a certain relationship of our psychic being with the world, and this relationship, or rather our consciousness of it, is not a chaotic connection between the ego and the universe. It is an organized and describable structure.

I do not see that the cortico-thalamic sensitivity, recently invented by the same ones who make these criticisms of James, allows for a satisfactory answer to the question. First, James's peripheric theory had a great advantage; it took into account only physiological disturbances which could be revealed directly or indirectly. The theory of cerebral sensitivity invokes an unverifiable cortical disturbance. Sherrington has made some experiments on dogs, and one can certainly praise his skill as an operator. But these experiments taken by themselves prove *absolutely nothing*.

From the fact that the *head of a dog* practically isolated from its body still gives signs of emotion, I do not see that one has the right to conclude that the *dog* experiences a complete emotion. Moreover, even supposing that the existence of a cortico-thalamic sensitivity were established, it would again be necessary to ask the previous question: can a physiological disturbance, *whatever it may be*, account for the *organized* character of emotion?

This is what Janet understood quite well, but expressed unfortunately, when he said that James, in his description of emotion, lacked the psychic. Janet, taking a strictly objective standpoint, wished to record only the external manifestations of emotion. But he thought that, even considering only the organic phenomena which one can describe and reveal from the exterior, these phenomena immediately admit of being classed in two categories, psychic phenomena, or behavior, and physiological phenomena. A theory of emotion which wishes to restore to the psychic its preponderant role should make of emotion a matter of behavior. But Janet, like James, was sensitive, despite everything, to the appearance of disorder which all emotion presents. Therefore, he makes emotion a less well adapted behavior, or, if one prefers, a behavior of disadaptation, a behavior arising from a setback.

When the task is too difficult and we cannot maintain the superior behavior which would be suitable to it, the psychic energy liberated is spent in another way: we maintain an inferior behavior which requires a lesser physiological tension. Let us take, for example, a young girl whose father has just told her that he has pains in his arms and that he is a little afraid of paralysis. She rolls on the floor, a prey to violent emotion, which returns a few days later with the same violence and finally forces her to seek the help of doctors. In the course of the treatment, she confesses that the idea of taking care of her father and leading the austere life of a sick-nurse had suddenly seemed unbearable. The emotion, therefore, represents in this instance a setback-behavior. It is a substitution for "sick-nurse-behavior-unable-to-be-endured." Likewise, in his work on *Obsession and Psychasthenia*, Janet cites the cases of several sick people who, having come to him to confess, could not get to the end of their confession and ended by bursting into sobs, sometimes even by having an attack of hysteria. There again, the behavior to be kept up is too difficult. The tears, the hysteria, represent a setback-behavior which is substituted for the first by diversion from its proper course. It is not necessary to insist; examples abound. Who does not remember having bantered with a friend, having remained calm as long as the contest seemed equal, and having become irritated the very moment he found nothing more to answer? Janet can therefore pride himself on having reintegrated the psychic into emotion; the consciousness which we take of emotion—which consciousness, moreover, is here only a secondary phenomenon* is no longer the simple correlative physiological disorder; it is the consciousness of a setback and a setback-behavior. The theory seems fascinating. It is certainly a *psychological* thesis and has a quite mechanistic simplicity. The phenomenon of derivation is nothing more than a change of path for freed nervous energy.

And yet, how many obscurities there are in these few

---

* But not an epiphenomenon: consciousness is the behavior of behavior.

notions which seem to be so clear. To consider the matter more closely, it is noticeable that Janet goes beyond James only by using implicitly a finality which his theory explicitly rejects. In effect, what is setback-behavior? Should we mean by that only the automatic substitution for a superior behavior that we cannot maintain? In that case, nervous energy could discharge itself at random and in accordance with the law of least resistance. But then the ensemble of active reactions would be less a setback-behavior than an absence of behavior. There could be a diffuse organic reaction, a disorder, in place of an adapted reaction. But is that not precisely what James has said? Does not emotion intervene for him precisely at the moment of an abrupt disadaptation, and does it not consist essentially of the ensemble of disorders which this disadaptation brings about in the organism? Doubtless, Janet puts more emphasis on the *setback* than James does. But what are we to understand by that? If we consider the individual as a system of behavior, and if the derivation occurs automatically, the setback is nothing; it does not exist; there is simply substitution of one behavior by a diffuse ensemble of organic manifestations. For emotion to have the psychic signification of a setback, consciousness must intervene and confer this signification upon it. It must keep the superior behavior as a possibility and must grasp the emotion precisely as a setback *in relation* to this superior behavior. But this would be to give to consciousness a constitutive role which Janet did not want at any price. If one wanted Janet's theory to retain some meaning, he would be led logically to adopt the position of M. Wallon. In an article in the *Revue des Cours et Conférences*, M. Wallon offers the following interpretation: assume a primitive nervous system, a child's. The ensemble of the new born infant's reactions to tickling, pain, etc., would always be governed by this system (shivering, diffuse muscular contractions, accelerations of the cardiac rhythm, etc.) and would then constitute a first organic adaptation, an inherited adaptation, of course. By what follows we would learn about conduct and would realize new set-ups, that is, new systems. But when in a new and difficult situation, we cannot find the adapted behavior which suits him, there would be a return to the primitive nervous system. It is evident that this theory represents the transposition of Janet's views on the level of pure behaviorism, since, in short, emotional reactions are regarded not as a pure disorder but as a lesser adaptation: the nervous system of the child, the first organized system of defensive reflexes, is disadapted in relation to the needs of the adult, but in itself it is a functional organization, analogous, for example, to the respiratory reflex. But it is also evident that this thesis is differentiated from that of James only by the supposition of an organic unity which would connect all the emotive manifestations. It goes without saying that James would have accepted the existence of such a system without any difficulty, if it had been proved. He would have held this modification of his own theory as of little importance because it was of a strictly physiological order. Therefore, Janet, if we keep to the terms of his thesis, is much nearer to James than he wished to say. He has failed in his attempt to reintroduce the "psychic" into emotion. He has not explained either why there are *various* forms of setback-behavior, why I may react to abrupt aggression by fear *or* anger. Moreover, almost all the examples he cites come back to slightly differentiated emotional upheavals (sobs, hysteria, etc.) which are much closer to what is properly called emotional shock than to qualified emotion.

But it seems that there is in Janet a subjacent theory of emotion—and, furthermore, of conduct in general—which would introduce finality without naming it. In his general discussions of psychasthenia or affectivity he insists, as we have said, on the automatic character of derivation. But in many of his descriptions he lets it be understood that the sick person throws himself into the inferior behavior *in order not* to maintain the superior behavior. Here it is the sick person himself who proclaims himself checked even before having undertaken the struggle, and the emotive behavior comes to *mask* the impossibility of maintaining the adapted behavior. Let us again take the example which we cited earlier: a sick girl comes to Janet; she wants to confide the secret of her turmoil, to describe her obsession minutely. But she is unable to; such social behavior is too hard for her. *Then* she sobs. But does she sob *because* she cannot say anything? Are her sobs vain attempts to act, a diffuse upheaval which represents the decomposition of too difficult behavior? Or does she sob precisely *in order not to say anything?* At first sight, the difference between these two interpretations seems slight; in both hypotheses there is behavior which is impossible to maintain; in both there is substitution for behavior by diffuse manifestations. Janet also passes easily from one to the other; that is what makes his theory ambiguous. But in reality, these two theories are separated by an abyss. The first, in effect, is purely mechanistic and—as we have seen—rather close to the essence of that of James. The second, on the contrary, really brings us something new; it alone really deserves the title of a psychological theory of the emotions; it alone sees emotion as behavior. That is because, if we reintroduce finality here, we can understand that emotional behavior is not a disorder at all. It is an organized system of means aiming at an end. And this system is called upon to mask, substitute for, and reject behavior that one cannot or does not want to maintain. By the same token, the explanation of the diversity of emotions becomes easy; they represent a particular subterfuge, a special trick, each one of them being a different means of eluding a difficulty.

But Janet gave us what he could. He was too uncertain, divided as he was between a spontaneous finalism and a fundamental mechanism. We shall not ask him to expound the pure theory of emotion-behavior. One finds a first draft of it in the disciples of Köhler, notably in Lewin* and Dembo.† Here is what P. Guillaume has written on the subject in his *Psychology of Form*:‡

"Let us take the simplest example: the subject is asked to reach an object placed on a chair, but without putting his foot outside a circle drawn on the ground. The distances are calculated so that the thing is very difficult or impossible to do directly, but one can resolve the problem by indirect means. . . . Here the force oriented toward the object takes on a clear and concrete meaning. Besides, in these problems there is an obstacle to the direct execution of the act; the obstacle may be material or moral; for example, it may be a rule which one is bound to observe. Thus, in our example, the circle which one must not overstep forms a barrier in the subject's perception from which there emanates a force directed in an opposite direction to that of the first.

"The conflict of the two forces produces a tension in the phenomenal field. . . . When the solution has been found, the successful act puts an end to his tension. There is a whole psychology of the act of replacement or substitution, of ersatz, to which the school of Lewin has made an interesting contribu-

---

* Lewin, "Vorsatz, Wille und Bedürfnis," *Psy. Forschung*, VII, 1926.

† Dembo, "Der Aerger als dynamisches Problem," *Psy. Forschung*, 1931, pp. 1-144.

‡ Bib. de Philosophie scientifique, pp. 138-142.

tion. Its form is very variable. The half-results attained may help to stabilize it. Sometimes the subject facilitates the act by freeing himself from some of the imposed conditions of quantity, quality, speed, and duration, and even by modifying the nature of his task. In other cases it is a matter of unreal, symbolic acts; one makes an evidently vain gesture in the direction of the act; one describes the act instead of doing it; one imagines fantastic, fictitious procedures (if I had . . . I would have to . . .) outside of the real or imposed conditions which would permit of its being accomplished. If the acts of substitution are impossible or if they do not produce sufficient resolution, the persistent tension manifests itself by the tendency to give up, to run away, or to retire into oneself in an attitude of passivity. We have said, in effect, that the subject finds himself submissive to the positive attraction of the goal, to the negative attraction of the barrier. Moreover, the fact of having agreed to submit to the test has conferred a negative value on all other objects in the field, in this sense, that all diversions foreign to the task are *ipso facto* impossible. The subject is therefore enclosed in some way in a circuit which is closed everywhere: there is only one positive way out, but it is closed by the specific barrier. This situation corresponds to the diagram below:

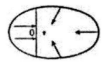

"*Escape* is only a brutal solution since one has to break the general barrier and accept a diminution of the self. Withdrawing into oneself, the *encystment* which raises a protective barrier between the hostile field and the self, is another equally feeble solution.

"The continuation of the test can end in conditions of emotional disorder, other still more primitive forms of the freeing of tensions. The attacks of sometimes very violent anger which occur in certain persons have been well studied in the work of T. Dembo. The situation undergoes a structural simplification. In anger, and doubtless in all other emotions, there is a weakening of the barriers which separate the deep and the superficial layers of the self and which normally assure control of actions by the deep personality and the mastery of the self; a weakening of the barriers between the real and unreal. Contrariwise, from the fact that action is blocked, tensions between the external and the internal continue to increase; the negative character extends uniformly to all objects in the field which lose their proper value. . . . The privileged direction of the goal having disappeared, the differentiated structure which the problem has imposed on the field is destroyed. . . . The particular facts, notably the varied physiological reactions, to which some psychologists have atributed a particular signification, are intelligible only on the basis of this combined conception of the topology of emotion."

We have now arrived, at the end of this long quotation, at a functional conception of anger. Anger is certainly neither an instinct nor a habit nor a reasoned calculation. It is an abrupt solution of a conflict, a way of cutting the Gordian knot. And we certainly come back to Janet's distinction between superior behavior and inferior or derived behavior. Only, this distinction now takes on its full meaning: it is we who put ourselves into a state of complete inferiority, because on this very low level our needs are fewer; we are satisfied, and with less expense. Being unable, in the state of high tension, to find the delicate and precise solution of a problem we act upon ourselves, we lower ourselves, and we transform ourselves into the kind of being who is satisfied with crude and less well adapted solutions (for example, tearing up the paper which gives the statement of the problem). Thus, anger appears here as an escape; the subject in anger resembles a man who, lacking the power to undo the knots of the ropes which bind him, twists and squirms about in his bonds. And the behavior of "anger," less well adapted to the problem than the superior—and impossible—behavior which would resolve it, is, however, precisely and perfectly adapted to the need of breaking the tension, of shaking off that leaden cloak which weighs on our shoulders. Henceforth, one will be able to understand the examples which we cited earlier: the psychasthenic who went to see Janet wanted to confess to him. But the task was too difficult. There she was in a narrow and threatening world which expected her to perform a precise act and which repulsed her at the same time. Janet himself indicated by his attitude that he was listening and waiting. But, at the same time, by his prestige, his personality, and so on, he repelled this confession. It was necessary to escape this intolerable tension, and the sick person could do so only by exaggerating her weakness and her confusion, by turning her attention from the act to be done in order to bring it back to herself ("How unhappy I am"), by transforming Janet, by her very attitude, from a judge to a comforter, by externalizing and enacting her very lack of power to talk, by canceling the precise necessity of giving such and such information about the heavy and undifferentiated pressure which the world exerted upon her. That was the moment for the sobs and the hysteria to appear. Likewise, it is easy to understand the fit of anger which seized me when I could no longer reply to someone with whom I had been bantering. Anger in this case had not quite the same role as in Dembo's example. It was a matter of carrying on the discussion on another plane: I was unable to be witty; I made myself formidable and intimidating. I wanted to inspire fear. At the same time I used derived (*ersätze*) means to conquer my opponent: abuse and threats which were *equivalents for* the witticism I could not find, and, by the abrupt transformation which I imposed upon myself, I became less exacting in my choice of means.

Yet we cannot be satisfied with the point we have reached. The theory of behavior-emotion is perfect, but in its very purity and perfection we can see its insufficiency. In all the examples we have cited, the functional role of emotion is undeniable. But as such it is also incomprehensible. I understand that for Dembo and the psychologists of form the passage from the state of inquiry to the state of anger is explained by the breaking of one form and the reconstitution of another. And I understand the breaking of the form "problem-without-a-solution" in a very strict sense; but how can I admit the appearing of the other form? It must be thought of as being clearly given as the substitute of the first. It exists only in relation to the first. Therefore there is a single process, namely, transformation of form. But I cannot understand this transformation without first supposing consciousness, which, alone, by its synthetic activity, can break and reconstitute forms ceaselessly. It alone can account for the finality of emotion. Besides, we have seen that the entire description of anger given by Guillaume, following Dembo, shows it to us as aiming to transform the aspect of the world. It is a matter of "weakening the barriers between the real and the unreal" and "destroying the differentiated structure which the problem has imposed upon the field." Splendid; but as soon as it is a question of setting up a connection from the world to the self, we can no longer be content with a psychology of form. We must evidently have recourse to consciousness. And moreover, in the last analysis, is that not what Guillaume has recourse to when he says that the angry person "weakens the barriers which separate the deep and superficial levels of the self"? Thus, the physiological theory of James has led us by its very inadequacy to Janet's theory of behavior, which, in turn, has led us to the functional theory of emotion-form, and this, in turn, sends us back to consciousness. That is what we should have begun with. It is now time to formulate the real problem.

2. THE PSYCHOANALYTIC THEORY

One can understand emotion only if he looks for a *significa-tion*. This signification is by nature of a functional order. We are therefore led to speak of a finality of emotion. We grasp this finality in a very concrete way by objective examination of emotional behavior. It is not at all a matter of a more or less obscure theory of emotion-instinct based on *a priori* prin-ciples or on postulates. The simple consideration of facts leads us to an empirical intuition of the finalist signification of emo-tion. If, on the other hand, we try to establish the essence of emotion as a fact of interpsychology in a full intuition, we grasp this finality as inherent in its structure. And all psychol-ogists who have reflected on James's peripheric theory have been more or less conscious of this finalist signification. This is what Janet adorns with the name "psychic." It is what psy-chologists or physiologists like Cannon and Sherrington tried to reintroduce into the description of emotive facts with their hypothesis of a cerebral sensitivity; again, this is what we find in Wallon or, more recently, in the psychologists of form. This finality supposes a synthetic organization of behavior which can be only the unconscious of the psychoanalysts or con-sciousness. But it would be rather easy, if it were necessary, to have a psychoanalytic theory of emotion-finality. One could, without too much trouble, show anger or fear to be means used by unconscious tendencies to satisfy themselves symbolically or to break a state of unbearable tension. One could account for this essential character of emotion as follows: one *undergoes* it; it takes one by surprise; it develops in accordance with its own laws and without our conscious spontaneity's being able to modify its course appreciably. This dissociation of the organized character of emotion, whose organizing theme one could cast into the unconscious, and of its inevitable character, which would be such only for the consciousness of the subject, would render about the same service on the plane of empirical psychology as the Kantian distinction between empirical character and noumenal character does on the metaphysical plane.

Psychoanalytic psychology has certainly been the first to put the emphasis on the signification of psychic facts; that is, it was the first to insist upon the fact that every state of consciousness is the equivalent of something other than itself. For example, the clumsy theft carried out by a person who is sexually obsessed is not simply a "clumsy theft." As soon as we consider it with the psychoanalysts as a phenomenon of self-punishment it sends us back to something other than itself. It sends us back to the first complex for which the sick person is trying to justify himself by punishing himself. One can see that a psychoanalytic theory of emotion could be possible. Does it not already exist? A woman has a phobia of bay-trees. As soon as she sees a cluster of bay-trees, she faints. The psychoanalyst discovers in her childhood a painful sexual incident connected with a laurel bush. Therefore, what will the emotion be in such a case? A phenomenon of refusal, of censure. Not of refusal *of the bay-tree*. A refusal to re-live the memory connected with the bay-tree. The emotion here is flight from the revelation to be made, as sleep is sometimes a flight from a decision to be made, as the sickness of some young girls is, for Stekel, a flight from marriage. Of course, emotion will not always be escape. One can already begin to see among the psychoanalysts an interpretation of anger as a symbolic gratification of sexual tendencies. And, of course, none of these interpretations is to be rejected. There can be no doubt that anger may *signify* sadism. That fainting from passive fear may signify flight, the search for a refuge, is certain, and we shall try to show the reason for it. What is in question here is the very principle of psychoanalytic explanation. That is what we should like to consider here.

The psychoanalytic interpretation considers the phenomenon of consciousness as the symbolic realization of a desire repressed by censorship. Let us note that for consciousness this desire *is not implicated in its symbolic realization*. Insofar as it exists by and in our consciousness, it is only what it appears to be: emotion, desire for sleep, theft, phobia of bay-trees, etc. If it were otherwise and if we had some consciousness, *even implicit*, of our real desire, we should be *dishonest*; the psychoanalyst does not mean it that way. It follows that the signification of our conscious behavior is entirely external to the behavior itself, or, if one prefers, the *thing signified* is entirely cut off from the *thing signifying*. The behavior of the subject is, in itself, what it is (if we call "in itself" what it is *for itself*), but it is possible to decipher it by appropriate techniques as a written language is deciphered. In short, the conscious fact is to the thing signified as a thing, the *effect* of a certain event, is to that event, for example, as the traces of a fire lit on the mountain are to the human beings who lit the fire. Human presences are not *contained* in the ashes which remain. They are connected with them by a bond of causality; the bond is *external*, the remains of the fire are *passive* in relation to this causal relationship as is every effect in relation to its cause. A consciousness which has not acquired the necessary technical knowledge would be unable to perceive these traces as *signs*. At the same time, these traces are what they are, that is, they exist in themselves outside of any signifying interpretation; they *are* half-calcinated pieces of wood; that is all.

May we admit that a fact of consciousness may be like a thing in relation to its signification, that is, may receive it from without like an external quality—as it is an external quality for the burnt wood to have been burned by men who wanted to warm themselves? It seems, at the start, that the first result of such an interpretation is to establish consciousness as a thing in relation to the thing signified; it is to admit that consciousness is established as a signification without being conscious of the signification which it establishes. There is a flagrant contradiction here, unless one does not consider consciousness as an existence like a stone or a cart. But in this case it is necessary to renounce entirely the Cartesian *cogito* and make of consciousness a secondary and passive phenomenon. Insofar as consciousness *makes itself*, it is never anything but what it appears to be. Therefore, if it possesses a signification it should contain it in itself as a structure of consciousness. This does not at all mean that this signification has to be perfectly explicit. Many degrees of consideration and clarity are possible. It means only that we should not examine consciousness from without as one examines the traces of the fire or the encampment, but from within, that one should find signification *in it*. If the *cogito* is to be possible, consciousness is itself the *fact*, the *signification*, and the *thing signified*.

The truth is that what makes an exhaustive refutation of psychoanalysis difficult is that the psychoanalyst does not consider signification as being conferred upon consciousness from without. For him there is always an internal analogy between the conscious fact and the desire which it expresses, since the *conscious fact symbolizes with the complex which is expressed.* And for the psychoanalyst this character of symbol is evidently not external to the fact of consciousness itself; it is constitutive. We are completely in agreement with him on this point: that symbolization is constitutive of symbolic consciousness will trouble no one who believes in the absolute value of the Cartesian *cogito.* But it must be understood that if symbolization is constitutive of consciousness, it is permissible to perceive that there is an immanent bond of *comprehension* between the symbolization and the symbol. Only, we shall have to agree upon what it is that consciousness *is constituted of* in symbolization. In that case, there is nothing behind it, and the relation between symbol, thing symbolized, and symbolization is an interstructural bond of consciousness. But if we add that consciousness symbolizes under the causal pressure of a transcendent fact which is the repressed desire, we again fall into the previously described theory which makes the relation of thing signified to thing signifying a causal relation. It is the profound contradiction of all psychoanalysis to introduce *both* a bond of causality and a bond of comprehension between the phenomena which it studies. These two types of connection are incompatible. Also, the psychoanalytic theoretician establishes transcendent bonds of rigid causality among the facts studied (in dreams, a pin cushion always *signifies* woman's breasts; entering a railway-carriage *signifies* performing the sexual act), whereas the practitioner is confident of getting successful results by studying, above all, the facts of consciousness in comprehension, that is, by seeking in a flexible way, the intra-conscious relationship between symbolization and symbol.

As for us, we do not reject the results of psychoanalysis when they are obtained by comprehension. We limit ourselves to denying any value and any intelligibility to its subjacent theory of psychic causality. And, moreover, we assert that to the extent to which the psychoanalyst makes use of *comprehension* to interpret consciousness, it would be better freely to recognize that everything which takes place in consciousness can receive its explanation only from consciousness itself. So we have returned to our point of departure: a theory of emotion which insists on the signifying character of emotive facts should seek this signification in consciousness itself. In other words, it is consciousness which *makes itself* consciousness, being moved to do so by the needs of an inner signification.

The fact is that partisans of psychoanalysis will immediately raise a difficulty of principle: if consciousness organizes emotion as a certain type of response adapted to an exterior situation, how does it come about, therefore, that it does not have consciousness of this adaptation? And it must be recognized that their theory accounts perfectly for the wedging between signification and consciousness, which ought not to astonish us since it is made precisely for that purpose. Better still, they will say, in most cases we struggle as a conscious spontaneity against the development of emotional manifestations; we try to master our fear, to calm our anger, to hold back our sobs. Thus, not only do we not have consciousness of the finality of emotion but we still repress emotion with all our strength, and it invades us in spite of ourselves. A phenomenological description of emotion owes it to itself to remove these contradictions.

3. A SKETCH OF A PHENOMENOLOGICAL THEORY

Perhaps what will help us in our investigation is a preliminary observation which may serve as a general criticism of all the theories of emotion which we have encountered (except, perhaps, Dembo's theory). For most psychologists everything takes place as if the consciousness *of* the emotion were first a reflective consciousness, that is, as if the first form of the emotion as a fact of consciousness were to appear to us as a modification of our psychic being or, to use everyday language, to be first perceived as a *state of consciousness*. And certainly it is always possible to take consciousness of emotion as the affective structure of consciousness, to say "I'm angry, I'm afraid, etc." But fear is not originally consciousness *of* being afraid, any more than the perception of this book is consciousness *of* perceiving the book. Emotional consciousness is, at first, unreflective, and on this plane it can be conscious of itself only on the non-positional mode. Emotional consciousness is, at first, consciousness *of* the world. It is not even necessary to bring up the whole theory in order clearly to understand this principle. A few simple observations may suffice, and it is remarkable that the psychologists of emotion have never thought of making them. It is evident, in effect, that the man who is afraid is afraid *of* something. Even if it is a matter of one of those indefinite anxieties which one experiences in the dark, in a sinister and deserted passageway, etc., one is afraid *of* certain aspects of the night, of the world. And doubtless, all psychologists have noted that emotion is set in motion by a perception, a representation-signal, etc. But it seems that for them the emotion then withdraws from the object in order to be absorbed into itself. Not much reflection is needed to understand that, on the contrary, the emotion returns to the object at every moment and is fed there. For example, flight in a state of fear is described as if the object were not, before anything else, a flight *from* a certain object, as if the object fled did not remain constantly present in the flight itself, as its theme, its reason for being, *that from which one flees.* And how can one talk about anger, in which one strikes, injures, and threatens, without mentioning the person who represents the objective unity of these insults, threats, and blows? In short, the affected subject and the affective object are bound in an indissoluble synthesis. Emotion is a certain way of apprehending the world. Dembo is the only one who has perceived this, though he gives no reason for it. The subject who seeks the solution of a practical problem is outside in the world; he perceives the world every moment through his acts. If he fails in his attempts, if he gets irritated, his very irritation is still a way in which the world appears to him. And, between the action which miscarries and the anger, it is not necessary for the subject to reflect back upon his behavior, to intercalate a reflexive consciousness. There can be a continuous passage from the unreflective consciousness "world-acted" (action) to the unreflective consciousness "world-hateful" (anger). The second is a transformation of the other.

To understand better the meaning of what is to follow, it

is necessary that the reader bear in mind the essence of *unre-flective behavior*. There is too great a tendency to believe that action is a constant passing from the unreflective to the reflective, from the world to ourself. We perceive the prob-lem (unreflectiveness-consciousness *of* the world); then we perceive ourself as having the problem to solve (reflection); on the basis of this reflection we conceive an action insofar as it ought to be carried on *by us* (reflection), and then we go into the world to carry out the action (unreflective), no longer considering anything but the object acted upon. Then, all new difficulties, all partial checks which might require a restriction of adaptation, again send us to the reflective plane. Hence, a constant going and coming, which is constitutive of action.

Now it is certain that we can reflect on our action. But an operation *on* the universe is carried out most often without the subject's leaving the unreflective plane. For example, at this moment I am writing, but I have no consciousness of writ-ing. Will it be said that habit has made me unconscious of the movements my hand is making as it forms the letters? That would be absurd. Perhaps I have the habit of writing *particu-lar* words in a *particular* order. In a general way, one should distrust explaining things by ascribing them to habit. In reality, the art of writing is not at all unconscious. It is a present struc-ture of my consciousness. Only, it is not conscious *of* itself. To write is to take an active consciousness *of the words* insofar as they are born under my pen. Not of words insofar as they are written *by me:* I intuitively grasp the words insofar as they have this structural quality of issuing *ex nihilo*, and yet of not being creators of themselves, of being passively created. At the very moment that I form one of them, I do not pay attention to each solitary stroke that my hand forms; I am in a special state of waiting, creative waiting; I wait for the word—which

I know in advance—to borrow the hand which writes and the strokes which it forms in order that it may realize itself. To be sure, I am not conscious of the words in the same way as when I look over someone's shoulders and read what he is writing. But that does not mean that I am not conscious of myself as writing. The essential differences are as follows: first, my intuitive apprehension of what my neighbor is writing is of the type called "probable evidence." I perceive the words which his hand forms well in advance of its having completely formed them. But at the very moment when, on reading "indep . . .," I intuitively perceive "independent," the word "independent" is given as a probable reality (in the manner of the table or the chair). Contrariwise, my intuitive perception of the words I am writing delivers them to me as certain. It is a matter of a somewhat special certainty; it is not certain that the word "certainty" which I am in the act of writing is going to appear (I may be disturbed, may change my mind, etc.), but it is certain that if it appears, it will appear as such. Thus the action constitutes a class of certain objects in a probable world. Let us say, if you will, that insofar as they are real, future objects, they are probable, but insofar as they are potentialities of the world, they are certain. In the second place, the words which my neighbor is writing make no demands; I contemplate them in their order of successive appearance as I would look at a table or a clothes-hanger. On the other hand, the words which I write are *exigencies*. The very way I perceive them through my creative activity constitutes them as such; they appear as potentialities *having to be realized*. Not having to be realized by *me*. The *I* does not appear here at all. I simply sense the traction which they exert. I feel their exigence objectively. I see them realizing themselves and at the same time demanding to be realized further. I may very well *think* that the very words which my neighbor is forming are demanding their realization from him. I do not *feel* this exigence. On the other hand, the exigence of the words which I form is directly present; it has weight and it is felt. They tug at my hand and guide it. But not in the manner of live and active little demons who might actually push and tug at it; they have a passive exigence. As to *my hand*, I am conscious of it in the sense that I see it directly as the instrument by which the words realize themselves. It is an object in the world, but at the same time, it is present and lived. Here I am at the moment hesitating: shall I write "therefore" or "consequently"? That does not at all imply that I stop and think about it. Quite simply, the potentialities "therefore" and "consequently" appear—as potentialities—and come into conflict. We shall try elsewhere to describe in detail the world acted upon. The thing that matters here is to show that action as spontaneous unreflective consciousness constitutes a certain existential level in the world, and that in order to act it is not necessary to be conscious of the self as acting—quite the contrary. In short, unreflective behavior is not unconscious behavior; it is conscious of itself non-thetically, and its way of being thetically conscious of itself is to transcend itself and to seize upon the world as a quality of things. Thus, one can understand all those exigences and tensions of the world which surrounds us. Thus, one can draw up a "hodological"* map of our *umwelt*, a map which varies as a function of our acts and needs. Only, in normal and adapted action, the objects "to be realized" appear as having to be realized in certain ways. The means themselves appear as potentialities which demand existence. This apprehension of the means as the only possible way to reach the end (or, if there are n means, as the only n pos-

---

* Lewin's expression.

sible means, etc.) can be called a pragmatistic intuition of the determinism of the world. From this point of view, the world around us—what the Germans call *umwelt*—the world of our desires, our needs, and our acts, appears as if it were furrowed with strict and narrow paths which lead to one or the other determined end, that is, to the appearance of a created object.

Naturally, there are decoys and traps scattered around here and there. This world might be compared to the moving plates of the coin-making machines on which the ball-bearings are made to roll; there are paths formed by rows of pins, and often, at the crossings of the paths, holes are pierced through. The ball-bearings must travel across a determined route, taking determined paths and without falling into the holes. This world is difficult. This notion of difficulty is not a reflective notion which would imply a relationship to me. It is there, on the world; it is a quality of the world which is given in the perception (exactly like the paths towards the potentialities and the potentialities themselves and the exigences of objects: books having to be read, shoes having to be assembled, etc.); it is the noematical correlative of our activity whether undertaken or only conceived.

At present, we can conceive of what an emotion is. It is a transformation of the world. When the paths traced out become too difficult, or when we see no path, we can no longer live in so urgent and difficult a world. All the ways are barred. However, we must act. So we try to change the world, that is, to live as if the connection between things and their potentialities were ruled not by deterministic processes, but by magic. Let it be clearly understood that this is not a game; we are driven against a wall, and we throw ourselves into this new attitude with all the strength we can muster. Let it also be understood that this attempt is not conscious of being such, for it would then be the object of a reflection. Before anything else, it is the seizure of new connections and new exigencies. The seizure of an object being impossible or giving rise to a tension which cannot be sustained, consciousness simply seizes it or tries to seize it otherwise. In itself there is nothing strange about this change in the direction of consciousness. We find a thousand examples of similar transformations in activity and perception. For example, to look for a face concealed in a picture puzzle ("Where is the gun?") is to lead ourselves perceptibly into the picture in a new way, to behave before the branches, the telegraph poles and the image *as* in front of a gun, to, realize the eye movements which we would make in front of a gun. But we do not grasp these movements as such. An intention which transcends them and whose hyle they constitute directs itself through them upon the trees and the poles which are seized as "possible guns" until suddenly the perception crystallizes and the gun appears. Thus, through a change of intention, as in a change of behavior, we apprehend a new object, or an old object in a new way. There is no need to start by placing ourselves on the reflective plane. The vignette's inscription serves directly as motivation. We seek the gun without leaving the unreflective plane. That is, a potential gun appears—vaguely localized in the image. The change of intention and behavior which characterizes the emotion must be conceived in the same manner. The impossibility of finding a solution to the problem objectively apprehended as a quality of the world serves as motivation for the new unreflective consciousness which now perceives the world otherwise and with a new aspect, and which requires a new behavior—through which this aspect is perceived—and which serves as hyle for the new intention. But the emotive behavior is not on the same plane as the other behaviors; it is not *effective*. Its end is not really to act upon the object as such through the agency of particular means. It seeks by itself to confer upon the object, and without modifying it in its actual structure, another quality, a lesser existence, or a lesser presence (or a greater existence, etc.). In short, in emotion it is the body which, directed by consciousness, changes its relations with the world in order that the world may change its qualities. If emotion is a joke, it is a joke we believe in. A simple example will make this emotive structure clear: I extend my hand to take a bunch of grapes. I cannot get it; it is beyond my reach. I shrug my shoulders, I let my hand drop, I mumble, "They're too green," and I move on. All these gestures, these words, this behavior are not seized upon for their own sake. We are dealing with a little comedy which I am playing *under* the bunch of grapes, through which I confer upon the grapes the characteristic of being "too green" which can serve as a substitute for the behavior which I am unable to keep up. At first, they presented themselves as "having to be picked." But this urgent quality very soon becomes unbearable because the potentiality cannot be realized. This unbearable tension becomes, in turn, a motive for foisting upon the grapes the new quality "too green," which will resolve the conflict and eliminate the tension. Only I cannot confer this quality on the grapes chemically. I cannot act upon the bunch in the ordinary ways. So I seize upon this sourness of the too green grapes by acting disgusted. I magically confer upon the grapes the quality I desire. Here the comedy is only half sincere. But let the situation be more urgent, let the incantatory behavior be carried out with seriousness; there we have emotion.

For example, take passive fear. I see a wild animal coming toward me. My legs give way, my heart beats more feebly, I turn pale, I fall and faint. Nothing seems less adapted than this behavior which hands me over defenseless to the danger.

And yet it is a behavior of *escape*. Here the fainting is a refuge. Let it not be thought that this is a refuge *for me*, that I am trying to save *myself* in order not to *see* the wild animal *any more*. I did not leave the unreflective level, but, lacking power to avoid the danger by the normal methods and the deterministic links, I denied it. I wanted to annihilate it. The urgency of the danger served as motive for an annihilating intention which demanded magical behavior. And, by virtue of this fact, I did annihilate it as far as was in my power. These are the limits of my magical action upon the world; I can eliminate it as an object of consciousness* itself. Let it not be thought that the physiological behavior of passive fear is pure disorder. It represents the abrupt realization of the bodily conditions which ordinarily accompany the transition from being awake to sleeping.

The flight into active fear is mistakenly considered as rational behavior. Calculation is seen in such behavior—quick calculation, to be sure—the calculation of someone who wants to put the greatest possible distance between himself and danger. But this is to misunderstand such behavior, which would then be only prudence. We do not flee in order to take shelter; we flee for lack of power to annihilate ourselves in the state of fainting. Flight is a fainting which is enacted; it is a magical behavior which consists of denying the dangerous object with our whole body by subverting the vectorial structure of the space we live in by abruptly creating a potential direction on the *other side*. It is a way of forgetting it, of denying it. It is the same way that novices in boxing shut their eyes and throw

---

* Or at least by modifying it; fainting is the transition to a dream consciousness, that is, "unrealizing."

themselves at their opponent. They want to eliminate the existence of his fists; they refuse to perceive them and by so doing symbolically eliminate their efficacy. Thus, the true meaning of fear is apparent; it is a consciousness which, through magical behavior, aims at denying an object of the external world, and which will go so far as to annihilate itself in order to annihilate the object with it.

Passive sadness is characterized, as is well known, by a behavior of oppression; there is muscular resolution, pallor, coldness at the extremities; one turns toward a corner and remains seated, motionless, offering the least possible surface to the world. One prefers the shade to broad daylight, silence to noise, the solitude of a room to crowds in public places or the streets. "To be alone with one's sorrow," as they say. That is not the truth at all. It is a mark of good character to seem to meditate profoundly on one's grief. But the cases in which one really cherishes his sorrow are rather rare. The reason is quite otherwise: one of the ordinary conditions of our action having disappeared, the world requires that we act in it and on it *without that condition.* Most of the potentialities which throng it (tasks *to* do, people *to*see, acts of daily life *to* carry out) have remained the same. Only the means of realizing them, the ways which cut through our "hodological space" have changed. For example, if I have learned that I am ruined, I no longer have the same means at my disposal (private auto, etc.) to carry them out. I have to substitute new media for them (to take the bus, etc.); that is precisely what I do not want. Sadness aims at eliminating the obligation to seek new ways, to transform the structure of the world by a totally undifferentiated structure. In short, it is a question of making of the world an affectively neutral reality, a system in total affective equilibrium, of discharging the strong affective charge from objects, of reducing them all to affective zero, and, by the same token, of apprehending them as perfectly equivalent and interchangeable. In other words, lacking the power and will to accomplish the acts which we had been planning, we behave in such a way that the universe no longer requires anything of us. To bring that about we can only act upon our self, only "dim the light," and the noematical correlative of this attitude is what we call *Gloom;* the universe is gloomy, that is, undifferentiated in structure. At the same time, however, we naturally take the cowering position, we "withdraw into ourselves." The noematical correlative of this attitude is *Refuge.* All the universe is gloomy, but precisely because we want to protect ourselves from its frightening and limitless monotony, we constitute any place whatever as a "corner." It is the only differentiation in the total monotony of the world: a stretch of wall, a bit of darkness which hides its gloomy immensity from us.

Active sadness can take many forms. But the one cited by Janet (the psychasthenic who became hysterical because she did not want to confess) can be characterized as a *refusal.* The question is, above all, one of a negative behavior which aims at denying the urgency of certain problems and substituting others. The sick person wanted Janet's feelings to be moved. That means she wanted to replace the attitude of impassive waiting which he adopted by one of affectionate concern. That was what she wanted, and she used her body to bring it about. At the same time, by putting herself into a state which made confession impossible, she cast the act to be performed out of her range. Thus, as long as she was shaken with tears and hiccups, any possibility of talking was removed. Therefore, the potentiality was not eliminated in this case; the confession remained "to be made." But she had withdrawn from the sick person; she could no longer *want* to do it, but only *wish* to do it some day. Thus, the sick person had delivered herself from the painful feeling that the act was *in her power*, that she was free to do it or not. Here the emotional crisis is the abandoning of responsibility. There is magical exaggeration of the difficulties of the world. Thus, the world preserves its differentiated structure, but it appears as unjust and hostile, because it demands *too much* of us, that is, more than it is humanly *possible* to give it. The emotion of active sadness in this case is therefore a magical comedy of importance; the sick person resembles servants who, having brought thieves into their master's home, have themselves tied up so that it can be clearly seen that they could not have prevented the theft. Only, here, the sick person is tied up by himself and by a thousand tenuous bonds. Perhaps it will be said that this painful feeling of freedom which he wants to get rid of is necessarily of a reflective nature. But we do not believe it, and all one need do is observe himself to be aware of this: it is the object which is given as having to be created *freely*, the confession which is given as both *having* to and *being able* to be made.

Of course, there are other functions and other forms of active sadness. We shall not insist upon anger, which we have already spoken of at some length and which, of all the emotions, is perhaps the one whose functional role is most evident. But what is to be said about joy? Does it enter into our description? At first sight it does not seem to, since the joyous subject does not have to defend himself against a change which belittles him, against a peril. But at the very beginning, we must first distinguish between joy-feeling, which represents a balance, an adapted state, and joy-emotion. But the latter, if we consider it closely, is characterized by a certain impatience. Let it be understood that we mean by that that the joyous subject behaves rather exactly like a man in a state of impatience. He does not stay in one place, makes a thousand plans which he immediately abandons, etc. In effect, it is because his joy has been aroused by the appearance of the object of his desires. He is informed that he has acquired a considerable sum of money or that he is going to see again someone he loves and whom he has not seen for a long time. But although the object is "imminent," it is not yet there, and it is not yet *his*. A certain amount of time separates him from the object. And even if it is there, even if the longed-for friend appears on the platform of the station, still it is an object which only yields itself little by little, though the pleasure we have in seeing it is going to lose its edge; we shall never get to the point of holding it there before us as our absolute property, of seizing it at one swoop as a totality (nor will we ever, at one swoop, realize our new wealth as an instantaneous totality. It will yield itself through a thousand details and, so to speak, by "abschattungen"). Joy is a magical behavior which tends by incantation to realize the possession of the desired object as instantaneous totality. This behavior is accompanied by the certainty that the possession will be realized sooner or later, but it seeks to anticipate this possession. The divers activities of joy, as well as muscular hypertension and slight vaso-dilatation, are animated and transcended by an intention which aims through them at the world. This seems easy; the object of our desires appears near and easy to possess. Each gesture is a further approbation. To dance and sing for joy represent symbolically approximate behavior, incantations. By means of these the object, which one could really possess only by prudent and, in spite of everything, difficult behavior, is possessed at one swoop—symbolically. Thus it is, for example, that a man who has just been told by a woman that she loves him, can start dancing and singing.

By doing this he abandons the prudent and difficult behavior which he would have to practice to deserve this love and make it grow, to realize slowly and through a thousand little details (smiles, little acts of attentiveness, etc.) that he possesses it. He even abandons the woman who, as a living reality, represents precisely the pole of all his delicate behavior. He grants himself a respite; he will practice them later. For the moment, he possesses the object by magic; the dance mimics the possession.

Yet we cannot be satisfied with these few remarks. They have allowed us to appreciate the functional role of emotion, but we still do not know very much about its nature.

We must first note that the few examples we have just cited are far from exhausting the variety of emotions. There can be many other kinds of fear, many other kinds of sadness. We merely state that they all are tantamount to setting up a magical world by using the body as a means of incantation. In each case the problem and the behavior are different. To grasp its significance and its finality it would be necessary to know and analyze each particular situation. Generally speaking, there are not four major types of emotion. There are many more, and it would be useful and fruitful to classify them. For example, if the fear of the timid person is suddenly moved to anger (a change of behavior motivated by a change of situation), this is not an ordinary type of anger; it is *fear* which has been *surpassed*. This does not at all mean that it is in some way reducible to fear. It simply retains the antecedent fear and makes it enter its own structure. It is only when one has been convinced of the functional structure of emotion that he will come to understand the infinite variety of emotional consciousness. On the other hand, it is proper to insist upon a fact of major importance: behavior pure and simple *is not emotion*, and pure and simple consciousness of this behavior is not emotion either. Indeed, if it were so, the finalist character of emotion would appear much more clearly, and on the other hand, consciousness would easily be able to free itself from it. Moreover, there are false emotions which are not behavior. If someone gives me a gift which only half interests me, it is possible that I may make an external show of intense joy, that I may clap my hands, that I may jump, that I may dance. However, all this is a comedy. I shall let myself be drawn into it a little, and it would be inexact to say that I *am not* joyful. However, my joy is not real. I shall drop it, I shall cast if off as soon as my visitor has parted. This is exactly what we shall call a *false* joy, bearing in mind that falseness is not a logical characteristic of certain propositions, but an existential quality. In the same way I can have false fear or false sadness. Nevertheless, these false states are distinguished from those of the actor. The actor mimics joy and sadness, but he *is neither* joyful *nor* sad because this kind of behavior is addressed to a fictitious universe. He mimics behavior, but he is not behaving. In the different cases of false emotion which I have just cited, the behavior is not sustained by anything; it exists by itself and is voluntary. But the situation is real, and we conceive it as demanding this behavior. Also, by means of this behavior we intend magically to invest real objects with certain qualities. But these qualities are false.

That need not mean that they are imaginary or that they must necessarily annihilate themselves later. Their falseness arises out of an essential weakness which *presents itself* as violence. The agreeableness of the object which was just given to me exists as an exigence much more than a reality; it has a sort of parasitic and tributary reality which I strongly feel. I know that I make it appear upon the object by a kind of fascination; let me cease my incantations and it will immediately disappear.

True emotion is quite otherwise; it is accompanied by belief. The qualities conferred upon objects are taken as true qualities. Exactly what is meant by that? Roughly this: the emotion is undergone. One cannot abandon it at will; it exhausts itself, but we cannot stop it. Besides, the behavior which boils down to itself alone does nothing else than sketch upon the object the emotional quality which we confer upon it. A flight which would simply be a journey would not be enough to establish the object as being horrible. Or rather it would confer upon it the formal quality of *horrible*, but not the matter of this quality. In order for us truly to grasp the horrible, it is not only necessary to mimic it; we must be spell-bound, flooded by our own emotion; the formal frame of the behavior must be filled with something opaque and heavy which serves as matter. We understand in this situation the role of purely physiological phenomena: they represent the *seriousness* of the emotion; they are phenomena of belief. They should certainly not be separated from behavior. At first, they present a certain analogy with it. The hyper-tension of fear or sadness, the vaso-constrictions, the respiratory difficulties, symbolize quite well a behavior which aims at denying the world or discharging it of its affective potential by denying it. It is then impossible to draw exactly a borderline between the pure difficulties and the behavior. They finally enter with the behavior into a total synthetic form and cannot be studied by themselves; to have considered them in isolation is precisely the error of the peripheric theory. And yet they are not reducible to behavior; one can stop himself from fleeing, but not from trembling. I can, by a violent effort, raise myself from my chair, turn my thought from the disaster which is crushing me, and get down to work; my hands will remain icy. Therefore, the emotion must be considered not simply as being enacted; it is not a matter of pure demeanor. It is the demeanor of a body which is in a certain state; the state alone would not provoke the demeanor; the demeanor without the state is comedy; but the emotion appears in a highly disturbed body which retains a certain behavior. The disturbance can survive the behavior, but the behavior constitutes the form and signification of the disturbance. On the other hand, without this disturbance, the behavior would be pure signification, and affective scheme. We are really dealing with a synthetic form; *in order to believe* in magical behavior it is necessary to be highly disturbed.

In order to understand clearly the emotional process with consciousness as the point of departure, it is necessary to bear in mind the twofold character of the body, which is, on the one hand, an object in the world and, on the other, something directly *lived* by consciousness. We can then grasp the essential point: emotion is a phenomenon of belief. Consciousness does not limit itself to projecting affective signification upon the world around it. It *lives* in the new world which it has just established. It lives in it directly; it is interested in it; it endures the qualities which behavior has set up. This signifies that when, with all paths blocked, consciousness precipitates itself into the magical world of emotion, it does so by degrading itself; it is a new consciousness facing the new world, and it establishes this new world with the deepest and most inward part of itself, with this point of view on the world present to itself without distance. The consciousness which is roused rather resembles the consciousness which is asleep. The latter, like the former, is thrown into a new world and transforms its body as synthetic totality in such a way that it can live and grasp this new world through it.

In other words, consciousness changes the body, or, if you

like, the body—as a point of view of the universe immediately inherent in consciousness—puts itself on the level of behavior. There we have the reason why physiological manifestations are, at bottom, very trivial disturbances; they resemble those of fever, of angina pectoris, of artificial overexcitement, etc. They simply represent the total and commonplace disturbance of the body as such (the behavior alone will decide whether the disturbance will be in "diminution of life" or in "enlargement"). In itself it is nothing; quite simply, it represents an obscuring of the point of view of consciousness on things *insofar* as consciousness realizes this obscuring and *lives it spontaneously*. Of course, we mean by this obscuring a synthetic totality and not something piecemeal. But on the other hand, as the body is a thing among things, a scientific analysis will be able to distinguish in the "biological-body" or the "thing-body" troubles localized in such or such an organ.

Thus the origin of emotion is a spontaneous and lived degradation of consciousness in the face of the world. What it cannot endure in one way it tries to grasp in another by going to sleep, by approaching the consciousness of sleep, dream, and hysteria. And the disturbance of the body is nothing other than the lived belief of consciousness, insofar as it is seen from the outside. Only it must be noted:

First, that consciousness does not thetically have consciousness of itself as degrading itself in order to escape the pressure of the world; it has only positional consciousness of the degradation of the world which takes place on the magical level. So it is non-thetically conscious of itself. It is to this extent and this extent only that one can say of an emotion that it is not sincere. There is therefore nothing surprising in the fact that the finality of the emotion is not placed by an act of consciousness at the core of the emotion itself. This finality, however, is not unconscious; it exhausts itself in the constitution of the object.

Second, that consciousness is caught in its own trap. Precisely because it lives the new aspect of the world by *believing* in it, it is caught in its own belief, exactly as in dreaming and in hysteria. Consciousness of the emotion is a captive but we do not necessarily mean thereby that anything whatever external to it might have enchained it. It is its own captive in the sense that it does not dominate this belief, that it strives to live, and it does so precisely because it lives it, because it is absorbed in living it. We need not conceive spontaneity of consciousness as meaning that it might always be free to deny something at the very moment that it posits this something. A spontaneity of this kind would be contradictory. Consciousness, by its very nature, transcends itself; it is therefore impossible for it to withdraw into itself so that it may suppose that it is outside in the object. It *knows* itself only in the world. And the doubt, by its very nature, can only be the constitution of an existential quality of the object, namely, the *dubious*, or a reflective activity of reduction; that is, the essential characteristic of a new consciousness directed upon the positional consciousness. Thus, just as consciousness sees the magical world into which it has cast itself, it tends to perpetuate this world in which it holds itself captive; the emotion tends to perpetuate itself. It is in this sense that one can call it undergone; consciousness becomes concerned about its emotion; it rises in value. The more one flees, the more frightened he is. The magical world is delineated, takes form, and then is compressed against the emotion and clasps it; the emotion does not wish to escape; it can attempt to flee the magical object, but to flee it is to give it a still stronger magical reality. And as for this very character of *captivity*—consciousness does not realize it in itself; it perceives it in objects; the objects are captivating, enchaining; they seize upon consciousness. Freedom has to come from a purifying reflection or a total disappearance of the affecting situation.

However, the emotion, such as it is, would not be so absorbing if it apprehended upon the object *only* the exact counterpart of what it is noetically (for example, a certain man is terrifying *at this time*, in *this* lighting, in such circumstances). What is constitutive of the emotion is that it perceives upon the object something which exceeds it beyond measure. There is, in effect, a world of emotion. All emotions have this in common, that they make a same world appear, a world which is cruel, terrible, gloomy, joyful, etc., but one in which the relationship of things to consciousness is always and exclusively magical. It is necessary to speak of a world of emotion as one speaks of a world of dreams or of worlds of madness, that is, a world of individual syntheses maintaining connections among themselves and possessing *qualities*. But every quality is conferred upon an object only by a passage to infinity. This grey, for example, represents the unity of an infinity of real and possible *abschattungen*, some of which are green-grey, green seen in a certain light, black, etc. Similarly, the qualities which emotion confers upon the object and the world it confers upon them *ad aeternum*. Of course, if I abruptly perceive an object as horrible, I am not explicitly affirming that it will remain horrible throughout eternity. But the very affirmation of the horrible as a substantial quality of the objects is already in itself a passage to infinity. The horrible is now within the thing, at the heart of the thing; it is its affective texture; it is constitutive of it.

Thus, an overwhelming and definitive quality of the thing

appears to us through the emotion. And that is what exceeds and maintains our emotion. The horrible is not only the present state of the thing; it is threatened for the future; it spreads itself over the whole future and darkens it; it is a revelation of the meaning of the world. "The horrible" means precisely that the horrible is a substantial quality; it means that there is the horrible in the world. Thus in every emotion a host of affective pretensions are directed toward the future to set it up in an emotional light. We live emotively a quality which penetrates us, which we suffer, and which exceeds us on every side; at once, the emotion ceases to be itself; it transcends itself; it is not a trivial episode of our daily life; it is intuition of the absolute.

This is what explains the delicate emotions. Through a behavior which is barely outlined, through a slight fluctuation of our physical state, we apprehend an objective quality of the object. The delicate emotion is not at all apprehensive about a slight unpleasantness, a modified wonder, a superficial disaster. It is an unpleasantness, a wonder, a disaster *dimly seen*, perceived through a veil. It is a diminution, one which gives itself out as such. But the object is there; it is waiting, and perhaps the next day the veil will be thrown aside, and we shall see it in broad daylight. Thus, one may be only very slightly affected by all this, if one means thereby the bodily disturbances or the behavior, and yet, through a slight depression, we may fear that our whole life will be disastrous. The disaster is total—we know it—it is profound; but as far as today is concerned, we catch only an imperfect glimpse of it. In this case, and in many others like it, the emotion ascribes more strength to itself than it really has, since, in spite of everything, we see through it and perceive a profound disaster. Naturally, the delicate emotions differ radically from the weak emotions whose affective grasp of the object is slight. It is the intention which differentiates delicate emotion from weak emotion because the behavior and the somatic state may be identical in both cases. But this intention is, in turn, motivated by the situation.

This theory of emotion does not explain certain abrupt reactions of horror and admiration which appear suddenly. For example, suddenly a grinning face appears flattened against the window pane; I feel invaded by terror. Here, evidently, there is no behavior to take hold of; it seems that the emotion has no finality at all. Moreover, there is, in a general way, something immediate about the perception of the *horrible* in certain faces or situations, and the perception is not accompanied by flight or fainting. Nor even by impulsions to flight. However, if one reflects upon it, it is a question of phenomena which are very particular but which are susceptible of an explanation which fits in with the idea we have just expounded. We have seen that, in emotion, consciousness is degraded and abruptly transforms the determined world in which we live into a magical world. But there is a reciprocal action: this world itself sometimes reveals itself to consciousness as magical instead of determined, as was expected of it. Indeed, we need not believe that the magical is an ephemeral quality which we impose upon the world as our moods dictate. Here is an existential structure of the world which is magical.

We do not wish to enlarge here upon this subject which we are reserving for treatment elsewhere. Nevertheless we can at present point out that the category "magical" governs the interpsychic relations of men in society and, more precisely, our perception of others. The magical, as Alain says, is "the mind dragging among things," that is, an irrational synthesis of spontaneity and passivity. It is an inert activity, a consciousness rendered passive. But it is precisely in this form that others appear to us, and they do so not because of our position in relation to them, not as the effect of our passions, but out of essential necessity. In effect, consciousness can be a transcendent object only by undergoing the modification of passivity. Thus, the meaning of a face is a matter of consciousness to begin with (and not a sign of consciousness), but an altered, degraded consciousness, which is, precisely, passivity. We shall come back to these remarks later and we hope to show that they obtrude themselves upon the mind. Thus, man is always a wizard to man, and the social world is at first magical. It is not impossible to take a deterministic view of the interpsychological world nor to build rational superstructures upon this magical world. But this time it is they which are ephemeral and without equilibrium; it is they which cave in when the magical aspect of faces, of gestures, and of human situations, is too strong. What happens, then, when the superstructures laboriously built by reason cave in and man finds himself once again abruptly plunged into the original magic? It is easy to guess; consciousness seizes upon the magical as magical; it forcibly lives it as such. The categories of "suspicious," of "alarming," designate the magical insofar as it is lived by consciousness, insofar as it urges consciousness to live it. The abrupt passage from a rational apprehension of the world to a perception of the same world as magical, if it is motivated by the object itself and if it is accompanied by a disagreeable element, is horror; if it is accompanied by an agreeable element it will be wonder (we cite these two examples; there are, of course, many other cases). Thus, there are two forms of emotion, according to whether it is we who constitute the magic of the world to replace a deterministic activity which cannot be realized, or whether it is the world itself which abruptly reveals itself as being magical. In horror, for example, we suddenly perceive the upsetting of the deterministic barriers. That face which appears at the pane—we do not first take it as belonging to a man who might open the door and with a few steps come right up to us. On the contrary, he is given, passive as he is, as acting at a distance. He is in immediate connection, on the other side of the window, with our body; we live and undergo his signification, and it is with our own flesh that we establish it. But at the same time it obtrudes itself; it denies the distance and enters into us. Consciousness, plunged into this magical world, draws the body along with it, insofar as the body is belief. It believes in it. The behavior which gives emotion its meaning is no longer *ours;* it is the expression of the face, the movements of the body of the other person which come to form a synthetic whole with the disturbance of our organism. Thus, we again find the same elements and the same structures as those we described a little while ago. Simply, the first magic and the signification of the emotion come from the world, not from ourself. Of course, magic as a real quality of the world is not strictly limited to the human. It extends to things insofar as they can be given as human (the disturbing interpretation of a landscape; of certain objects of a room which retains the traces of a mysterious visitor) or as they bear the mark of the psychic. Besides, of course, this distinction between the two great types of emotion is not absolutely rigorous; there are often mixtures of the two types and most emotions are not pure. It is in this way that consciousness, by realizing through spontaneous finality a magical aspect of the world, can create the opportunity to manifest itself as a real magical quality. And reciprocally, if the world is given as magical in one way or another it is possible for consciousness to specify and complete the constitution of this magic, diffuse it everywhere, or, on the contrary, gather it up and concentrate it on a single object.

At any rate, it should be noted that emotion is not an accidental modification of a subject which would otherwise be plunged into an unchanged world. It is easy to see that every emotional apprehension of an object which frightens, irritates, saddens, etc., can be made only on the basis of a total alteration of the world. In order that an object may in reality appear *terrible*, it must realize itself as an immediately and magical presence *face to face* with consciousness. For example, the face which appeared behind the window ten yards from me must be lived as immediately present to me in its menacing. But this is possible only in an act of consciousness which destroys all the structures of the world which might *reject* the magical and reduce the event to its proper proportions. For example, the window as "*object which must first be broken,*" the ten yards as "*distance which must first be covered,*" must be annihilated. This does not at all mean that consciousness in its terror *brings* the face *closer* in the sense that it *would reduce* the distance from the face to my body. To reduce the distance is still to reckon with the distance. Likewise, as long as the frightened subject can think that "the window can be broken easily, it can be opened from the outside," he is only giving rational interpretations which he proposes out of fear. In reality, the window and the distance are perceived "*at the same time*" in the act by which consciousness perceives the face behind the window. But in the very act of perceiving it they are relieved of their character of necessary *instruments*. They are perceived otherwise. The distance is no longer perceived as distance, because it is no longer perceived as "that which must first be travelled." It is perceived as the unitary *basis* of the horrible. The window is no longer perceived as "*that which must first be opened.*" It is perceived as the *frame* of the horrible face. And in a general way regions are set up around me *on the basis of which* the horrible manifests itself. For the horrible *is not possible* in the deterministic world of instruments. The horrible can appear only in the kind of world whose existents are magical by nature and whose possible recourses against the existents are magical. This is rather well shown in the universe of the dream where doors, locks, walls, and arms are not recourses against the menaces of the thief or the wild animal because they are perceived in a unitary act of horror. And as the act which disarms them is the same as the one which creates them, we see the murderers cross these walls and doors. In vain do we press the trigger of our revolver—the shot does not go off. In short, to perceive any object whatsoever as horrible is to perceive it on the basis of a world which reveals itself as *already* being horrible.

Thus, consciousness can "be-in-the-world" in two different ways. The world can appear to it as a complex of instruments so organized that if one wished to produce a determined effect it would be necessary to act upon the determined elements of the complex. In this case, each instrument refers to other instruments and to the totality of instruments; there is no absolute action or radical change that one can immediately introduce into this world. It is necessary to modify a particular instrument and this by means of another instrument which refers to other instruments and so on to infinity. But the world can also appear to it as a non-instrumental totality, that is, modifiable by large masses and without an intermediary. In this case, the categories of the world will act upon consciousness immediately. They are present to it *without distance* (for example, the face which frightens us through the window acts upon us *without instruments;* there is no need for the *window* to open, for a man to leap into the *room* and walk upon the *floor*). And, reciprocally, consciousness aims at combating these dangers or modifying those objects without distance and without instruments by absolute and massive modifications of the world. This aspect of the world is entirely coherent; it is the *magical* world. We shall call emotion an abrupt drop of consciousness into the magical. Or, if one prefers, there is emotion when the world of instruments abruptly vanishes and the magical world appears in its place. Therefore, it is not necessary to see emotion as a passive disorder of the organism and the mind which comes *from the outside* to disturb the psychic life. On the contrary, it is the return of consciousness to the magical attitude, one of the great attitudes which are essential to it, with appearances of the correlative world, the magical world. Emotion is not an accident. It is a mode of existence of consciousness, one of the ways in which it *understands* (in the Heideggerian sense of "Verstehen") its "being-in-the-world."

A reflective consciousness can always direct itself upon emotion. In this case emotion appears as a structure of consciousness. It is not pure and inexpressible quality as is brick-red or the pure impression of grief—as it ought to be according to James's theory. It has a meaning; it *signifies something for my psychic life*. The purifying reflection of the phenomenological reduction can perceive the emotion insofar as it constitutes the world in a magical form. "I find it hateful *because* I am angry."

But this reflection is rare and necessitates special motivations. Ordinarily, we direct upon the emotive consciousness an accessory reflection which certainly perceives consciousness as consciousness, but insofar as it is motivated by the object: "I am angry *because* it is hateful." It is on the basis of this reflection that the passion will constitute itself.

CONCLUSION

The purpose of the theory of emotion which we have just outlined is to serve as an experiment for the establishment of a
phenomenological psychology. Of course, since it is an *example*, we are prevented from giving it the development which it
requires.* On the other hand, since it was necessary to make
a clear sweep of ordinary psychological theories of emotion,
we moved gradually from the psychological considerations
of James to the idea of signification. A phenomenological
psychology which was sure of itself and which had first set
up a fresh area would begin at the very start by fixing in an
eidetic image, the essence of the psychological fact which it
was investigating. This is what we have tried to do for the *mental image* in a work which will soon appear. But despite these
reservations of detail we hope that we have managed to show
that a psychic fact like emotion, which is usually held to be
a lawless disorder, has a proper signification and cannot be
grasped in itself without the understanding of this signification. At present we should like to mark the limits of this psychological research.

---

* We should very much like our suggestions to stimulate the writing, from this point
of view, of complete monographs on joy, sadness etc. We have here furnished only the
schematic directions for such monographs.

We have said in our introduction that the signification of a fact of consciousness comes down to this: that it always indicates the total human reality which *becomes* moved, attentive, perceiving, willing, etc. The study of emotions has quite verified this principle: an emotion refers back to what it signifies. And, in effect, what it signifies is the totality of the relationships of the human reality to the world. The passage of emotion is a total modification of "being-in-the-world" according to the very particular laws of magic. But at once we see the limits of such a description; the psychological theory of emotion supposes a preliminary description of affectivity insofar as the latter constitutes the being of the human reality; that is, insofar as it is constitutive of *our* human reality of being affective human reality. In this case, instead of starting from a study of the emotion or the inclinations which might indicate a human reality not yet elucidated as the ultimate term of all research, an ideal term, moreover, and in all likelihood, beyond the reach of anyone who begins with the empirical, the description of affect would take place *on the basis* of the human reality described and fixed by an *a priori* intuition. The various disciplines of phenomenological psychology are *regressive*, and yet the term of their regression is *for them* a pure ideal. Those of pure phenomenology are, on the contrary, progressive. It will doubtless be asked why it is expedient in these conditions to use these two disciplines simultaneously. It seems that pure phenomenology would be sufficient. But if phenomenology can prove that emotion is in essence a realization of human reality insofar as it is *affection*, it will be impossible for it to show that human reality must necessarily manifest itself in *such* emotions. That there are such and such emotions, and only these, manifests without any doubt the *factitiousness* of human existence. It is this factitiousness which makes necessary a regular recourse to the empirical; it is this which, in all likelihood, will prevent psychological regression and phenomenological progression from ever coming together.

Part IV

THE ROLE OF THE IMAGE IN MENTAL LIFE

1. THE SYMBOL*

The image serves neither as illustration nor as support for thought. It is in no way different from thought. An imaginative consciousness includes knowledge and intentions, and it may also include words and judgments. And by this we do not mean that a judgment can be made *on* the image, but that, in the very structure of the image, judgments can enter in a special form, namely in the imaginative form. For instance, if I want to represent to myself the stairway of a house which I have not mounted for a long time, I at first "see" a stairway of white stone. Several steps will appear before me in a fog. But I am not satisfied, something is missing. I hesitate for a moment, I burrow in my memories, but without emerging from the imaginative attitude; then, all of a sudden, with the clear impression of engaging myself, of assuming my responsibilities, I cause to appear before me a rug with copper rods on the stone steps. A thought process occurred here, a free and spontaneous decision was made. But this decision did not pass through a stage of pure knowledge or of a simple ver-

---

* In this essay it will be convenient for us to use some constructions and expressions which appear to endow the unreal object with the power of causality over consciousness. This is to be taken only metaphorically. It is easy to reconstruct the veritable processes. For instance, an image has no persuasive power but we persuade ourselves by the very act by which we construct the image.

bal formulation. The act in which I was engaged, the act of affirmation, was precisely an imaginative act. My assertion consisted exactly of conferring on the object of my image the quality "recovery of a cover." And this quality I caused to appear *on* the object. But this act is evidently a judgment since, as the researches of the Wurzburg school have so well shown, the essential characteristic of the judgment is the *decision*. Into the imaginative consciousness there enters therefore a particular sort of judgment; imaginative assertions. In a word (later on we shall see that even reasoning may occur in imagery, that is, necessary connections of imaginative consciousness), the ideational elements of an imaginative consciousness are the same as those of the consciousness to which the name of thoughts is usually given. The difference lies essentially in a general attitude. What we ordinarily designate as *thinking* is a consciousness which affirms this or that quality of its object but without realizing the qualities on the object. The *image*, on the contrary, is a consciousness that aims to produce its object: it is therefore constituted by a certain way of judgment and feeling of which we do not become conscious as such but which we apprehend *on* the intentional object as this or that of its qualities. In a word: the function of the image is *symbolic*.

For the past several years much has been written, about symbolic thinking, no doubt under the influence of psychoanalysis. What struck one in these writings was the conception of the image as a material trace, an inanimate element, which later plays the role of symbol. Most psychologists look upon thinking as a selective and organizing activity which fishes for its images in the unconscious to arrange them and combine them according to circumstances: the thought stays strictly on the outside of the images it gathers together, which may be compared to a checker player who moves his pieces on the checkerboard so as to bring about a certain combination. Each combination is a symbol.

We cannot accept a conception according to which the symbolic function is added to the image from the outside. It seems to us, and we hope that we have already made it somewhat obvious, that the image is symbolic in essence and in its very structure, that the symbolic structure of the image cannot be suppressed without destroying the image itself.

But what exactly is a symbol? How is the symbol to be distinguished from the sign or the illustration? A critical analysis of the outstanding but little-known works of Flach on "the symbolic schemes in the thought process"* will enable us to answer this question.

"I have noticed," writes Flach, "that from time to time, when I wanted to clarify the data of a problem or even to understand some propositions which were definitely useful for my thinking, there came to the fore some more or less vivid representations but which always brought along with them the solution of the problem, the comprehension of the phrase."

These representations appear with the act of comprehension, properly so called. They do not accompany the mere memory of a proposition or of a problem. They cannot be voluntarily produced. If an attempt is made to produce them, all that comes to the fore is what Flach calls "illustrations of thinking,"† that is, the "thin engraving" of Binet. If a scheme is to appear it must be aimed at directly—all of the subject's effort must be directed to the understanding of a word or a proposition. But are all acts of comprehension accompanied

---

* A. Flach, "Ueber Symbolische Schemata im produktiven Denkprozess," *Arch. f. Ges. Psych. Bd.* LII, p. 369 *et seq.*

† Denkillustrierungen.

by schemes? Flach does not think so. He notes that there are no schemes in very weak mental effort. "We obtained no schemes when work was very easy or when subjects could solve the problem by recourse to memory. In such cases we found at times a verbal-motor reaction and at times simple illustrations."

These schemes possess an essential trait: they "have no meaning in themselves but only a symbolic one." If a subject makes a sketch of the scheme that has just appeared to him the sketch appears deprived of meaning in the eyes of an uninformed observer. That is, these images possess *all the basic traits* called for by an exact representation of thinking in its concrete structure—and *only these traits*.

This is what distinguishes them from other sorts of images, called by Flach, as we have seen, "illustrations of thinking" and defined by him as follows:

"By this I understand that what they make sensible is an illustration of the object whose relations with thought are fortuitous, external, and of a purely associative order."

We can guess that in the illustrations there is at one and the same time more or less than thinking.

"Experiment 53: the subject asked to give a short and essential account of Zola at a horse race. The experimenter asks whether the subject knows what relationship this representation has with the account asked for and the subject answers that one day he read a detailed description of a journey in *Nana* and that since then the image regularly arises at the name of Zola."

But note, on the other hand, several symbolic schemes (sketches, diagrams, outlines) from the accounts of the experiments of Flach. Flach presented his subjects with common terms, generally abstract ones, which they were to try to understand:

"7. Exchange: I gave my thoughts the form of a ribbon (bands). Here is a ribbon which represents the circular process of the exchange. The movement of the curve is a spiral because in the exchange the one acquires what the other loses. The inequality of the curves should explain the gain and the loss involved in every exchange. The ribbon appeared on the field."

This scheme, says Flach, is interesting as being the one which represents in logic two concepts whose extensions (or comprehensions) have a common part. But here it is a question in logic of a particular determination that is involved.

"14. Compromise: It is the association of two men. I had the representation of two bodies gliding towards each other, sideways. Their form was vague but it was two bodies—one on the right, the other on the left—which sucked up each other. The body was solid and had some protuberances which it pushed ahead and which disappeared in each other. Then, there was only *one* body. But what is surprising is that the body did not increase much in size. It was a bit larger than each of the parts but smaller than the two combined. It was a greyish green, had a dirty greyish green color. At the same time I made the movement with my hands."

"22. Baudelaire: I saw immediately, in the open space, on an absolutely dark bottom, a spot of blue-green color, of the color of vitriol and as if thrown there with one wide stroke of the brush. The spot was longer than broad—perhaps twice as long as broad. Immediately I knew that this color must express morbidity, the kind of decadence which characterizes Baudelaire. I study whether this image can be applied to

Wilde or Huysmans. Impossible: I feel a strong resistance, as if something contrary to logic were proposed to me. This image belongs only to Baudelaire and from this moment on, will represent that poet to me."

"27. Proletariat: I had a strange image, a flat and black area and, underneath, a sea flowing dimly, an endless wave, something like a dark and thick mass rolling with unwieldy vagueness. What did the mass signify? Extension in the entire world; something like a latent dynamism."

The schemes in general have but one meaning, that of the thought they symbolize:

"This intuitive image expresses nothing else than a system of conceptual relationships which are grasped while the subject sees them as determined relationships between the sensory data. These relations, as sensory data, present themselves as *a priori* determinations of space.

"In symbolic schemes a thought is always grasped, due to the fact that the conceptual relations that constitute it are lived intuitively and, as far as I could ascertain, as spatial data. Whereas in the cases illustrating thought, space has the role of a receptacle, a background, or a substratum and functions as a stage on which they are placed, yet when it is a matter of symbolic representations, it has, on the contrary, a clarifying role: spatial determinations and figurations do not exist. They are but the supports and essential concretization of abstract relationships. It is by the spatialization of these relationships that the abstract content of thought is seized. By means of simple limitations, of condensations, by indications of the directions or by a particular rhythm of a region of space, an abstract thought can specify its content. Here is an example: When we asked: what do you understand by altruism, the subject had the representation of a direction, the fact of going towards another thing which is not given. . . ."

Flach adds that we must distinguish between the preceding cases "and those in which an ideal abstract content is as if localized in a determined region of space without the thought being characterized by that localization. These localizations are then nothing else than contact points for the thought, which they tie to spatial determinations and which can thus rest on them as on real objects."

What remains to explain is the source of these symbolic schemes. It is on this point, we must admit, that Flach is most unsatisfactory. He retricts himself, or nearly so, to looking upon the symbolic scheme as a creation of "*Sphaerenbewusstsein*."*

"It is, as a whole, on the level of the consciousness of direction without words, the stage in which we endeavor to give expression to and define in words the essence of an objective content that we have precisely lived subjectively (internalized) and that we nevertheless possess in some manner more or less intuitive. Then it often happens that, in its main outlines, thought emerges as a scheme from its all-inclusive wrapper."

But why does the symbolic scheme appear and in which cases? How does it build itself up? What is its relationship to pure knowledge, to the pure act of comprehension? What does it mean for a comprehension to realize itself by the intermediary of a symbol? And just what is the symbolic function of the scheme? These are the questions Flach leaves unanswered. We must then take up again after him the study

---

* "Consciousness of spheres." An expression used especially by psychologists of the Würzburg school and which designates a certain condition of pure knowledge, prior to the image—and, by extension, thought, as understood by the psychologist.

of these symbolic schemes and see what further conclusions we can draw about them.

We have seen that acts of ready comprehension or consciousness of pure meaning are not accompanied by schemes. The scheme accompanies the effort of intellection, properly so called, and it presents in the form of a spatial object the results of this effort. Nevertheless, it would have been interesting to know whether all the acts, beginning with a certain degree of difficulty, are translated into a scheme, or whether there can occur intellections (understanding, perception) without images. The results of Mesmer's experiments enable us to complete the work of Flach on this point; there are many cases in which understanding occurs without imagery, by simply words, *in* the words; examples can also be found of a direct and pure understanding without imagery or words. But in the latter case it rather seems that the understanding stopped on the way, that one stopped short of a complete development. But what fails to reach the end is not the imaginative phase: in every case we have been able to study, the subjects are aware of having been short on words. We can therefore affirm that there are two classes of comprehension: *a pure comprehension* (whether or not supported by signs) and an *imaginative comprehension* (which also may or may not make use of words). Since we cannot admit that this division is the effect of chance we must suppose that there is a functional difference between the two types of comprehension. Numerous observations have, in fact, permitted us to conclude that the use of the one or the other of these comprehensions was not governed by the object. I have often verified, for instance, that, depending on the circumstances, I could understand the same phrase by means of schemes or without any help at all.

These observations permit us to formulate a first problem more clearly: granted that there are two ways of understanding and that these two ways can be applied regardless of the object of consciousness, what are the motives which can lead consciousness to operate an understanding in one or the other of these ways? These motives must be looked for in the very structure of antecedent consciousnesses and not in the objects. In a word, an imaginative comprehension is always a part of a temporal form to be described, in which consciousness takes a certain position in relation to its object. It is this position we must ascertain; we can ask ourselves for which intentional attitude of consciousness comprehension will operate in the imaginative way and what is the functional relation of the symbolic scheme to that attitude. But it is not easy to determine immediately the nature of that attitude and we must at first make a deeper study of the idea of symbolic schemes.

We see at once that the symbolic scheme is constructed as follows: a knowledge, which we must still investigate, penetrates and unites into a synthetic act a kinaesthetic analogue to which at times there is joined an effective analogue. These determinations of psychological space are none other, in fact, than impressions of movement apprehended imaginatively. Everything we have said concerning movement . . . is applicable to experiments 7 and 13 as we reported above. Experiments 14 and 21, which we also cited, show very clearly the way in which the affective analogue is added in a new synthesis to the kinaesthetic analogue. The purpose of the latter is to express as clearly as possible the rational structure, the concept to be understood. The non-kinaesthetic element of the analogue is more difficult to characterize. It nevertheless translates the personal reaction of the subject to the concept;

but it translates it as a quality of the concept since it occurs itself as a quality of the scheme. In this connection experiment 14 is very instructive:

". . . It was moldy green, it had a dirty moldy green color." According to Flach himself, this person had to give a "dirty" color to her scheme because she was compelled by her surroundings to incessantly renew an arrangement which appeared to her immoral and humiliating. Whatever one may think of this interpretation which is psychoanalytical, it is quite typical that the art of Baudelaire is symbolized by a blot the color of vitriol. As we noted above, the affective analogue presents itself as representing ineffable sensations. In the two cases we cited, it serves as a substitute of a color. The rational elements of the concept, on the contrary, are translated into a form, that is, a movement.

With the scheme thus constituted, we should ask ourselves whether it is true that it is the sense of the concept or of the proposition to be understood that is read *on* the scheme. Flach claims repeatedly that "the essential characteristic of these schemes is that the thinking proceeds *on* these images, *beginning* with these images. . . . The image appears first and only then the thinking . . . which indicates that I thought on the occasion of that image."

And, in truth, several statements of his subjects ("Thought followed immediately, which I read in the image . . ."), seem to confirm this. But is this possible? What this view comes to when clearly expressed is this: first the symbolic image appears, when the subject tries to understand—and the subject deciphers this image and finds in it just the meaning he is looking for. The essence of the effort to understand would thus consist of constructing the schemes.

Now we must note that according to this hypothesis when

the subject constructs the scheme he does not yet understand it. And we ask how, under these circumstances, was he able to produce a symbolic representation which can have, according to Flach's own terms, "all the basic traits of the idea he is to understand." This could happen only provided an unconscious understanding preceded the conscious understanding. But in that case, if the image occurs first and is then deciphered, how can the subject interpret it correctly? We have seen, in fact, that an uninformed observer is unable to understand a symbolic schema without an explanation unless he is shown a sketch of it. We are then called upon to suppose that the unconscious understanding is transformed behind the scheme into conscious understanding. But in that case the role of the scheme is superfluous. But shall we claim, as does Flach, that in the scheme the idea is "lived intuitively" before it is understood? But, we repeat that the construction of the scheme implies the comprehension of the idea. We do not mean to say, of course, that understanding occurs first and then construction. But it is very evident that comprehension is realized in and by construction. The structure of the concept to be understood serves as the rule for the elaboration of the scheme and one becomes conscious of this rule by the very fact of applying it. So that once the scheme is constructed there is nothing more to understand. What could have deceived some subjects and Flach himself is that, if we do not limit ourselves to understand for ourselves only, if we desire to transmit the result of our thinking by discourse, we must transport ourselves on another level and express by means of verbal signs what we had grasped as spatial relations. This transcription which naturally takes understanding for granted nevertheless calls for some effort of adaptation which, in certain cases, could be mistaken for understanding itself.

Everything we have just said could be expressed more simply: . . . we could say that it is impossible to find in the image anything more than what was put into it; in other words, the image teaches nothing. Consequently, it is impossible that understanding operates on the already constructed image. A similar conclusion follows from the illusion of immanence. The image cannot, as a matter of fact, have for its function helping understanding. But understanding can in certain cases adopt the imaginative structure. The image-object appears in such a case as the simple intentional correlative of the very act of comprehension.

But at what point will understanding assume the symbolic form? To answer this question it is enough to remind ourselves of the typical make-up of a symbolic scheme. A scheme is either a form in movement, or a static form. Both cases involve a visual imaginative apprehension of kinaesthetic sensation. We saw . . . how this apprehension works. We saw that the sensible element as such is framed by a protention and a retention. By protention we are finally thrown back to a knowledge which presents itself as protention and which is transformed into retention as the movement flows out. The constitution of the symbolic scheme therefore sends us back to the knowledge as to its origin. What knowledge is involved here?

Understanding is not pure reproduction of a meaning. It is an act. In making itself manifest, this act envisions a certain object and this object is, in general, a truth of judgment or a conceptual structure. But this act does not start from nothing. For instance, I may try to understand the word "man" but not its corresponding German "*Mensch*" unless I know German. Every word in terms of which I can make an effort to understand is therefore shot through and through with a knowledge which is nothing other than the recollection of past understandings. We know that Descartes draws a distinction between ideas and the recollection of ideas. Knowledge is in some manner a recollection of ideas. It is empty, it implies past and future understandings but is itself not an understanding. It is evident that when Flach presented his subjects with the words they were to understand, the understanding began with this knowledge: it proceeded from the knowledge to the act. It is then at the level of the knowledge that the nature of understanding is decided. In accordance with the intention of the knowledge, this comprehension will be imaginative or not, that is, the knowledge will or will not change into a protention followed by a synthetic movement. In a word, the essential factor we have to describe is that intentionality which appears in the knowledge and which finally constructs the symbolic scheme. Why does it debase the knowledge?

Does it do so in order to facilitate the understanding? This we have already answered above: the image teaches nothing. The understanding attains its end as *an image*, but not *by* the image. . . . We shall see, moreover, that the scheme, far from helping intellection, often checks and deflects it. But if we return to an analysis of Flach's experiments it may help us to understand the function of the image.

Let us give an account of experiment 27. The subject who is asked to give the meaning of the word "proletariat," sees "a flat and black area, and, below it, a sea rolling vaguely." What can lead us astray here, and what seems to have deceived Flach, is a faulty interpretation of the idea of symbol. Flach seems to believe in fact that this scheme is the *symbol* of proletariat, that is, that his subject, in producing this symbol, intends to represent his idea by means of lines and colors. This image will therefore present itself as a schematic representation of the content of the idea "proletariat," as a means of making the inventory of that content. In other words, the image would still be a sign. But to this view we can object, first, that it is impossible to see the reason why the subject should want to make such a construction. Secondly, and above all, we need but produce one of these schemes for ourselves and observe it to convince ourselves that the schemes in no way perfom the role of sign and representation. No doubt there is a representative in the scheme: it is the affective-motor analogue by means of which we apprehend the form and its color. But the scheme itself is no longer an analogue: it itself is an object having a meaning. That "flat and dark area" with that "vaguely rolling sea" is neither a sign nor a symbol for the proletariat. It *is* the proletariat in person. Here we reach the real meaning of the symbolic scheme: the scheme is the object of our thought giving itself to our consciousness. So the function of the scheme as such is in no way to help the understanding; it functions neither as expression nor as support, nor as exemplification. We expressly declare, using an indispensable neologism, that the role of the scheme is that of *presentifier*.

. . . We defined *pure knowledge* as consciousness of a rule. But let us add, it is "an ambiguous consciousness which is given as both a consciousness without any relational structure of the object and as a consciousness full of a state of the subject." In a word, just as we called it pre-objective, it can be called pre-reflexive. It brings to the subject instructions concerning its own capacities ("Yes, I know . . ., I could know," etc.) but this does not appear fully as a spontaneous activity of ideation and the relation which makes the object of the knowledge appear at times as an objective relation and at times as a rule for obtaining ideas. This state without equilibrium can become debased into imaginative knowledge: in which case all reflection disappears. It can also become a pure reflective consciousness, that is, posit itself for itself as consciousness of a rule. In that case the meaning of a word will be grasped on the reflective level as the content of a concept and the meaning of a phrase as judgment. On this level, reasoning still appears as a succession of ideas which are generated from the very depth of their innerness, the premises appear as the operating rules for forming the conclusion, and the psychic motivation clothes the following form: "If I posit that A implies B and that B implies C, in order to be consistent, I must posit that A implies C." It is in considering the reflexive nature of classical reasoning that formal logic defined itself as the study of the condition "of the agreement of mind with itself." All this mental activity moves on the reflective level, the ideas appear as ideas at the same time that they are forming themselves. Consciousness is separated from the object while it is reasoning. It can rejoin it at the level of the conclusion, provided it converts this latter into a non-reflective affirmation. This reflexive ideation is not accompanied by images. In the first place, images are here useless; secondly, if they should appear as image consciousnesses of image and not as object consciousnesses, they would lose their meaning.

But ideation can operate entirely on the non-reflective plane: all that is needed is that the pure knowledge become debased into imaginative knowledge, that it lose its pre-reflective character in order to become unhesitatingly non-reflective. In that case, all thought becomes consciousness of things and not consciousnesses of itself. To understand a word is no longer to apprehend a concept: it is to realize an essence; the comprehension of the judgment bears upon the objective content which the Germans call *Sachverhalt*. This non-reflective plane may be called the *plane of presences* because of the attitude assumed by consciousness: it behaves in fact as if it were *in the presence* of the objects which it judges; that is to say, it seeks to apprehend that thing and to formulate ideas on it as an external object. To understand a word at that moment amounts to constructing before consciousness the corresponding thing. To understand "proletariat" consists in constructing the proletariat, and making it appear to consciousness. The form in which this something will appear will naturally be a spatial form, because a consciousness can effectuate a presence only as a spatial form. But this spatialization is not desired for its own sake. In reality what operates here in consciousness is the natural confusion between transcendence and externality. Instructed to understand the word "proletariat" or the phrase "Nature imitates art," we attempt to refer to the things themselves in order to contemplate them; in other words, the first step of consciousness is to turn to intuition. The understanding of the word occurs therefore as a sudden appearance of the object. So that the spatial determinations are not signs or images of the structural relations which constituted the thing: they are apprehended as these relations themselves. They are these relations constituted by a knowledge which incorporated itself into a series of movements. But, naturally, the object is not really constituted, it is here only "as an image" and consequently it presents itself as absent. Correlatively the attitude of consciousness is not that of observation, that is, the presence of the object as an image teaches him nothing since the constitution of the object as an image is already the understanding. Nevertheless the final thoughts will occur as reactions of consciousness to the transcendent object, that is, as the results of contemplation, as they unroll by a normal track from the original comprehension. We shall shortly investigate the mechanism of this thought as an image and see that, if the construction of the scheme changes nothing in the phenomenon of comprehension, the final thoughts are changed in their essence by the fact that they have been motivated by an original thought as an image.

2. SYMBOLIC SCHEMES AND ILLUSTRATIONS OF THOUGHT

Before defining the symbolic schemes Flach distinguishes between them as follows:

1. *Simple illustrations of thoughts* which can appear, according to him, together with a symbolic scheme but which can never express more than one example.

2. *Schematic representation* of Messer ("It was neither lion nor tiger, I was aware of a hairy skin"). The symbolic scheme is not the image of a definite concrete object forming something indefinite.

3. *Diagrams* which represent schematically, for instance, which something is missing: schematic representations are therefore illustrations of somewhat hazy thoughts contain-the days of the week, the months of the year.

"What the diagram has in common with the symbolic scheme is the fact that the diagram represents spatially an abstract and unextended object. But there is nothing else here than a definite localization in space. This localization serves as a mooring, an attachment, an orientation for our memory, but plays no role in our thought."

4. *Synaesthesias and synopsies*, that is, images aroused regularly by hearing proper names, vowels, etc.

5. *Auto-symbolic phenomena*. This is the name Silberer gives* to hypnagogic visions that symbolize an immediately preceding thought. Flach recognizes two types of hypnagogic symbolization. The first contains symbols which are close to symbolic schemes. In the second there are simple illustrations of thought.

The essential distinction Flach draws between illustrations, schematic representations, diagrams, synaesthesias, auto-symbolic phenomena, on the one hand, and symbolic schemes, on the other, comes in the main to this: The former do not express thought, they are connected with ideation by external ties and are moreover quite loose (what is roughly known as ties of *association*), the latter are a direct product of thought and its expression on the level of the image. This amounts to admitting that there are images which have a symbolic function and others that have no function of any sort, whether as survivals, fortuitous connections, or stereotypes. Below the level of symbolic schemes Flach places the "engravings" of Binet.

We do not share his opinion. The image is a consciousness. If this principle is accepted what meaning does the association of ideas retain? Association occurs as a causal linkage between two consciousnesses: one consciousness cannot be aroused *from the outside* by another consciousness: but it arises by itself by its own intentionality, and the only tie that can connect it with the previous consciousness is that of *motivation*. Consequently we must no longer speak of automatisms and stereotypes. Binet and the Würzburg psychologists tend to

---

* Herbert Silberer, *Der Traum*, Stuttgart, 1919.

construct the image, over against thought, as a phenomenon deprived of meaning. But if the image is a consciousness, it must have its own meaning, as does every other sort of consciousness. Its appearance in the course of thought is never the effect of a chance connection: it plays a role. This role is undoubtedly easier to determine in the case of the symbolic scheme than in that of the engraving. But if our premises are correct, there must be a function for all images which do not occur as schemes.

Diagrams are quite readily reduced to symbolic schemes. Flach almost admits this when, after having distinguished most diagrams from symbolic schemes and having denied them any other function than that of an "orientation for our memory," makes an exception of diagrams whose structure betrays a dominant preoccupation of the subject. Apropos of a diagram representing the month of the year, for instance, when the subject was asked why three months were missing, the answer was: "Because in my childhood there were three months of anxiety out of every year."

This diagram is evidently symbolic. But is this not the case with every diagram, although somewhat more discreetly so? For many subjects the months are completely given but arranged in an ascending, descending, broken, bent, straight, etc., order. All these arrangements have a meaning which corresponds most often to the way in which the year is divided by the professional vocation of the subject. In a word, the diagrams which represent the months or the days of the week for the subject express regularly the way in which the succession of the months or the days appear to the subject: that is, the year or the week appears in its concrete structure. The same is true of syntheses, that is, for those cases, for instance, in which a vowel arouses in the subject a certain color. Synaesthesia never occurs as the product of a pure association. The color occurs as the *sense* of the vowel.

"A man forty years of age, experiences very definite colors for a, o, and u, but not for i; he understands that if need be the sound can be seen white or yellow, but he feels that in order to find it red one must have a distorted mind or a perverted imagination."*

When Flourney tries to explain synaesthesias by what he calls "identity of emotional basis," he does not take into account the sort of logical resistance one experiences when one attempts to change the color aroused by a vowel. This happens because the color occurs at the sound "in person" just as the "vague sea" occurs as the proletariat in person. Naturally what we have here is a consciousness which is more affective than intellectual and the image attributes the personal reaction of the subject to the vowel. Besides, it is hard to see why Flach, who admits the symbolic meaning of the color in his discussion of Experiment 14 ("arrangement . . . he had a dirty color, greenish grey") or of experiment 21 ("Baudelaire . . . a spot of blue-green color, of the color of vitriol") will not admit this in the case of synaesthesia. Moreover, what difference is there between experiment 21 "Baudelaire" and a simple synaesthesia, other than in complexity? No doubt that the symbolic scheme is generally built up as a spatial determination. But this is simply due to the fact that purely intellectual comprehensions are more readily translated into movements. Knowledge, as we have seen, directly impregnates kinaesthetic sensations. But there is also a comprehension "of the heart," and it is this comprehension that expresses itself by synopsies.

Finally, it is fitting to show that images which present all the

---

* Cited by Flourney, *Des phénomènes de synopsie*, p. 65.

features of "engraving" can play the role of a symbolic scheme. This Flach himself recognized: when one of his subjects was asked to furnish him with a brief description of the philosophy of Fichte, he pictured "the self creating the non-self in order to go beyond it" as a worker pounding a wall with a hammer; and Flach is compelled to admit that this illustration of thought is functionally similar to a scheme.

So if we brush aside the phenomenon of auto-symbolism, which is so uncertain and difficult to investigate, a first examination leads to the following conclusions: first, that the realm of the symbolic scheme is wider than Flach assumes and we must admit into it all the neighboring phenomena which Flach tried to side-track; secondly, the distinction between scheme and engraving is not well marked: these are rather limited cases connected by transitory forms; they should not therefore be looked upon as exercising radically different functions.

We must, however, face the fact that when a scheme is compared to an illustration considerable differences are found between these two sorts of images. Let us suppose I am asked to define the historical period known as the Renaissance in a few words. It may happen that I produce an indefinite image of movement, something like a stream of water which expands and wanes; I may also see the opening out of a flower. In both cases we call my image a symbolic scheme. There is no doubt more in the second case than in the first: in addition to a symbolic meaning, the image has another meaning which can be grasped from without, as, for instance, if the subject makes a drawing of his image. But this supplementary meaning is not thought of for its own sake: in the degree to which it is conscious it is still a quality I confer upon the subject.

But I can also produce another sort of image: for instance: on hearing the word Renaissance, I may "see" the David of

Michelangelo. The essential difference in this case is that David *is not* the Renaissance. We should also note that this difference cannot be verified from without. Only the subject can say whether the image is symbolic of the Renaissance or whether, in some way, it is a *lateral* image; only he can inform us if the David of Michelangelo is thought of for itself or as a symbol. Let us suppose that the David of Michelangelo is apprehended for itself. In this very apprehension there must be a particular intention, since it is the apprehension itself which could be symbolic. The symbolizing apprehension gives David the meaning of "Renaissance"; the non-symbolizing apprehension constitutes it as the "statue of Michelangelo to be found in such and such a museum in Florence, etc." If my first aim was to give a brief definition of what I understood by "Renaissance," I must recognize that my thought deviated. But this deviation could not arise on the level of the constituted image; it is on the level of the knowledge, at the very level of the process of ideation that the change of direction operates; and, this change, far from being aroused by the appearance of the image, is the indispensable condition for its appearance. It is therefore a spontaneous deviation which thought gives to itself and which cannot be the effect of chance or of some external compulsion; this deviation must have a functional meaning. Why has a thought which seeks to discover the content of the concept "Renaissance" made this hook, why has it delayed to form the image of that statue?

It is advisable that we undertake a description of how this image appears to me. We notice, first, that it occurs as linked by the unity of the same quest to the anterior productions of consciousness, in a word, this David does not present itself simply as such but as a step towards the understanding of the term "Renaissance." And this very term of step is a rubric for the total of the contradictory meanings of the statue. In one sense, in fact, it presents itself as a unity among others, the collection of which constitutes the total extension of the term being studied. It is a point of departure for a systematic review of all the works of art I may know which were produced at the time of the Renaissance. But, from another side, the image attempts to hold us upon itself: in this very David I could find the solution of the problem I am investigating. David, without presenting himself explicitly as the Renaissance, pretends vaguely to conceal in himself the meaning of that period, as happens, for instance, when we say that by visiting the castle in Berlin one will understand the meaning of the Prussia of Bismarck. At the end of this pretension and, by a sort of participation, the envisioned statue can appear as *being* the Renaissance.

Only, this way of *being* the Renaissance cannot have the purity of that of a symbolic scheme. In the scheme, in fact, the spatial determinations have no other meaning than that of the concept they represent, or if, perchance, they have a meaning of their own (flower, the worker pounding with a hammer), this meaning has value only within the limits of the concept symbolized and as a more subtle means to make it appear. For David, on the contrary, the manner of appearing as David is wholly independent of the Renaissance. The very meaning of David *as David* goes back to a mass of ideas which cannot be of service here. This statue by Michelangelo presents itself to me as the David I have seen in the course of my journey in Italy, as the work of a sculptor some of whose other works I also know, as an artistic production which I can class among others, etc., and finally, as a unique event in my life, from the beginning of which I can reconstruct a whole atmosphere, a whole past epoch. All this is, of course, not specified, it is an affective meaning which could be developed. But it is enough for this David who, in some way, *is* or *tends to be* "the Renaissance" to appear also as something which can divert my thought and carry me far from my actual task, in short, as the correlative of a consciousness which can lose its equilibrium and slip perhaps into revery. So that the statue seems rather *to be* the Renaissance by a mystic tie of participation.

At the end of this brief description we arrive at the conclusion that the image as an illustration is produced as the first groping of a lower thought, and that the ambiguities concerning its meaning are due to the uncertainties of a thought which has as yet not risen to a clear vision of a concept. It seems to us, in fact, that our first response to an abstract question, even though it may correct itself immediately, is always—at least as an answer to the question—a lower response, at once prelogical and empirical. This response is at the same time without unity because the thought is uncertain and hesitates between several means—all of them insufficient—to produce a concept. Socrates asked Hippias: "What is Beauty?" and Hippias answered: "It is a beautiful woman, a beautiful horse, etc." This answer seems to us to make not only an historical step in the development of human thought but also a necessary step (as well as the habit of reflection can curtail it) in the production of a concrete individual thought. This first response of thought naturally takes on the form of an image. Many persons, when questioned about the nature of Beauty, form an image of Venus de Milo, and this is as if they answered: "Beauty is the Venus de Milo."

But this is only one of the aspects of the image as an illustration: it is formed in addition by an unintelligent thought, which rapidly attempts to cast the greatest amount of knowledges on the question presented; it is as if we were to say: "Beauty? Well: the Venus de Milo, for instance . . .," without going any further because of the contradictory tendencies which make up the image. So here we see a second way that thought has of representing a concept for itself: it is simply the sum of the unities of the class it designates.

But the very fact that these knowledges (Venus de Milo, David, etc.) present themselves under an imagined form and not purely verbal indicates more and better. Place someone in a hall in a museum in which there are several masterpieces of the Renaissance and ask him to give you a short account of that artistic epoch and it is a safe bet that before answering he will cast a quick glance at one of the statues and paintings. Why? This he could not answer himself: it is an attempt to observe, to return to the thing itself and to examine it; it is the primary data of experience, a way of confirming a naïve empiricism which is also one of the lower stages of thought. In the absence of these masterpieces the reaction would be the same the statue of David *would be evoked*, that is, thought would assume the form of imaginative consciousness. Only thought itself does not know whether the object it presents to itself in such haste *is* beauty or only a *sample* of beautiful things or whether one could derive an idea of the concept "beauty" by examining it. The result of these uncertainties is an image which sets itself up for its own sake and also as a step in understanding. From this point on thought will suddenly leave this course by means of real understanding, and by a creative effort will consider the Renaissance itself as present in person: it is then that the scheme appears. It is then not the role of the image that changes, which is always the correlative of a consciousness; but the nature of the thought. From the onset of the image as an illustration, two roads are always possible: one by which thought loses itself in revery as it abandons its first assignment, and another which leads it to understanding as such. It is this ever-possible annihilation of thought at the level of the image that has impressed some psychologists like Binet and led them to the conclusion that the image was an obstruction for thought. But it is thought itself that is responsible for this unbalance of thought, and not the image.

3. IMAGE AND THOUGHT

We shall not seek to know whether all non-reflective thought assumes the form of the image. We are satisfied with having shown that the image is like an incarnation of non-reflective thought. Imaginative consciousness represents a certain type of thought: a thought which is constituted in and by its object. Every new thought concerning this object will present itself, in the imaginative consciousness, as a new determination apprehended on the object. But it is naturally only quasi-apprehensions that are involved here. The thought does not, in fact, establish itself on the object; it rather *appears as the object*. If the development of an idea occurs in the form of a series of imaginative consciousnesses that are synthetically linked, it will imbue the object as an image with a sort of vitality. It will appear now under one aspect, now under another, now with this determination, now with some other. To judge that a coachman whose face one imagines vaguely had a moustache is to see his face appear as having a moustache. There is an imaginative form of the judgment which is nothing else than the addition to the object of new qualities, accompanied by the feeling of venturing, promising, or of assuming responsibilities. These few observations enable us to suggest a solution of the problem of the relationships of the image to the concept. If we think imaginatively of some individual objects it will be these objects themselves that will appear to our consciousness. They will appear as they are, that is, as spatial realities with determinations of form, color, etc. But they will never have the individuality and unity which characterize objects of perception. There will be some distortions, a sort of deep-seated vagueness, lack of definiteness . . . At the same time, the object presents itself as not being here in body, as an *absent object*. Whatever it may be, it is the form that thought takes on in order to appear to our consciousness. If we think right now of a class like "horse," "man," etc., it is the class itself that will appear to us. It is, of course, but rarely that we think of a class all alone. Most of the time our thoughts are of the relationships between classes. We can say rightly that the thought of an isolated concept is always the result of artificial practices. But such thought is, however, always possible and it can occur in three ways: in the first, we do not know direction of the looked-for concept or we approach it indirectly. In this case our first approximations will present themselves under the form of individual objects belonging to the extension of that concept. If I try to think the concept "man," I could orient myself by producing the image of a particular man or the image of the geography that represents the white man, etc. In the preceding chapter we attempted to give an account of this type of thought. But it is also possible that our thought grasps the concept itself directly. In this second case the concept could appear as an object in space. But this object will not be individualized, it will not be this or that man, but *man*, the class turned into a man. The object of our imaginative consciousness will naturally be an undetermined man, who has nothing in common with the composite image of Galton, but whose indetermination will be the essence itself. It will be like the fleeting consciousness of having a man before one without either being able, or even wanting, to know his appearance, his color, his height, etc. This way of getting to the concept in extension is, no doubt, a very low level of thought. But if, in the third place, we get to the concept all at once in comprehension, that is, as a system of relations, it will then appear to us a collection of pure spatial determinations which will have no other function than *to permit it;* that is, it will take the form of a symbolic scheme. But some concepts like "man," "horse," etc. are too charged with sensible and too poor in logical content to enable us to rise often to this third stage of thought. The symbolic scheme appears only with an effort of comprehension, that is on the occasion of abstract thought. These three ways in which the concept appears to non-reflective thought correspond therefore to the three clearly-defined attitudes of consciousness. In the first I orient myself, I look about me. In the second, I remain among the objects but I call forth the very class, the collection of these objects as such in my consciousness. In the third, I completely turn away from things (as a unity or a collection) to their relations. The relationships between the concept and image therefore present no problem. In fact, there are no concepts and no images. But there are two ways in which the concept can appear: as a pure thought on the reflective level and on the non-reflective level as an image.

But a more serious question arises: in the image, thought itself becomes a thing. Will this not cause thought to undergo profound modifications? Can we admit that a purely reflective thought and a spatialized thought have exactly the same meaning; is not thought as an image, an internal form of thought? We must distinguish between two cases, and this way that thought has of being a prisoner of a spatial representation carries different consequences for the ultimate course of consciousness, depending on whether the latter (consciousness) supports reluctantly this imprisonment and seeks to free itself from it, or whether it permits itself to be absorbed by the image like water by sand. In the first case the subject is conscious of the insufficiency of this way of thinking at the very moment he forms the image and seeks to free himself from it. Here is an interesting observation of R. A., a professor of philosophy:

"I had the impression of clearly understanding the main thought of Brunschvicg in reading the pages of *L'Orientation du Rationalisme*, which resumes the thought of Schopenhauer: 'There is no object excepting for the spectator.' When going beyond the order of knowledge. Mr. Brunschvicg, in the very order of being, brings forth the two correlative realities (subject and object) of a spiritual activity, of an original course, I thought I had grasped the final point of his thought and I recalled an image that illustrated, in some way, my intellectual effort. In the center, a kind of schematic, geometric representation of a movement and then, beyond, from the two sides of this moving line, two symmetrical points or rather two small circles very similar to the circle of a target. This image was not, of course, in the forefront of consciousness. Nevertheless I noticed it but felt it to be insufficient because still tainted with some materiality, but it seemed to me that my impression of understanding sprang mainly from the movement of thought to grasp the image and to go beyond it. I felt that if I could think of the spiritual equivalent of that image without the help of any sensible representation, then I would have truly understood M.Brunschvicg because I would have had to see 'with the eyes of the heart' the nature and the spirit (in the second sense), emerge out of this spiritual and creative primitive urge."*

The description of R. A. does not permit us to doubt that

---

* I have met other instances among a number of scholars and professors of this effort to surpass the image at the very moment when it is formed. I had an especially interesting report from M. L. deR., a student of philosophy.

we are in the presence of a symbolic scheme. . . . But the consciousness of R. A. contains an additional determination which we have not found up to now in any of the descriptions of Flach: the scheme is itself but provisional, insufficient as a step to be surpassed. But did we not say that the symbolic scheme was the essence it represented? How then is it possible that it should present itself at the same time as being and as not being this essence (the genesis in a spiritual movement of subject-object combination)? It seems, however, that this structure of consciousness is very common among philosophers, that is, among men who are very much in the habit of "thinking about thinking" as Goethe said, that is, who have delved deeply into the immaterial nature of thinking, who know by long experience that it escapes every attempt to picture it, to define it, to capture it, and who consequently resort to comparisons and metaphors reluctantly and cautiously when they speak of it. The symbolic scheme therefore appears, for them, as but superficial and very deceptive. No doubt it is completely there, but in a form which can deceive. As a result, the scheme presents itself as something external to thought which itself appears as something which cannot be exhausted by anything "external" which it may adopt, and finally, as radically incongruous with its appearances.

As a result, the investigator can have two attitudes in relation to his own thinking. He can either be contented with seizing the scheme as a possible direction, as the open door to a series of further investigations, the indication of nature through which to grasp some material aspects. In this case, the scheme possesses a characteristic dynamism which derives from the fact that it permits its own over-extension. But, at the same time, *understanding* is not given in act; it is only outlined as possible, as being at the point of the deliverance (enfranchisement) of all images. Very often the comprehension is only that: the scheme plus the idea that one could—that one should—go further.

Or else the subject actually carries out the operations which are to liberate his thought from their materialistic obstacle. It disengages itself from the scheme, while entirely retaining the thought. But if it remains in the non-reflective attitude, that is, if it is only conscious *of* the object (particular or universal essence, relationships between essences, etc.), on which it forms thoughts, it can turn away from a symbolic scheme only to construct another, and so on to infinity. It will stop sooner or later in these operations. But this cessation remains without importance if the subject stays aware of the unsatisfactory nature of all imagery, whose importance we have just seen, if he can say to himself at the moment when he stops himself what Gide wants to write at the end of *The Counterfeiters:* "Could be continued." In that case, the essence searched for appears as not being in any of the forms it has assumed, nor in the infinity of those it might have assumed. It is *different*, radically different. And, from the very fact that the subject *does not cease to affirm this heterogeneity*, all these imagined coatings, all these schemes are without danger for thought. But thought, although we could express ourselves upon it without keeping account of the images in which it reveals itself, is never directly accessible to us, if we have once taken the imaginative attitude in forming it. We will always go from image to image. Comprehension is a movement which is never ending, it is the reaction of mind to an image by another image, to this one another image, and so on, in a straight line, to infinity. To substitute for this infinite regression the simple intuition of a thought calls for a radical change in attitude, a veritable revolution, that is, passing from the non-reflective plane to that of the reflective. On this plane thought presents itself as thought at the very time that it appears: and so it is completely transparent to itself. But we can never discover any connecting path which permits us to elevate ourselves progressively from non-reflective to reflective thought, that is, from the idea as an image to the idea as idea. The simple act of intellection on the reflective plane has for its correlative the infinitive idea of approximations through symbols on the non-reflective plane. The result of this equivalence is that the two processes, on the two planes, are equivalents for the progress of knowledge.

It is altogether different when the scheme absorbs thought and presents itself as *being* itself the essence or the relationship to be determined. *Non-reflective thought is a possession.* To think of an essence, relationship, is on this plane to produce them "in flesh and bone," to constitute them in their living reality . . . and at the same time to see them, to possess them. But, at the same time, it is to constitute them *under a certain form* and to consider this form as expressing their nature, as *being their* nature. Here thought encloses itself in the image and the image presents itself as adequate to the thought. There follows a warping—possible at any moment—of the further course of consciousness. In fact, the object under consideration (essence, relation, a complex of relations, etc.), does not present itself only as an ideal structure: it is also a material structure. Or rather ideal and material structure are but one. But the material structure implies certain determinations of space, certain symmetries; certain relations of position, and sometimes even the existence of things and persons. . . . While the evolution of these determinations remains governed by the *ideal sense* of the image, while the transformations of the scheme remain commanded by those of thought, the development of the idea is not altered. But this subordination of material structures to the ideal structures is possible only if the material structures are grasped as not exhausting the ideal structures, as if a relative independence were posited between the two. . . . But in the very great majority of cases the material structure occurs as *being*, the ideal structure, and the development of the figure, of the scheme, in its spatial nature is given as exactly identical with the development of the idea. We can see the danger; a slight preference is enough, it is enough to consider for a moment for themselves the spatial relations of the scheme and to permit them to affirm themselves or to modify themselves in accordance with the laws of belonging to spatiality: the thought is hopelessly warped, we no longer follow the idea directly, we think by analogy. It has appeared to us that this imperceptible debasement of thought was one of the most common causes of error, particularly in philosophy and in psychology.

In the imaginative attitude, in fact, we find ourselves in the presence of an object which presents itself as an analogue to those which can appear to us in perception. This object, in as much as it is constituted as a *thing* (pure determinations of geometric space, common object, plant, animal, person), is the correlative of a certain knowledge (empirical—physical or biological, laws—or *a priori*—geometric laws), which has served to constitute it but which has not exhausted itself in that constitution. This knowledge presides at the ultimate developments of the image, it is this knowledge which orients them in this or that direction, which resists when we want to modify the image arbitrarily. In short as soon as I constitute the image of an object, the object has a tendency to behave as an image in the same way that other objects of the same class do in reality. Flach cites some fine examples, but does not seem to grasp their importance. "The subject imagines, for instance, balls thrown in the air. He then feels in his arms the resistance of the air to the rising of the balls. We have made no deeper studies on synaesthesias since it is established that these phenomena really belong to intuition and do not form an important characteristic of the symbolic scheme as such. They apply as well to cases of illustrations of thought by simple association."

In this excellent example cited by Flach no associations are, in fact, involved, but rather the interpretation of a knowledge which becomes conscious of itself only in the form of an image. All that the subject clearly envisions is the trajectory of the balls tossed in the air. But he cannot think of this trajectory without at the same time thinking of the resistance of the air; although this resistance was not deliberately thought of, the body imitates it as the indispensable complement of the object. Left to itself, the image thus has its own laws of development, and these depend in their turn on the knowledge which has served to constitute it. Here is an observation that will enable us to see this more clearly:

"I wanted to speak of an automobile that climbed hills easily and I was searching for an expression which would describe this abstract idea—unformulated—that would be comical: 'It climbs the hills as if it were pulled up by a weight, as if it were falling towards the top and not the bottom.' I had an image. I saw the automobile climbing a hill; I had the feeling that it was climbing by itself and without a motor. But I just could not imagine this reversing of the weight: the image resisted and offered me but an equivalent: I had the vague feeling of the presence on top of the hill of an ill-defined object, a sort of loadstone, that pulled the automobile. Since this image was not the one I had wanted to produce, there resulted from it a wavering and I could not find the adequate expression. I had therefore to look for a subterfuge and I said: 'One is obliged to check the ascent.' This introduction of a new element modified my image and gave it an entirely different nuance, while its elements nevertheless remained the same; instead of being pulled by a loadstone, the same automobile climbed the hill by itself: it was no longer a machine but a living being which was moving spontaneously and whose ardor I had to control."

In this example the subject wanted to construct, as an intermediary between the abstract thought "reversing of the weight" and his verbal expression, a concrete image the substance of which would have passed into the discourse. But this image would not permit itself to be constructed because it is nature to contradict the concrete knowledge that had presided at its formation; its searched-for structure had been missing, one slid to the right or left, one struck the living automobile-beast, the magnetized automobile, but this reversed weight, although conceived, was not grasped as in an image. From these concrete laws that presided at the individual development of every image, nothing is more typical than the transformation of the automobile into a living being after the phrase "one is obliged to check the ascent." This automobile which must be checked in its ascent ceased being a machine due to this very command. The mere fact of imagining this restraint and these circumstances completed itself spontaneously by the annexation to the machine which was being restrained with a sort of living force. Thus, although the mind is always free to vary no matter which element of the image, we must not believe that the mind could change, at the same time, *all* the elements at its pleasure. All happens as if the transformations of the image were sufficiently rigorous by the laws of *compassibility*. These laws cannot be determined *a priori* and depend upon the knowledge which enter into combination.

Let us now return to our problem: when I produce, in the course of my reflections, an image of the type of those Flach calls "symbolic" (whether of a scheme or any other representation), it seems that there is a conflict in this image between what it is and what it represents, between the possibilities of development which come to it from the idea it embodies, and its own dynamism. On the one hand stones, a hammer, a flower could be symbols of a mass of abstract essences; on the other, this flower, these stones, this hammer, have their own nature and tend to develop into an image in keeping with this nature. When I conserve this dissatisfaction with images of which we have spoken at the very heart of the images, the thought does not suffer from this ambiguity because I leave no time for the image to develop in accordance with its own laws, I leave it as soon as I formed it; I am never satisfied with it. Always ready to be engulfed in the materiality of the image, thought runs away by gliding into another image, this one into another, and so on. But in the majority of cases, this defiance of the image, which is like a recollection of reflection, does not appear. In that case, the laws of development that belong to the image are often confused with the laws of the essence that is under consideration. If that essence appears as a stone that is rolling down an incline, this descent of the stone, which draws all its necessity from my physical knowledge, develops and reinforces the symbol, confers upon it its rigor. The following instance will show the dangers of this substitution. "I would have liked to convince myself of the idea that every oppressed person or every oppressed group draws from the very oppression from which it suffers the strength to destroy it. But I had the clear impression that such a theory was arbitrary and I felt a sort of annoyance. I made a new effort to think: at this very moment there arose the image of a compressed force. At the same time I felt the latent force in my muscles. It was going to break out the more violently the more compressed it was. In a moment I felt to the point of certainty the necessity of the idea of which I could not persuade myself the moment before."*

We see what is involved here: the oppressed *is* the force. But on the other hand, *on* the compressed force we can already read with confidence the strength with which it will be discharged: a compressed force represents clearly potential energy. This potential energy is evidently that of the oppressed, since the oppressed *is* the force. Here we see clearly the contamination between the laws of the image and those of the essence represented. This idea of potential energy which increases in proportion to the force exercised on the object, is the force which *presents* it, it is upon it that it can be apprehended. Change the term of comparison, and substitute an organism for the force, and you will have the absolutely inverse intuition, something which could be expressed in the phrase: "The oppression demeans and debases those who suffer from it." But the image of the force left to itself and envisaged purely and simply as an image of force, would not be enough to convince us. No doubt that the force gathers strength. But never enough to get rid of the load which weighs upon it, because the force it gathers is *always inferior* to that which compresses it. The conclusion we then draw from the image will be this: "The oppressed gains in strength and in value from the very fact of the oppression, but it will never get rid of its yoke." In fact, as I could explain it to myself, in reproducing in myself the scheme of the force, there is more. The image is falsified by the meaning: the energy that gathers in the compressed force is not felt as a pure passive storing, but as a living force, one

---

* Observation of R. S., a student.

which increases *with time*. Here the image of the force is no longer a simple image of force. It is more of something indefinable: an image of a living force. Here there is no doubt a contradiction, but . . . there is no image without an inherent contradiction. It is in and by this very contradiction that the impression of evidence arises. The image thus carries within itself a persuasive power which is spurious and which comes from the ambiguity of its nature.

4. IMAGE AND PERCEPTION

At the beginning of this book* we showed the difficulties raised by every attempt to interpret perception as an amalgam of sensations and images. We now understand why these theories are inadmissible: for the image and the perception, far from being two elementary psychical factors of similar quality and which simply enter into different combinations, represent the two main irreducible attitudes of consciousness. It follows that they exclude each other. . . . When Peter is envisioned as an image by means of a picture it means that the painting is no longer *perceived*. But the structure of images called "mental" is the same as that of images whose analogue is external: the formation of an imaginative consciousness is accompanied, in this as in the former case, by an annihilation of a perceptual consciousness, and vice versa. As long as I am *looking* at this stable I cannot form an image of Peter; but if the unreal Peter arises before me all of a sudden, the table which is before my eyes disappears, leaves the scene. These two objects, the real table and the unreal Peter, can alternate only as correlative of radically distinct consciousness; how then, under these conditions could the image cooperate to form the perception?

It is then evident that I always *perceive more and other-*

---

* *L'Imaginaire.*

wise than I *see*. It is this contestable fact—and which seems to us to constitute the very structure of perception—that the psychologists of the past tried to explain by introducing images into perception, that is, by supposing that we complete the strictly sensory material by projecting unreal qualities on the objects. This explanation naturally demanded the possibility of a strict assimilation between image and sensations—at least theoretically so. If it is true as we have tried to show, that there is here an enormous contradiction, we must look for some new hypothesis. We will limit ourselves to indicating the possible directions of research.

In the first place, the works of Köhler, Wertheimer, and Koffka permit us henceforth to explain certain anomalous constants of perception by the persistence of formal structures during our change of position. A thorough study of these forms would permit us, no doubt, to understand why we perceive *in a different way* than we see.

We must now explain why perception includes *more*. The problem would be more simple if we would once and for all give up that creature of reason which we know as pure sensation. We could then say, with Husserl, that perception is the act by which consciousness puts itself in the presence of a temporal-spatial object. Now, into the very constitution of that object there enters a mass of pure intentions which do not posit new objects which determine the present object in relation to aspects not now perceived. For instance, it is well understood that this ash-tray before me has a "bottom," that it rests *by means of this bottom* on the table, that this bottom is of white porcelain, etc. These various facts are derived from either a mnemic knowledge, or from ante-predicative inferences. But what we should note well is that this knowledge, whatever its source may be, remains unformed: not that it is unconscious but it sticks to the object, it is grounded in the act of perception. What is envisioned is never the invisible aspect itself of the object, but that visible aspect of the thing to which the invisible one corresponds, namely, the upper surface of the ash-tray in that its very structure as the upper surface implies the existence of a "bottom." It is evidently these intentions which supply perception with its fullness and its richness. Without them, Husserl rightly observes, mental contents would remain "anonymous." But they are not less radically heterogeneous in imaginative consciousness: they do not become formulated, posit nothing apart and limit themselves to projecting into the object as a constituting structure qualities which are hardly determined, all but simple possibilities of development (like that fact that a chair should have two other legs than those seen, that the arabesques of the mural tapestry should extend all the way behind the closet, that the man I see from behind should also be seen from in front, etc.). We see that what is involved here is neither an image that has dropped into the unconscious nor that of an image that has been subdued.

These intentions can no doubt give rise to images and this is the very source of the error which we have exposed. They are the very condition of every image concerning objects of perception, in the sense in which all knowledge is the condition of corresponding images. Only, if I wish to represent for myself the mural tapestry *behind* the cupboard, the pure intentions implied in the perception of the visible arabesques will have to detach themselves, to posit themselves for themselves, to *express* themselves, to *debase* themselves. At the same time they will stop to ground themselves on the perceptual act and become a *sui generis* act of consciousness. So also, the hidden arabesques will no longer be a quality of the visible arabesques—namely, as *having a sequel, of continuing without interruption.* But they will rather appear as isolated to consciousness, as an autonomous object.

There is therefore in perception the charm of an infinity of images; but these can rise only at the cost of the annihilation of perceptual consciousness.

In summary, we can say that the imaginative attitude represents a special function of mental life. If such an image appears, in place of simple words, of verbal thoughts or pure thoughts, it is never the result of a chance association: it is always an inclusive and *sui generis* attitude which has a meaning and a use. It is absurd to say that an image can harm or check thought, or then this must be understood to mean that thought hurts itself, loses itself in windings and byways; implying that as a matter of fact there is no opposition between image and thought but only the relation of species to a genus which it subsumes. Thought takes the image form when it wishes to be intuitive, when it wants to ground its affirmations on the *vision* of an object. In that case, it tries to make the object appear before it, in order to *see* it, or better still, to *possess* it. But this attempt, in which all thought risks being bogged down, is always a defeat: the objects become affected with the character of unreality. This means that our attitude in the face of the image is radically different from our attitude in the face of objects. Love, hate, desire, will, are quasi-love, quasi-hate, etc., since the observation of the unreal object is a quasi-observation.

Part V

WHAT IS WRITING?

No, we do not want to "engage" painting, sculpture, and music "too," or at least not in the same way. And why would we want to? When a writer of past centuries expressed an opinion about his craft, was he immediately asked to apply it to the other arts? But today it's the thing to do to "talk painting" in the argot of the musician or the literary man and to "talk literature" in the argot of the painter, as if at bottom there were only one art which expressed itself indifferently in one or the other of these languages, like the Spinozistic substance which is adequately reflected by each of its attributes.

Doubtless, one could find at the origin of every artistic calling a certain undifferentiated choice which circumstances, education, and contact with the world particularized only later. Besides, there is no doubt that the arts of a period mutually influence each other and are conditioned by the same social factors. But those who want to expose the absurdity of a literary theory by showing that it is inapplicable to music must first prove that the arts are parallel.

Now, there is no such parallelism. Here, as everywhere, it is not only the form which differentiates, but the matter as well. And it is one thing to work with color and sound, and another to express oneself by means of words. Notes, colors, and forms are not signs. They refer to nothing exterior to themselves. To be sure, it is quite impossible to reduce them strictly to themselves, and the idea of a pure sound, for example, is an abstraction. As Merleau-Ponty has pointed out in *The Phenomenology of Perception*, there is no quality of sensation so bare that it is not penetrated with signification. But the dim little meaning which dwells within it, a light joy, a timed sadness, remains immanent or trembles about it like a heat mist; it *is* color or sound. Who can distinguish the green apple from its tart gaiety? And aren't we already saying too much in naming "the tart gaiety of the green apple"? There is green, there is red, and that is all. They are things, they exist by themselves.

It is true that one might, by convention, confer the value of signs upon them. Thus, we talk of the language of flowers. But if, after the agreement, white roses signify "fidelity" to me, the fact is that I have stopped seeing them as roses. My attention cuts through them to aim beyond them at this abstract virtue. I forget them. I no longer pay attention to their mossy abundance, to their sweet stagnant odor. I have not even perceived them. That means that I have not behaved like an artist. For the artist, the color, the bouquet, the tinkling of the spoon on the saucer, are *things*, in the highest degree. He stops at the quality of the sound or the form. He returns to it constantly and is enchanted with it. It is this color-object that he is going to transfer to his canvas, and the only modification he will make it undergo is that he will transform it into an *imaginary* object. He is therefore as far as he can be from considering colors and signs as a *language*.*

What is valid for the elements of artistic creation is also valid for their combinations. The painter does not want to cre-

---

* At least in general. The greatness and error of Klee lie in his attempt to make a painting both sign and object.

ate a thing.* And if he puts together red, yellow, and green, there is no reason for the ensemble to have a definable signification, that is, to refer particularly to another object. Doubtless this ensemble is also inhabited by a soul, and since there must have been motives, even hidden ones, for the painter to have chosen yellow rather than violet, it may be asserted that the objects thus created reflect his deepest tendencies. However, they never express his anger, his anguish, or his joy as do words or the expression of the face; they are impregnated with these emotions; and in order for them to have crept into these colors, which by themselves already had something like a meaning, his emotions get mixed up and grow obscure. Nobody can quite recognize them there.

Tintoretto did not choose that yellow rift in the sky above Golgotha to *signify* anguish or to *provoke* it. It is anguish and yellow sky at the same time. Not sky of anguish or anguished sky; it is an anguish become thing, an anguish which has turned into yellow rift of sky, and which thereby is submerged and impasted by the proper qualities of things, by their impermeability, their extension, their blind permanence, their externality, and that infinity of relations which they maintain with other things. That is, it is no longer *readable*. It is like an immense and vain effort, forever arrested half-way between sky and earth, to express what their nature keeps them from expressing.

Similarly, the signification of a melody—if one can still speak of signification—is nothing outside of the melody itself, unlike ideas, which can be adequately rendered in several ways. Call it joyous or somber. It will always be over and

---

* I say "create," not "imitate," which is enough to squelch the bombast of M. Charles Estienne who has obviously not understood a word of my argument and who is dead set on tilting at shadows.

above anything you can say about it. Not because its passions, which are perhaps at the origin of the invented theme, have, by being incorporated into notes, undergone a transubstantiation and a transmutation. A cry of grief is a sign of the grief which provokes it, but a song of grief is both grief itself and something other than grief. Or, if one wishes to adopt the existentialist vocabulary, it is a grief which does not *exist* any more, which *is*. But, you will say, suppose the painter does houses? That's just it. He *makes* them, that is, he creates an imaginary house on the canvas and not a sign of a house. And the house which thus appears preserves all the ambiguity of real houses.

The writer can guide you and, if he describes a hovel, make it seem the symbol of social injustice and provoke your indignation. The painter is mute. He presents you with *a* hovel, that's all. You are free to see in it what you like. That attic window will never be the symbol of misery; for that, it would have to be a sign, whereas it is a thing. The bad painter looks for the type. He paints the Arab, the Child, the Woman; the good one knows that neither the Arab nor the proletarian exists either in reality or on his canvas. He offers a workman, a certain workman. And what are we to think about a workman? An infinity of contradictory things. All thoughts and all feelings are there, adhering to the canvas in a state of profound undifferentiation. It is up to you to choose. Sometimes, high-minded artists try to move us. They paint long lines of workmen waiting in the snow to be hired, the emaciated faces of the unemployed, battlefields. They affect us no more than does Greuze with his "Prodigal Son." And that masterpiece, "The Massacre of Guernica," does any one think that it won over a single heart to the Spanish cause? And yet something is said that can never quite be heard and that would take an infinity of words to express. And Picasso's long harlequins, ambiguous and eternal, haunted with inexplicable meaning, inseparable from their stooping leanness and their pale diamond-shaped tights, are emotion become flesh, emotion which the flesh has absorbed as the blotter absorbs ink, and emotion which is unrecognizable, lost, strange to itself, scattered to the four corners of space and yet present to itself.

I have no doubt that charity or anger can produce other objects, but they will likewise be swallowed up; they will lose their name; there will remain only things haunted by a mysterious soul. One does not paint significations; one does not put them to music. Under these conditions, who would dare require that the painter or musician engage himself?

On the other hand, the writer deals with significations. Still, a distinction must be made. The empire of signs is prose; poetry is on the side of painting, sculpture, and music. I am accused of detesting it; the proof, so they say, is that *Les Temps Modernes* publishes very few poems. On the contrary, this is proof that we like it. To be convinced, all one need do is take a look at contemporary production. "At least," critics say triumphantly, "you can't even dream of engaging it." Indeed. But why should I want to? Because it uses words as does prose? But it does not use them in the same way, and it does not even *use* them at all. I should rather say that it serves them. Poets are men who refuse to *utilize* language. Now, since the quest for truth takes place in and by language conceived as a certain kind of instrument, it is unnecessary to imagine that they aim to discern or expound the true. Nor do they dream of *naming* the world, and, this being the case, they name nothing at all, for naming implies a perpetual sacrifice of the name to the object named, or, as Hegel would say, the name is revealed as the inessential in the face of the thing which is essential. They do not speak, neither do they keep still; it is something different. It has been said that they wanted to destroy the "word" by monstrous couplings, but this is false. For then they would have to be thrown into the midst of utilitarian language and would have had to try to retrieve words from it in odd little groups, as for example "horse" and "butter" by writing "horses of butter."*

Besides the fact that such an enterprise would require infinite time, it is not conceivable that one can keep oneself on the plane of the utilitarian project, consider words as instruments, and at the same time contemplate taking their instrumentality away from them. In fact, the poet has withdrawn from language-instrument in a single movement. Once and for all he has chosen the poetic attitude which considers words as things and not as signs. For the ambiguity of the sign implies that one can penetrate it at will like a pane of glass and pursue the thing signified, or turn his gaze toward its *reality* and consider it as an object. The man who talks is beyond words and near the object, whereas the poet is on this side of them. For the former, they are domesticated; for the latter they are in the wild state. For the former, they are useful conventions, tools which gradually wear out and which one throws away when they are no longer serviceable; for the latter, they are natural things which sprout naturally upon the earth like grass and trees.

But if he dwells upon words, as does the painter with colors and the musician with sounds, that does not mean that they have lost all signification in his eyes. Indeed, it is signification alone which can give words their verbal unity. Without it they are frittered away into sounds and strokes of the pen. Only, it too becomes natural. It is no longer the goal which is always out of reach and which human transcendence is always aiming

---

* This is the example cited by Bataille in *Inner Experience*.

at, but a property of each term, analogous to the expression of a face, to the little sad or gay meaning of sounds and colors. Having flowed into the word, having been absorbed by its sonority or visual aspect, having been thickened and defaced, it too is a thing, increate and eternal.

For the poet, language is a structure of the external world. The speaker is in *a situation* in language; he is invested with words. They are prolongations of his meanings, his pincers, his antennae, his eyeglasses. He maneuvers them from within; he feels them as if they were his body; he is surrounded by a verbal body which he is hardly aware of and which extends his action upon the world. The poet is outside of language. He sees words inside out as if he did not share the human condition, and as if he were first meeting the word as a barrier as he comes toward men. Instead of first knowing things by their name, it seems that first he has a silent contact with them, since, turning toward that other species of thing which for him is the word, touching them, testing them, palping them, he discovers in them a slight luminosity of their own and particular affinities with the earth, the sky, the water, and all created things.

Not knowing how to use them as a *sign* of an aspect of the world, he sees in the word the *image* of one of these aspects. And the verbal image he chooses for its resemblance to the willow tree or the ash tree is not necessarily the word which we use to designate these objects. As he is already on the outside, he considers words as a trap to catch a fleeing reality rather than as indicators which throw him out of himself into the midst of things. In short, all language is for him the mirror of the world. As a result, important changes take place in the internal economy of the word. Its sonority, its length, its masculine or feminine endings, its visual aspect, compose for him a face of flesh which *represents* rather than expresses signification. Inversely, as the signification is *realized*, the physical aspect of the word is reflected within it, and it, in its turn, functions as an image of the verbal body. Like its sign, too, for it has lost its pre-eminence; since words, like things, are increate, the poet does not decide whether the former exist for the latter or vice-versa.

Thus, between the word and the thing signified, there is established a double reciprocal relation of magical resemblance and signification. And the poet does not *utilize* the word, he does not choose between diverse acceptations; each of them, instead of appearing to him as an autonomous function, is given to him as a material quality which merges before his eyes with the other acceptation.

Thus, in each word he realizes, solely by the effect of the poetic *attitude*, the metaphors which Picasso dreamed of when he wanted to do a matchbox which was completely a bat without ceasing to be a matchbox. Florence is city, flower, and woman. It is city-flower, city-woman, and girl-flower all at the same time. And the strange object which thus appears has the liquidity of the *river*, the soft, tawny ardency of *gold*, and finally abandons itself with *propriety* and, by the continuous diminution of the silent *e*, prolongs indefinitely its modest blossoming.* To that is added the insidious effect of biography. For me, Florence is also a certain woman, an American actress who played in the silent films of my childhood, and about whom I have forgotten everything except that she was as long as a long evening glove and always a bit weary and always

---

* This sentence is not fully intelligible in translation as the author is here associating the component sounds of the word Florence with the signification of the French words they evoke. Thus: FL-OR-ENCE, *fleuve* (river), *or* (gold), and *décence* (propriety). The latter part of the sentence refers to the practice in French poetry of giving, in certain circumstances, a syllabic value to the otherwise silent terminal *e*.—Tr.

chaste and always married and misunderstood and whom I loved and whose name was Florence.

For the word, which tears the writer of prose away from himself and throws him into the midst of the world, sends back to the poet his own image, like a mirror. This is what justifies the double undertaking of Leiris who, on the one hand, in his *Glossary*, tries to give certain words a *poetic definition*, that is, one which is by itself a synthesis of reciprocal implications between the sonorous body and the verbal soul, and, on the other hand, in a still unpublished work, goes in quest of remembrance of things past, taking as guides a few words which for him are particularly charged with affectivity. Thus, the poetic word is a microcosm.

The crisis of language which broke out at the beginning of this century is a poetic crisis. Whatever the social and historical factors, it manifested itself by attacks of depersonalization of the writer in the face of words. He no longer knew how to use them, and, in Bergson's famous formula, he only half recognized them. He approached them with a completely fruitful feeling of strangeness. They were no longer his; they were no longer he; but in those strange mirrors, the sky, the earth, and his own life were reflected. And, finally, they became things themselves, or rather the black heart of things. And when the poet joins several of these microcosms together the case is like that of painters when they assemble their colors on the canvas. One might think that he is composing a sentence, but this is only what it appears to be. He is creating an object. The words-things are grouped by magical associations of fitness and incongruity, like colors and sounds. They attract, repel, and "*burn*" one another, and their association composes the veritable poetic unity which is the *phrase-object*.

More often the poet first has the scheme of the sentence in his mind, and the words follow. But this scheme has nothing in common with what one ordinarily calls a verbal scheme. It does not govern the construction of a signification. Rather, it is comparable to the creative project by which Picasso, even before touching his brush, prefigures in space the *thing* which will become a buffoon or a harlequin.

> *To flee, to flee there, I feel that birds are drunk But,*
> *oh, my heart, hear the song of the sailors.*
>
> *(Fuir, là-bas fuir, je sens que des oiseaux sont ivres*
> *Mais ô mon coeur entends le chant des matelots.)*

This "but" which rises like a monolith at the threshold of the sentence does not tie the second verse to the preceding one. It colors it with a certain reserved nuance, with "private associations" which penetrate it completely. In the same way, certain poems begin with "and." This conjunction no longer indicates to the mind an operation which is to be carried out; it extends throughout the paragraph to give it the absolute quality of a *sequel*. For the poet, the sentence has a tonality, a taste; by means of it he tastes for their own sake the irritating flavors of objection, of reserve, of disjunction. He carries them to the absolute. He makes them real properties of the sentence, which becomes an utter objection without being an objection *to* anything precise. He finds here those relations of reciprocal implication which we pointed out a short time ago between the poetic word and its meaning; the ensemble of the words chosen functions as an *image* of the interrogative or restrictive nuance, and vice-versa, the interrogation is an image of the verbal ensemble which it delimits.

As in the following admirable verses:

> *Oh seasons! Oh castles!*
> *What soul is faultless?*
> *(O saisons! O châteaux!*
> *Quelle âme est sans dédfaut?)*

Nobody is questioned; nobody is questioning; the poet is absent. And the question involves no answer, or rather it is its own answer. Is it therefore a false question? But it would be absurd to believe that Rimbaud "meant" that everybody has his faults. As Breton said of Saint-Pol Roux, "If he had meant it, he would have said it." Nor did he *mean* to say something else. He asked an absolute question. He conferred upon the beautiful word "soul" an interrogative existence. The interrogation has become a thing as the anguish of Tintoretto became a yellow sky. It is no longer a signification, but a substance. It is seen from the outside, and Rimbaud invites us to see it from the outside with him. Its strangeness arises from the fact that, in order to consider it, we place ourselves on the other side of the human condition, on the side of God.

If this is the case, one easily understands how foolish it would be to require a poetic engagement. Doubtless, emotion, even passion—and why not anger, social indignation, and political hatred?—are at the origin of the poem. But they are not *expressed* there, as in a pamphlet or in a confession. Insofar as the writer of prose exhibits feelings, he illustrates them; whereas, if the poet injects his feelings into his poem, he ceases to recognize them; the words take hold of them,

penetrate them, and metamorphose them; they do not signify them, even in his eyes. Emotion has become thing; it now
has the opacity of things; it is compounded by the ambiguous
properties of the vocables in which it has been enclosed. And
above all, there is always much more in each phrase, in each
verse, as there is more than simple anguish in the yellow sky
over Golgotha. The word, the phrase-thing, inexhaustible as
things, everywhere overflows the feeling which has produced
them. How can one hope to provoke the indignation or the
political enthusiasm of the reader when the very thing one
does is to withdraw him from the human condition and invite
him to consider with the eyes of God a language that has been
turned inside out? Someone may say, "You're forgetting Pierre
Emmanuel." Not a bit! They're the very ones I was going to
give as examples.*

---

* If one wishes to know the origin of this attitude toward language, the following are
a few brief indications.

Originally, poetry creates the *myth*, while the prose-writer draws its *portrait*. In reality,
the human act, governed by needs and urged on by the useful is, in a sense, a *means*.
It passes unnoticed, and it is the result which counts. When I extend my hand *in order
to* take up my pen, I have only a fleeting and obscure consciousness of my gesture; it
is the pen which I see. Thus, man is alienated by his ends. Poetry reverses the relationship: the world and things become inessential, become a pretext for the act which
becomes its own end. The vase is there so that the girl may perform the graceful act
of filling it; the Trojan War, so that Hector and Achilles may engage in that heroic
combat. The action, detached from its goals, which become blurred, becomes an act of
prowess or a dance. Nevertheless, however indifferent he might have been to the success of the enterprise, the poet, before the nineteenth century, remained in harmony
with society as a whole. He did not use language for the end which prose seeks, but he
had the same confidence in it as the prose-writer.

With the coming of bourgeois society, the poet puts up a common front with the
prose-writer to declare it unlivable. His job is always to create the myth of man, but
he passes from white magic to black magic. Man is always presented as the absolute
end, but by the success of his enterprise he is sucked into a utilitarian collectivity. The
thing that is in the background of his act and that will allow transition to the myth is
thus no longer success, but defeat. By stopping the infinite series of his projects like a
screen, defeat alone returns him to himself in his purity. The world remains the ines-

sential, but it is now there as a pretext for defeat. The finality of the thing is to send man back to himself by blocking the route. Moreover, it is not a matter of arbitrarily introducing defeat and ruin into the course of the world, but rather of having no eyes for anything but that. Human enterprise has two aspects: it is both success and failure. The dialectical scheme is inadequate for reflecting upon it. We must make our vocabulary and the frames of our reason more supple. Some day I am going to try to describe that strange reality, History, which is neither objective, nor ever quite subjective, in which the dialectic is contested, penetrated, and corroded by a kind of antidialectic, but which is still a dialectic. But that is the philosopher's affair. One does not ordinarily consider the two faces of Janus; the man of action sees one and the poet sees the other. When the instruments are broken and unusable, when plans are blasted and effort is useless, the world appears with a childlike and terrible freshness, without supports, without paths. It has the maximum reality because it is crushing for man, and as action, in any case, generalizes, defeat restores to things their individual reality. But, by an expected reversal, the defeat, considered as a final end, is both a contesting and an appropriation of this universe. A contesting, because man *is worth more* than that which crushes; he no longer contests things in their "little bit of reality," like the engineer or the captain, but, on the contrary, in their "too full of reality," by his very existence as a vanquished person; he is the remorse of the world. An appropriation, because the world, by ceasing to be the tool of success, becomes the instrument of failure. So there it is, traversed by an obscure finality; it is its coefficient of adversity which serves, the more human insofar as it is more hostile to man. The defeat itself turns into salvation. Not that it makes us yield to some "beyond," but by itself it shifts and is metamorphosed. For example, poetic language rises out of the ruins of prose. If it is true that the word is a betrayal and that communication is impossible, then each word by itself recovers its individuality and becomes an instrument of our defeat and a receiver of the incommunicable. It is not that there is *another thing to* communicate; but the communication of prose having miscarried, it is the very meaning of the word which becomes the pure incommunicable. Thus, the failure of communication becomes a suggestion of the incommunicable, and the thwarted project of utilizing words is succeeded by the pure disinterested intuition of the word. Thus, we again meet with the description which we attempted earlier in this study, but in the more general perspective of the absolute valorization of the defeat, which seems to me the original attitude of contemporary poetry. Note also that this choice confers upon the poet a very precise function in the collectivity: in a highly integrated or religious society, the defeat is masked by the State or redeemed by Religion; in a less integrated and secular society, such as our democracies, it is up to poetry to redeem them.

Poetry is a case of the loser winning. And the genuine poet chooses to lose, even if he has to go so far as to die, in order to win. I repeat that I am talking of contemporary poetry. History presents other forms of poetry. It is not my concern to show their connection with ours. Thus, if one absolutely wishes to speak of the engagement of the poet, let us say that he is the man who engages himself to lose. This is the deeper meaning of that tough-luck, of that malediction with which he always claims kinship and which he always attributes to an intervention from without; whereas it is his deepest choice, the source, and not the consequence of his poetry. He is certain of the total

But even if the poet is forbidden to engage himself, is that a reason for exempting the writer of prose? What do they have in common? It is true that the prosewriter and the poet both write. But there is nothing in common between these two acts of writing except the movement of the hand which traces the letters. Otherwise, their universes are incommunicable, and what is good for one is not good for the other. Prose is, in essence, utilitarian. I would readily define the prose-writer as a man who *makes use* of words. M. Jourdan made prose to ask for his slippers, and Hitler to declare war on Poland. The writer is a *speaker;* he designates, demonstrates, orders, refuses, interpolates, begs, insults, persuades, insinuates. If he does so without any effect, he does not therefore become a poet; he is a writer who is talking and saying nothing. We have seen enough of language inside out; it is now time to look at it right side out.*

---

defeat of the human enterprise and arranges to fail in his own life in order to bear witness, by his individual defeat, to human defeat in general. Thus, he contests, as we shall see, which is what the prose-writer does too. But the contesting of prose is carried on in the name of a greater success; and that of poetry, in the name of the hidden defeat which every victory conceals.

* It goes without saying that in all poetry a certain form of prose, that is, of success, is present; and, vice-versa, the driest prose always contains a bit of poetry, that is, a certain form of defeat; no prose-writer is *quite* capable of expressing what he wants to say; he says too much or not enough; each phrase is a wager, a risk assumed; the more cautious one is, the more attention the word attracts; as Valéry has shown, no one can understand a word to its very bottom. Thus, each word is used simultaneously for its clear and social meaning and for certain obscure resonances—let me say, almost for its physiognomy. The reader, too, is sensitive to this. At once we are no longer on the level of concerted communication, but on that of grace and chance; the silences of prose are poetic because they mark its limits, and it is for the purpose of greater clarity that I have been considering the extreme cases of pure prose and pure poetry. However, it need not be concluded that we can pass from poetry to prose by a continuous series of intermediate forms. If the prose-writer is too eager to fondle his words, the *eidos* of "prose" is shattered and we fall into highfalutin nonsense. If the poet relates, explains, or teaches, the poetry becomes *prosaic;* he has lost the game. It is a matter of complex structures, impure, but well-defined.

The art of prose is employed in discourse; its substance is by nature significative; that is, the words are first of all not objects but designations for objects; it is not first of all a matter of knowing whether they please or displease in themselves, but whether they correctly indicate a certain thing or a certain notion. Thus, it often happens that we find ourselves possessing a certain idea that someone has taught us by means of words without being able to recall a single one of the words which have transmitted it to us.

Prose is first of all an attitude of mind. As Valéry would say, there is prose when the word passes across our gaze as the glass across the sun. When one is in danger or in difficulty he grabs any instrument. When the danger is past, he does not even remember whether it was a hammer or a stick; moreover, he never knew; all he needed was a prolongation of his body, a means of extending his hand to the highest branch. It was a sixth finger, a third leg, in short, a pure function which he assimilated. Thus, regarding language, it is our shell and our antennae; it protects us against others and informs us about them; it is a prolongation of our senses, a third eye which is going to look into our neighbor's heart. We are within language as within our body. We *feel* it spontaneously while going beyond it toward other ends, as we feel our hands and our feet; we perceive it when it is the other who is using it, as we perceive the limbs of others. There is the word which is lived and the word which is met. But in both cases it is in the course of an undertaking, either of me acting upon others, or the other upon me. The word is a certain particular moment of action and has no meaning outside of it. In certain cases of aphasia the possibilities of acting, of understanding situations, and of having normal relations with the other sex, are lost.

At the heart of this aphasia the destruction of language

appears only as the collapse of one of the structures, the finest and the most apparent. And if prose is never anything but the privileged instrument of a certain undertaking, if it is only the poet's business to contemplate words in a disinterested fashion, then one has the right to ask the prose-writer from the very start, "What is your aim in writing? What undertakings are you engaged in, and why does it require you to have recourse to writing?" In any case this undertaking cannot have pure contemplation as an end. For, intuition is silence, and the end of language is to communicate. One can doubtless *pin down* the results of intuition, but in this case a few words hastily scrawled on paper will suffice; it will always be enough for the author to recognize what he had in mind. If the words are assembled into sentences, with a concern for clarity, a decision foreign to the intuition, to the language itself, must intervene, the decision of confiding to others the results obtained. In each case one must ask the reason for this decision. And the common sense which our pedants too readily forget never stops repeating it. Are we not in the habit of putting this basic question to young people who are thinking of writing. "Do you have anything to say?" Which means: something which is worth the trouble of being communicated. But what do we mean by something which is "worth the trouble" if it is not by recourse to a system of transcendent values?

Moreover, to consider only this secondary structure of the undertaking, which is what the *verbal moment* is, the serious error of pure stylists is to think that the word is a gentle breeze which plays lightly over the surface of things, which grazes them without altering them, and that the speaker is a pure *witness* who sums up with a word his harmless contemplation. To speak is to act; anything which one names is already no longer quite the same; it has lost its innocence.

If you name the behavior of an individual, you reveal it to him; he sees himself. And since you are at the same time naming it to all others, he knows that he is *seen* at the moment he *sees* himself. The furtive gesture which he forgot while making it, begins to exist beyond all measure, to exist for everybody; it is integrated into the objective mind; it takes on new dimensions; it is retrieved. After that, how can you expect him to act in the same way? Either he will persist in his behavior out of obstinacy and with full knowledge of what he is doing, or he will give it up. Thus, by speaking, I reveal the situation by my very intention of changing it; I reveal it to myself and to others *in order* to change it. I strike at its very heart, I transpierce it, and I display it in full view; at present I dispose of it; with every word I utter, I involve myself a little more in the world, and by the same token I emerge from it a little more, since I go beyond it toward the future.

Thus, the prose-writer is a man who has chosen a certain method of secondary action which we may call action by disclosure. It is therefore permissible to ask him this second question: "What aspect of the world do you want to disclose? What change do you want to bring into the world by this disclosure?" The "engaged" writer knows that words are action. He knows that to reveal is to change and that one can reveal only by planning to change. He has given up the impossible dream of giving an impartial picture of Society and the human condition. Man is the being toward whom no being can be impartial, not even God. For God, if He existed, would be, as certain mystics have seen Him, in a *situation* in relationship to man. And He is also the being Who can not even see a situation without changing it, for His gaze congeals, destroys, or sculpts, or, as does eternity, changes the object in itself. It is in love, in hate, in anger, in fear, in joy, in indignation, in admiration, in hope, in despair, that man and the world reveal themselves *in their truth*. Doubtless, the engaged writer can be mediocre; he can even be conscious of being so; but as one can not write without the intention of succeeding perfectly, the modesty with which he envisages his work should not divert him from constructing it *as if* it were to have the greatest celebrity. He should never say to himself "Bah! I'll be lucky if I have three thousand readers," but rather, "What would happen if everybody read what I wrote?" He remembers what Mosca said beside the coach which carried Fabrizio and Sanseverina away, "If the word Love comes up between them, I'm lost." He knows that he is the man who names what has not yet been named or what dares not tell its name. He knows that he makes the word "love" and the word "hate" *surge up* and with them love and hate between men who had not yet decided upon their feelings. He knows that words, as Brice-Parrain says, are "loaded pistols." If he speaks, he fires. He may be silent, but since he has chosen to fire, he must do it like a man, by aiming at targets, and not like a child, at random, by shutting his eyes and firing merely for the pleasure of hearing the shot go off.

. . . We may conclude that the writer has chosen to reveal the world and particularly to reveal man to other men so that the latter may assume full responsibility before the object which has been thus laid bare. It is assumed that no one is ignorant of the law because there is a code and because the law is written down; thereafter, you are free to violate it, but you know the risks you run. Similarly, the function of the writer is to act in such a way that nobody can be ignorant of the world and that nobody may say that he is innocent of what it's all about. And since he has once engaged himself in the universe of language, he can never again pretend that he can not speak.

Once you enter the universe of significations, there is nothing you can do to get out of it. Let words organize themselves freely and they will make sentences, and each sentence contains language in its entirety and refers back to the whole universe. Silence itself is defined in relationship to words, as the pause in music receives its meaning from the group of notes around it. This silence is a moment of language; being silent is not being dumb; it is to refuse to speak, and therefore to keep on speaking. Thus, if a writer has chosen to remain silent on any aspect whatever of the world, or, according to an expression which says just what it means, to *pass over* it in silence, one has the right to ask him a third question: "Why have you spoken of this rather than that, and—since you speak in order to bring about change—why do you want to change this rather than that?"

All this does not prevent there being a manner of writing. One is not a writer for having chosen to say certain things, but for having chosen to say them in a certain way. And, to be sure, the style makes the value of the prose. But it should pass unnoticed. Since words are transparent and since the gaze looks through them, it would be absurd to slip in among them some panes of rough glass. Beauty is in this case only a gentle and imperceptible force. In a painting it shines forth at the very first sight; in a book it hides itself; it acts by persuasion like the charm of a voice or a face. It does not coerce; it inclines a person without his suspecting it, and he thinks that he is yielding to arguments when he is really being solicited by a charm that he does not see. The ceremonial of the mass is not faith; it disposes the harmony of words; their beauty, the balance of the phrases, *dispose* the passions of the reader without his being aware and orders them like the mass, like music, like the dance. If he happens to consider them by themselves, he loses the meaning; there remains only a boring seesaw of phrases.

In prose the aesthetic pleasure is pure only if it is thrown into the bargain. I blush at recalling such simple ideas, but it seems that today they have been forgotten. If that were not the case, would we be told that we are planning the murder of literature, or more simply, that engagement is harmful to the art of writing? If the contamination of a certain kind of prose by poetry had not confused the ideas of our critics, would they dream of attacking us on the matter of form, when we have never spoken of anything but the content? There is nothing to be said about form in advance, and we have said nothing. Everyone invents his own, and one judges it afterward. It is true that the subjects suggest the style, but they do not order it. There are no styles ranged a priori outside of the literary art. What is more engaged, what is more boring than the idea of attacking the Jesuits? Yet, out of this Pascal made his *Provincial Letters*. In short, it is a matter of knowing what one wants to write about, whether butterflies or the condition of the Jews. And when one knows, then it remains to decide how one will write about it.

Often the two choices are only one, but among good writers the second choice never precedes the first. I know that Giraudoux has said that "the only concern is finding the style; the idea comes afterwards"; but he was wrong. The idea did not come. On the contrary, if one considers subjects as problems which are always open, as solicitations, as expectations, it will be easily understood that art loses nothing in engagement. On the contrary, just as physics submits to mathematicians new problems which require them to produce a new symbolism, in like manner the always new requirements of the social and the metaphysical engage the artist in finding a new language and new techniques. If we no longer write as they did in the eighteenth century, it is because the language of Racine and Saint-Evremond does not lend itself to talking about locomotives or the proletariat. After that, the purists will perhaps forbid us to write about locomotives. But art has never been on the side of the purists.

If that is the principle of engagement, what objection can one have to it? And above all *what objection has been made to it?* It has seemed to me that my opponents have not had their hearts in their work very much and that their articles contain nothing more than a long scandalized sigh which drags on over two or three columns. I should have liked to know *in the name of what*, with what conception of literature, they condemned engagement. But they have not said; they themselves have not known. The most reasonable thing would have been to support their condemnation on the old theory of art for art's sake. But none of them can accept it. That is also disturbing. We know very well that pure art and empty art are the same thing and that aesthetic purism was a brilliant maneuver of the bourgeois of the last century who preferred to see themselves denounced as philistines rather than as exploiters. Therefore, they themselves admitted that the writer had to speak about something. But about what? I believe that their embarrassment would have been extreme if Fernandez had not found for them, after the other war, the notion of the *message*. The writer of today, they say, should in no case occupy himself with temporal affairs. Neither should he set up lines without signification nor seek solely beauty of phrase and of imagery. His function is to deliver messages to his readers. Well, what is a message?

It must be borne in mind that most critics are men who

have not had much luck and who, just about the time they were growing desperate, found a quiet little job as cemetery watchmen. God knows whether cemeteries are peaceful; none of them are more cheerful than a library. The dead are there; the only thing they have done is write. They have long since been washed clean of the sin of living, and besides, their lives are known only through other books which other dead men have written about them. Rimbaud is dead. So are Paterne Berrichon and Isabelle Rimbaud. The trouble makers have disappeared; all that remains are the little coffins that are stacked on shelves along the walls like urns in a columbarium. The critic lives badly; his wife does not appreciate him as she ought to; his children are ungrateful; the first of the month is hard on him. But it is always possible for him to enter his library, take down a book from the shelf, and open it. It gives off a slight odor of the cellar, and a strange operation begins which he has decided to call reading. From one point of view it is a possession; he lends his body to the dead in order that they may come back to life. And from another point of view it is a contact with the beyond. Indeed, the book is by no means an object; neither is it an act, nor even a thought. Written by a dead man about dead things it no longer has any place on this earth; it speaks of nothing which interests us directly. Left to itself, it falls back and collapses; there remain only ink spots on musty paper. And when the critic reanimates these spots when he makes letters and words of them, they speak to him of passions which he does not feel, of bursts of anger without objects, of dead fears and hopes. It is a whole disembodied world which surrounds him, where human feelings, because they are no longer affecting, have passed on to the status of exemplary feelings and, in a word, of *values*. So he persuades himself that he has entered into relations with an intelligible world which is like the truth of his daily sufferings. And their reason for being. He thinks that nature imitates art, as for Plato the world of the senses imitates that of the archetypes. And during the time he is reading, his everyday life becomes an appearance. His nagging wife, his hunchbacked son, they too are appearances. And he will put up with them because Xenophon has drawn the portrait of Xantippe and Shakespeare that of Richard the Third.

It is a holiday for him when contemporary authors do him the favor of dying. Their books, too raw, too living, too urgent, pass on to the other shore; they become less and less affecting and more and more beautiful. After a short stay in Purgatory they go on to people the intelligible heaven with new values. Bergotte, Swann, Siegfried and Bella and Monsieur Teste are recent acquisitions. He is waiting for Nathanaël and Ménalque. As for the writers who persist in living, he asks them only not to move about too much, and to make an effort to resemble from now on the dead men they will be. Valéry, who for twenty-five years had been publishing posthumous books, managed the matter very nicely. That is why, like some highly exceptional saints, he was canonized during his lifetime. But Malraux is scandalous.

Our critics are Catharians. They don't want to have anything to do with the real world except eat and drink in it, and since it is absolutely necessary to have relations with our fellow-creatures, they have chosen to have them with the defunct. They get excited only about classified matters, closed quarrels, stories whose ends are known. They never bet on uncertain issues, and since history has decided for them, since the objects which terrified or angered the authors they read have disappeared, since bloody disputes seem futile at a distance of two centuries, they can be charmed with balanced periods, and everythinghappens for them as if all literature were only a vast tautology and as if every new prose-writer had invented a new way of speaking only for the purpose of saying nothing.

To speak of archetypes and "human nature"—is that speaking in order to say nothing? All the conceptions of our critics oscillate from one idea to the other. And, of course, both of them are false. Our great writers wanted to destroy, to edify, to demonstrate. But we no longer retain the proofs which they have advanced because we have no concern with what they mean to prove. The abuses which they denounced are no longer those of our time. There are others which rouse us which they did not suspect. History has given the lie to some of their predictions, and those which have been fulfilled became true so long ago that we have forgotten that they were at first flashes of their genius. Some of their thoughts are utterly dead, and there are others which the whole human race has taken up to its advantage and which we now regard as commonplace. It follows that the best arguments of these writers have lost their effectiveness. We admire only their order and rigor. Their most compact composition is in our eyes only an ornament, an elegant architecture of exposition, with no more practical application than such architectures as the fugues of Bach and the arabesques of the Alhambra.

We are still moved by the passion of these impassioned geometries when the geometry no longer convinces us. Or rather by the representation of the passion. In the course of centuries the ideas have turned flat, but they remain the little personal objectives of a man who was once flesh and bone; behind the reasons of reason, which languish, we perceive the reasons of the heart, the virtues, the vices, and that great pain that men have in living. Sade does his best to win us over, but we hardly find him scandalous. He is no longer anything but a soul eaten by a beautiful disease, a pearl-oyster. The *Letter on the Theater* no longer keeps anyone from going to the theater, but we find it piquant that Rousseau detested the art of the drama. If we are a bit versed in psychoanalysis, our pleasure is perfect. We shall explain the *Social Contract* by the Oedipus complex and *The Spirit of the Laws* by the inferiority complex. That is, we shall fully enjoy the well-known superiority of live dogs to dead lions. Thus, when a book presents befuddled thoughts which appear to be reasons only to melt under scrutiny and to be reduced to heart beats, when the teaching that one can draw from it is radically different from what its author intended, the book is called a message. Rousseau, the father of the French Revolution, and Gobineau, the father of racism, both sent us messages. And the critic considers them with equal sympathy. If they were alive, he would have to choose between the two, to love one and hate the other. But what brings them together, above all, is that they are both profoundly and deliciously wrong, and in the same way: they are dead.

Thus, contemporary writers should be advised to deliver messages, that is, voluntarily to limit their writing to the involuntary expression of their souls. I say involuntary because the dead, from Montaigne to Rimbaud, have painted themselves completely, but without having meant to—it is something they have simply thrown into the bargain. The surplus which they have given us unintentionally should be the primary and professed goal of living writers. They are not to be forced to give us confessions without any dressing, nor are they to abandon themselves to the too-naked lyricism of the romantics. But since we find pleasure in foiling the ruses of Chateaubriand or Rousseau, in surprising them in the secret places of their being at the moment they are playing at being the public man, in distinguishing the private motives from their most universal assertions, we shall ask newcomers to procure us this pleasure deliberately. So let them reason, assert, deny, refute, and prove; but the cause they are defending must be only the apparent aim of their discourse; the deeper goal is to yield themselves without seeming to do so. They must first disarm themselves of their arguments as time has done for those of the classic writers; they must bring them to bear upon subjects which interest no one or on truths so general that readers are convinced in advance. As for their ideas, they must give them an air of profundity, but with an effect of emptiness, and they must shape them in such a way that they are obviously explained by an unhappy childhood, a class hatred, or an incestuous love. Let them not presume to think in earnest; thought conceals the man, and it is the man alone who interests us. A bare tear is not lovely. It offends. A good argument also offends, as Stendhal well observed. But an argument that masks a tear—that's what we're after. The argument removes the obscenity from the tears; the tears, by revealing their origin in the passions, remove the aggressiveness from the argument. We shall be neither too deeply touched nor at all convinced, and we shall be able to yield ourselves in security to that moderate pleasure which, as everyone knows, we derive from the contemplation of works of art. Thus, this is "true," "pure" literature, a subjectivity which yields itself under the aspect of the objective, a discourse so curiously contrived that it is equivalent to silence, a thought which debates with itself, a reason which is only the mask of madness, an Eternal which lets it be understood that it is only a moment of History, a historical moment which, by the hidden side which it reveals, suddenly sends back a perpetual lesson to the eternal man, but which is produced against the express wishes of those who do the teaching.

When all is said and done, the message is a soul which is made object. A soul, and what is to be done with a soul? One contemplates it at a respectful distance. It is not customary to show one's soul in society without an imperious motive. But, with certain reserves, convention permits some individuals to put theirs into commerce, and all adults may procure it for themselves. For many people today, works of the mind are thus little straying souls which one acquires at a modest price; there is good old Montaigne's, dear La Fontaine's, and that of Jean-Jacques and of Jean-Paul and of delicious Gérard. What is called literary art is the ensemble of the treatments which make them inoffensive. Tanned, refined, chemically treated, they provide their acquirers with the opportunity of devoting some moments of a life completely turned outward to the cultivation of subjectivity. Custom guarantees it to be without risk. Montaigne's skepticism? Who can take it seriously since the author of the *Essays* got frightened when the plague ravaged Bordeaux? Or Rousseau's humanitarianism, since "Jean-Jacques" put his children into an orphanage? And the strange revelations of *Sylvie*, since Gérard de Nerval was mad? At the very most, the professional critic will set up infernal dialogues between them and will inform us that French thought is a perpetual colloquy between Pascal and Montaigne. In so doing he has no intention of making Pascal and Montaigne more alive, but of making Malraux and Gide more dead. Finally, when the internal contradictions of the life and the work have made both of them useless, when the message, in its imponderable depth, has taught us these capital truths, "that man is neither good nor bad," "that there is a great deal of suffering in human life," "that genius is only great patience," this melancholy cuisine will have achieved its purpose, and the reader, as he lays down the book, will be able to cry out with a tranquil soul, "All this is only literature."

But since, for us, writing is an enterprise; since writers are alive before being dead; since we think that we must try to be as right as we can in our books; and since, even if the centuries show us to be in the wrong, this is no reason to show in advance that we are wrong; since we think that the writer should engage himself completely in his works, and not as an abject passivity by putting forward his vices, his misfortunes and his weaknesses, but as a resolute will and as a choice, as this total enterprise of living that each one of us is, it is then proper that we take up this problem at its beginning and that we, in our turn, ask ourselves: "*Why* does one write?"

Part VI

ESSAYS IN AESTHETICS

1. THE VENETIAN PARIAH

Jacopo's Shenanigans

Nothing. His life is an enigma: A few dates, a few facts, and then the cackling of ancient writers. But courage: *Venice speaks to us.* Her voice is that of a perjured witness, now shrill, now whispering, always marked by periods of silence. Tintoretto's life story, the portrait painted during his lifetime by his native city, is tinged with unrequited animosity. The Doge's City reveals her contempt for the most celebrated of her sons. Nothing is stated outright; there are hints, suggestions, remarks made in passing. This inflexible hatred has the inconsistency of sand; it takes the form, not so much of outspoken aversion, as of coldness, moroseness, insidious ostracism. And this is just what we would expect. Jacopo fights a losing battle against a vast adversary, grows tired, surrenders, dies. That is the sum and substance of his life. We can study it in all its somber nakedness if for an instant we push aside the brushwood of slander that blocks our passage.

First, the birth of the dyer's son in 1518. Venice immediately insinuates that fate has marked him from the outset: "About 1530 the youth started to work in Titian's studio as an apprentice but was dismissed a few days later when the illustrious quinquagenarian discovered his genius." This anecdote reappears in book after book with astounding regularity. It might be argued that it does little credit to Titian—and this is indeed the case—not *today*, at any rate, not in our eyes. But when Vasari reports it in 1567, Titian has been reigning for half a century, and nothing is more respectable than long impunity. Then too, according to the customs of his time, Titian has his own studio, where he is second only to God in the conduct of his affairs and has every right to dismiss an employee. In such circumstances his victim is presumed guilty; marked by fate, contagious perhaps, he is presumed to have the evil eye. Here for the first time the gilded legend of Italian painting is threatened by an ill-fated childhood. But the lesson to be learned from his alleged dismissal must come later. The voice of Venice never lies provided that we know how to interpret it; we can listen once our ears have been properly attuned. At this point we suspend judgment but call attention to the improbability of the facts.

That Titian was not good-natured is well known. But Jacopo was twelve. At twelve talent is nothing and anything will obliterate it; patience and time are required to mold nascent skill and change it into talent; no artist at the pinnacle of his fame—not even the most supercilious—would take umbrage at a small boy. But suppose that the master, jealous, dismissed his apprentice. That amounts to assassination of him. The curse of a national celebrity weighs heavily, very heavily. More especially as Titian lacks the candor to make known his true motives; he is king, he frowns and from this moment on all doors are closed to the black sheep. He is forever barred from the profession.

A blacklisted child is something of a rarity. Our interest

quickens. We are eager to find out how he managed to overcome his handicap. Vain desire, for here the thread of the nar-
rative breaks at the same time in every single book and we are
confronted by a conspiracy of silence. No one will tell us what
happened to him between the age of twelve and twenty. Some
writers attempted to fill the void by imagining that he had
learned the art of painting independently. But they were in an
even better position than we to know that he could not have
done so, for at the beginning of the sixteenth century painting
is still a complicated, rather ceremonious technique; unduly
fettered by formulas and rites, it is a skill rather than an art,
proficiency rather than knowledge, a set of procedures rather
than a method. Professional rules, secret traditions—everything contributes toward making the apprenticeship a social
obligation and a necessity. The biographers' silence betrays
their embarrassment. Unable to reconcile the precocious
notoriety of young Robusti and excommunication, they throw
a veil of darkness on the eight years that separate the two. We
can be certain that no one has rejected Jacopo; and since he has
not perished from languor and scorn in his father's dye-shop,
he must have worked normally and regularly in the studio of
a painter about whom we know nothing except that *he was
not* Titian. In closed, suspicious guilds hatred is retroactive;
if the mysterious beginning of Jacopo's life seems a premoni-
tion of its mysterious end, if a curtain raised to show a disaster miraculously arrested is lowered on a disaster unattended
by any miracle, this is because Venice rearranged everything
afterwards to make his childhood consonant with his old age.
Nothing happens and nothing ends; birth mirrors death and
between the two lies scorched earth; everything is consumed
by the curse.

We pass beyond these mirages and find our view unobstructed all across the horizon. An adolescent emerges, dashes away at high speed in search of glory. The year is 1539; Jacopo has left his patron to set up his own studio; he is now a *past master*. The young employee has won independence, fame, a clientele; now it is his turn to hire workers, apprentices. This much is certain: in a city filled with painters, where an economic crisis threatens to strangle the market, becoming a master at the age of twenty is the exception to the rule; merit alone is not enough, nor work, nor tact; one must also have a run of good luck. Everything is in Robusti's favor. Paolo Cagliari is ten, Titian sixty-two; between the unknown child and the old man who will surely die before long many good painters might be found, but only Tintoretto holds out the promise of excellence; in his generation, at any rate, he has no rival and therefore he finds the road before him open. He does in fact pursue this road for several years: his commissions multiply, he enjoys the public's favor as well as that of patricians and intellectuals; Aretino deigns to congratulate him in person.* The young man is endowed with supernatural gifts which Providence reserves for adolescents who are to die, but he does not die and his woes begin: The old monarch Titian manifests a startling longevity, continuing all the while to vent his hatred on his young challenger and finally resorting to the malicious ruse of officially designating as his successor, to the surprise of no one, Veronese; Aretino's condescension turns to bitterness; critics lash out, censure, chide, castigate—in short, they behave like modern critics. This matters little so long as Jacopo retains the public's favor. But suddenly the wheel turns. At thirty, confi-

---

* Because of the influence which he exercised over kings, diplomats and artists through his writings, Pietro Aretino (1492-1556) has been called the first journalist. Curiously, the amoral publicist whose services went to the highest bidder counted Titian among his devoted friends. (Translator's notes are indicated by an asterisk.)

dent of his means, he asserts himself, paints *The Miracle of St. Mark* and puts himself, his whole self, into the painting. It is characteristic of him to astound, to strike hard and impose his will by surprise. In this instance, however, he will be the first to be caught off guard; his work dumbfounds his contemporaries but it also scandalizes them. He finds impassioned detractors but not impassioned defenders; behind the scenes we can detect a cabal: Frustration.* Face to face, united and separated by the same feeling of uneasiness, Venice and her painter contemplate but no longer understand each other. "Jacopo has not lived up to the promises of his adolescence," says the city. And the artist remarks, "To deceive them, all I had to do was reveal myself. So *I* was not what they loved!" Mutual grudges widen the gap between them, breaking one thread in the Venetian woof.

The pivotal year is 1548. *Before*, the gods are for him; *afterwards*, against. No great misfortunes are associated with his persistent bad luck—just enough little ones to lead him to the brink of despair. The gods smiled on the child only to bring about the downfall of the man. Jacopo suddenly undergoes radical change and becomes the frantic, harassed outlaw, Tintoretto. *Before*, we know nothing about him except that he worked relentlessly, for fame is not easily acquired at the age of twenty. *Afterwards* his tenacity turns to rage; he wants to produce, to produce without ceasing, to sell, to crush his rivals by the number and dimensions of his canvases. There is a certain element of desperation in his forced effort, for until his death Robusti works against the clock without ever revealing whether he is trying to find himself through his

---

* Ridolfi even maintains that the Scuola San Marco refused the canvas and that Tintoretto had to take it back to his studio.

work or to escape from himself through excessive activity. "Lightning Tintoretto" sails under a black flag, and for this swift pirate all means are fair, with a marked preference for unfair advantages. Disinterested whenever disinterest pays off, he lowers his eyes, refuses to name a price, repeats like a child, "It will be whatever you wish." But those Neapolitan rascals are in a better position than anyone else to know the value of their wares; they expect the customer to fleece himself through his generosity.

On other occasions he offers his merchandise at cost in order to close a transaction, only to make other more advantageous sales as a result of the initial emergency contract. On learning that the Crociferi are going to offer a commission to Paolo Cagliari, he feigns ignorance of everything and offers them his services. They essay a polite refusal: "Thank you, but we want something Veronese." And he: "Something Veronese?* Well and good. And who is going to do it?" Somewhat taken aback, they reply: "Why, we thought that Paolo Cagliari had been designated . . ." And Tintoretto now expresses his amazement: "Cagliari? The idea is fantastic. I'll paint you something Veronese. And for less." Signed and sealed. He resorted to the same gambit twenty times, painting *in the style of* Pordenone, *in the style of* Titian, always for less.

How can he cut costs? That is the question that torments him. One day he finds the contemptible but ingenious answer that will wreck a tradition. The masters are accustomed to having their canvases copied; their studios execute replicas and sell them at inflated prices, thereby creating a second market for their paintings. To win over their clientele, Jacopo will offer

---

* The spacious architectural quality of the paintings of Veronese (Paolo Cagliari, 1528-1588) is typical of his school.

them *better paintings for less*. He eliminates sketches; he will allow others to draw their inspiration from his canvases but not to copy them; through simple, invariable procedures his collaborators will produce something new but not original. They will need only to rearrange the composition, put the left on the right and the right on the left, substitute an old man for a woman who can be used again in another context. Such operations require some training but no more time than simple copying. Tintoretto candidly proclaims: "In my studio one can acquire an original work for the price of a reproduction."

When his canvases are spurned, he gives them away. On May 31, 1564, at the Scuola San Rocco the Brotherhood decides to beautify its conference hall by placing a painting in the central oval of the ceiling. Paolo Cagliari, Jacopo Robusti, Schiavone, Salviati and Zucearo are invited to submit sketches. Tintoretto bribes servants, obtains the exact measurements. He had already worked for the Brotherhood and I do not rule out the hypothesis that he found accomplices even within the *Banca e Zonta*. On the day set, each painter exhibits his sketch. When Robusti's turn comes, he electrifies them all. He climbs up a ladder, removes a section of pasteboard, and reveals above their heads a dazzling painting, already in place, already finished. Pandemonium. "A drawing is easily misunderstood," he explained. "While I was about it, I preferred to see it through. But if my work is displeasing to you, gentlemen, I will give it to you. Not to you, but to San Rocco, your patron, who has done so much for me." This forced their hand and the rascal knew it, for the rules of the Brotherhood prohibited their refusing religious donations. All that remained was for them to make the episode a matter of record in the Scuola: "On this day the undersigned Jacopo Tintoretto, painter, presented to us a painting; he asks no remuneration, promises to complete the work if requested to do so, and states that he is satisfied with it." And the undersigned wrote in his turn: "*Io Jachomo Tentoretto pintor contento et prometo ut supra.*"

Satisfied? Why not? His gift spreads panic among his competitors, opens to him every door of the Scuola, places its vast, barren walls at the mercy of his brush and finally brings him an annual pension of a hundred ducats. So satisfied is he, in short, that he repeats the gambit in 1571. At the Doge's Palace this time. Authorities, wishing to commemorate the battle of Lepanto, organize a contest. Instead of a sketch Tintoretto brings a canvas and presents it as a gift. It is accepted with gratitude; shortly thereafter he sends his bill.

In his base but charming shenanigans one is tempted to see, perhaps, a trait attributable more to morals than to character. We might with some degree of accuracy say that ostentation was characteristic not of Tintoretto but of his century. If an attempt were made to condemn him on the basis of these anecdotes I know everything that might be said in his defense. The most telling argument is that no one at that time could *work for himself.* Today paintings are in demand; then painters were for sale. They lined the market place like the *bracchiante* in the southern towns; buyers came, examined all of them, singled out one and took him to their church, their *scuola* or their *palazzo.* Artists had to make themselves available, to advertise themselves as our directors do, to accept just any work in the same way that our directors accept just any scenario in the foolish hope of using it to display their talents. Everything was under contract: the subject, number, quality, and sometimes even the attitude of the figures, and the dimensions of the canvas; these were complemented by restrictions imposed by traditions relating to religion and to taste. Their clients had their moods just as our producers have their whims. And their clients—alas!—they, too, had their sudden inspirations; at their bidding, everything had to be reworked. In the palace of the Medici, Benozzo Gozzoli was for a long time knowingly tortured by idiotic patrons; and we need only compare Tintoretto's *Paradise* in the Louvre with the one in the Doge's Palace to understand the magnitude of the pressures to which he was subjected. Intransigence, rejection of compromise, the superb choice of misery were out of the question since the artist had to provide for his family and keep his studio in operation, as present-day machines are. In sum, he had to renounce painting or to paint according to instructions. No one can blame Tintoretto for wishing to become rich. As a matter of fact, toward the middle of his life he was never out of work, never lacked money. This utilitarian artist followed the principle that nothing is done for nothing, that painting would be a mere pastime unless it produced some income. At long last, as we shall see, he will buy a comfortable plebeian house in a residential district. This purchase will crown his career, exhaust his savings, leave the Robusti children with only a ludicrous heritage to divide: the contents of his studio, a diminishing clientele, and the house itself, which is passed on to the oldest son, then to his son-in-law. Twelve years after the death of her husband, Faustina recalls bitterly that he left his family in need; she has every reason to complain, for the deceased had his own way. He liked money, of course, but in the American way. He saw in it nothing more than the external sign of success. At the bottom, this contract chaser sought only one thing: the means of practicing his craft. There is also an element of justice in his shenanigans, for they would be inconceivable without his professional talent, hard work, and speed. His speed gives him an advantage, for to paint a good picture he requires only the time taken by others to make bad sketches.

Furthermore, if he plagiarized Veronese, the latter repaid him in kind. Their reciprocal borrowings must be viewed through the eyes of their contemporaries. For many of their contemporaries the greatest painters are those who have met the test of certain social criteria; they are personalities defined by collective judgment. We are interested in a particular painting at first, and then in the particular man who painted it; we hang Matisse on our walls. But contrast our view with that of the Crociferi: they were not interested in Cagliari; they wanted a certain style that appealed to the senses, trifles, inoffensive and harmonious pomp; they knew a trademark, a slogan. A painting signed Veronese is certain to please. That is what they wanted, nothing else. Cagliari could produce better works and proved it when he painted his *Terrible Crucifixion*,* but he was too shrewd a businessman to squander his genius. Under such conditions we could hardly blame Tintoretto for appropriating at times a style that belonged exclusively to no one. After all, he made an honest proposal: "You want something trite and lifelike I will provide it."

I am aware of the tastes of his age. My aim here is not to judge him but to determine whether his age could identify itself with him without discomfort. And on this point the evidence is explicit: his conduct shocked his contemporaries and turned them against him. A little disloyalty would perhaps have been tolerated, but Tintoretto went too far; throughout Venice a single complaint was voiced: "He goes too far!" Even in that commercial city such shrewdness in commerce is unique. At the Scuola San Rocco, when he stole their commission, his colleagues barked so loudly that he felt obliged to appease them: the establishment had other ceilings and walls, the work had only begun; as for him, now that his gift had been accepted, he would disappear, leaving the field open to the most worthy of them. His unfortunate rivals soon discover that he is lying

---

* It is in the Louvre. The irony is that he was inspired by the *real* Robusti.

like a pagan, for the Scuola will become his fief, and as long as he lives, no other painter will ever cross the threshold. They had surely not waited for this occasion to begin hating him. It is worth noting, however, that the scandal occurs in 1561 and that the first *Life* of Tintoretto appears in 1567. The shortness of the interval between the two events further enlightens us concerning the origin and significance of the ugly rumors collected by Vasari.* Calumnies on the part of jealous rivals? They were all extremely jealous of each other; why, then, are calumnies heaped on Robusti alone unless he is the "foul smell" of the artists, unless he represents in the eyes of each and all the collective and magnified faults of his fellow men? Furthermore, even his clients seem shocked by his conduct. Not all of them, no. But he has made numerous enemies in high places. Zammaria de Zigninoni, a member of the San Rocco Brotherhood, promises fifteen ducats for decorative works under the express condition that Jacopo not be given the commission. The records of the Brotherhood suggest, moreover, that the *Banca e Zonta* held a few tense and somewhat unceremonious meetings in the Scuola in connection with the restricted donation and Jacopo's gambit; an agreement was reached but Zigninoni kept his ducats. Nor do the officials always seem kindly disposed toward him. In 1571, Tintoretto contributes his *Battle of Lepanto;* in 1577 the painting is destroyed by fire; when the question of replacing it arises, he has every reason to believe that the government will call on him. Not at all. He is deliberately passed over and preference is shown instead to the mediocre Vincentino. It might be argued that his canvas had met with disfavor. But that is hardly plausible, for Jacopo always treads softly when working

---

* The celebrated painter, architect and biographer published his *Lives of Excellent Painters, Sculptors, and Architects* in 1550. The date generally given for the revised edition is 1568.

for the officials; he "paints like Titian," disguising his own style. Besides, after 1571 the government gave him several commissions. No, the Venetian authorities have no intention of depriving themselves of his services; they simply want to punish him for his rascality. In short, there is unanimity: he is a disloyal colleague, a maverick painter, and there is bound to be something unsavory about him since he is without friends. Sweet troubled souls who use the dead to edify the living and especially yourselves, try if you will to find in his excesses the glittering proof of his passion. The fact is that passions are as diverse as people: ravenous and contemplative, dreamy and practical, abstract, dawdling, apprehensive, rash—a hundred others. I will call Tintoretto's passion practical, apprehensive-recriminatory and ravenous-rash. The more I reflect on his ludicrous gambits, the more I become convinced they were born of an ulcerated heart. What a nest of vipers! There we find everything: the delirium of pride and the folly of humility, chained ambition and unchained confusion, harsh rebukes and persistent bad luck, the goad of success and the lash of failure. His life is the story of an opportunist tormented by fear; it has a healthy, sprightly beginning; the offensive is well staged until the hard blow of 1548; after this the rhythm quickens, goes out of control, lights the fires of hell. Jacopo will fight on until the time of his death, knowing that he will not win. Opportunism and anguish, those are the two biggest vipers. If we wish truly to know him, we must have a closer look at them.

The Puritans of the Rialto

No one is a cynic. To be discouraged in the absence of discouragement is the diversion of saints. Only up to a certain point, however, for these chaste and generous creatures stigmatize their lechery and denounce their avarice. If they discover their real gangrene—saintliness—they look for justification, like all guilty creatures. *Tintoretto* is no saint; he knows that everyone in town condemns his conduct; he persists only because he thinks that he is right and they are wrong. And let no one come up and say that he is aware of his genius, for a genius—this is ironical but true—knows his courage but not his worth. Nothing is more wretched than sullen temerity that reaches for the moon and writhes in defeat; first comes pride, without proofs or pedigrees; when it matures into madness we can call it genius if we choose, but I fail to see that very much is gained thereby. No, to justify his piracy Tintoretto pleads neither limited originality nor unlimited aspirations. He defends his rights, claiming that he has been wronged whenever a commission goes to one of his colleagues. Left to himself, he would have covered every wall in the city with his paintings; no *cameo* would have been too vast, no *sotto portico* too obscure for him to illuminate. He would have covered the ceilings, people would have walked across his most beautiful images, his brush would have spared neither the façades of the palaces that line the Canale Grande nor the gondolas, nor perhaps the gondoliers. The man imagines that he was born with the privilege of transforming his city single-handed, and a good case can be drawn up in his favor.

When he begins his apprenticeship painting is on the wane. In Florence the crisis is manifest; Venice, as always, is silent or hypocritical, but we know for a certainty that the authentic Rialtan sources of inspiration have dried up. At the end of the fifteenth century the city is deeply affected by the passing of Antonello da Messina. His death marks a turning point; afterwards painters are imported. I am not saying that they are brought in from distant regions but simply that the most famous painters come from the mainland: Giorgione, from Castelfranco; Titian, from Pieve di Cadore; Paolo Cagliari and Bonifazio dei Pitati, from Verona; Palma Vecchio, from Sarinalta; Girolamo Vecchio and Paris Bordone, from Treviso; Andrea Schiavone, from Zara; and others still. As a matter of fact, this aristocratic republic is primarily a technocracy and has always been bold enough to recruit specialists from far and wide and clever enough to treat them as her own. Moreover, this is the time when the Republic of Venice, checked at sea and threatened by coalitions on the continent, turns to the hinterlands and tries through conquests to assert her might. Most of the new immigrants are from annexed territories. Venice betrays her anxiety by importing artists on a massive scale. When we recall that the artists of the Quattrocento were for the most part born inside the walls of the city or in Murano, we cannot suppress the notion that after the extinction of the Vivarini and Bellini families and after the death of Carpaccio, the resurgence of her generations of artists would not have been possible without a blood transfusion.

Painting is like all the other crafts in that the patriciate is responsible for facilitating the immigration of good artisans and—to prove what might be called their cosmopolitan chauvinism—for making the Republic of the Doges into a melting pot. In the eyes of his distrustful and jealous aristocracy, foreigners make the best Venetians; their adoption of Venice is proof of inspiration just as aloofness signals a weak character. We can be sure that the local artisans did not look upon the newcomers in the same way. Why should they? For them the newcomers represent foreign competition. They are tactful enough not to complain, and they carry on as if nothing were wrong; but there are conflicts, inescapable evidences of tension, charges and countercharges stemming from wounded pride. Forced to bow to the technical superiority of the alien settlers, the natives hide their humiliation by expanding their prerogatives. They agree to take second place to the most skilled, to the most expert, but only in return for a sacrifice: their birthright must remain intact. Only a Rialtan can claim Venice as his own; while Germans are better glaziers, they can never boast that they are true Venetians. Before their disappearance the great painters of the Quattrocento had the bitter experience of seeing the public turn away from them and bestow their favors on young intruders who scorned them. For example Titian, the outsider, leaves one of the Bellini brothers for the other—Gentile for Giovanni—in pursuit of still another outsider, Antonello, the meteor that rent the sky and the water of the lagoon twenty years earlier. Tiziano Vecellio has no need of Giovanni; what he seeks in him is a reflection; he proves this by soon abandoning the master of the disciple and joining Giorgione's school, for the third alien seems to the second to be the true heir to the first. Tiziano and Giorgio belong to the same generation; the pupil may even be older than the teacher. Did the Bellini brothers realize on that day that they had served their time? And what did Giovanni's true disciples say? And the others, the last representatives of the Murano school, what did they think? Many of them were youngsters or men still in their prime; the influence of Antonello da Messina had reached all of them through Giovanni Bellini; colors and light came from Messina, but their acclimatization was effected by Giovanni; through him they had become Venetian. The young artists staked their honor on remaining faithful but were strangled by their fidelity. They did their best to adapt to new conditions without abandoning the rather crude techniques that they had been taught, but to do so was to accept mediocrity. They must have felt bitter resentment on seeing two young intruders join forces, break with the indigenous tradition, rediscover the secrets of a Sicilian, and effortlessly carry painting to its highest perfection. Giovanni still reigns, however, and the fame of this admirable artist spreads throughout northern Italy. The barbarian invasion begins during his latter years and triumphs after his death in 1516.

At the height of the invasion, the greatest painter of the century is born in the heart of the occupied city, in an alley on the Rialto. A somber plebeian pride, always humiliated, always rebuffed, constantly in waiting, seizes upon the opportunity, infiltrates the heart of the sole Rialtan with a remnant of talent, emboldens and inflames it. We recall that he springs directly from neither the working class nor the bourgeoisie. His father is a successful artisan, a member of the petty bourgeoisie, who takes pride in not working for others. As the son of a working man Jacopo would perhaps have remained the obscure collaborator of an artist; as the son of an independent craftsman, however, he has to become a master or a failure. He will pass through the ranks but is prevented by his class and family status from stopping along the way. That he fails to leave good impressions in the studio where he serves his apprenticeship is understandable, for his aim on entering the studio was to leave it as soon as possible to reclaim the place already reserved for him in the social hierarchy. Then, too, Schiavone (or Bordone or Bonifazio dei Pitati—they are all the same) must have looked upon him as an intruder while Jacopo considered his master an alien or a thief. The Little Dyer is a *native* and Venice is his birthright. Had he been a mediocre painter, he would have remained modest and resentful; but he is brilliant and knows it, and he will take second place to no one. Aliens, in the eyes of a Rialtan, have nothing to protect them other than their professional worth; if Jacopo outshines them as a painter, they will have to disappear, even if this means their assassination. No one paints or writes without a mandate; would anyone dare if "*I* were not the Other"?* Jacopo is given a mandate by a toiling population to redeem through his art the privileges of a purebred Venetian. That explains his unscrupulous conduct. Popular recrimination fills his heart with an abiding desire to reassert a claim; he has been given the task of winning recognition of his rights; whoever champions such a just cause can use any means to succeed—he will show no mercy, give no quarter. His misfortune results from the fact that his struggle against the undesirables brings him into conflict with the patriciate and its policy of assimilation of foreigners in the name of the indigenous artisans. When he shouted in the streets, "Veronese to Verona!" it was the government that he was calling in question. Realizing this, he hesitates, then resumes his obstinate course, exhibiting a curious mixture of flexibility and inflexibility. As a prudent subject of a police state he always gives in, or pretends to; as an *indigenous* citizen of the most beautiful of all cities, his arrogance is boundless; he can even be servile without losing his ankylosis of pride. Everything is to no avail. His schemes against those protected by the aristocracy are thwarted by his impatience or by his incurable bluntness, or they backfire. Now we see the rancor of the Republic in a new light. The subject asks essentially only for what would probably have been accorded him, but his perverse submissiveness nettles the authorities, and they consider

---

* "The Other" occupies a central position in the existential world: "The Other is not only the one whom I see but the one *who sees me*" and makes it possible for me to "recognize that I am" as he sees me; I do not choose to be what I am for the Other, "but I can try to be for I myself what I am for the Other, by choosing myself as I appear to the Other." Quoted from "The Other and His Look" in Justus Streller's *To Freedom Condemned* (New York; Philosophical Library, 1960).

him a rebel. Or at the very least they are suspicious of him, and their suspicions are well founded. The consequences of his impetuousness are worth examining.

First, the studied and almost sadistic violence which I will call lack of self-restraint. Born among the underlings who endured the weight of a superimposed hierarchy, he shares their fears and their tastes; we find their prudence even in his presumptuousness. His neighbors, alert, courageous, somewhat suspicious of outsiders, have helped him to establish a system of values, shown him the dangers that life holds in store, pointed out the hopes that are permitted and those that are prohibited. Specific, limited opportunities, a foreseeable destiny, a future already visible in its general outlines, being imprisoned inside a transparency like a tiny flower inside a glass paperweight—all this kills dreams. One desires only what is possible; this is a mitigating circumstance that enrages fools and excites far-fetched but ephemeral ambitions. Jacopo's ambition suddenly asserts itself. . . . There is a means and there is an end in view which is the prescribed task; one can rise above the heaviest low-lying mists and touch the rigid, luminous membrane of the ceiling; there are other ceilings, membranes that grow progressively clearer and more delicate, and at the very top, perhaps, is the blue of the sky. But what does this matter to Tintoretto; each has his own soaring range and his own habitat. Tintoretto knows that he is talented; he has been told that his talent is his capital. By putting his capacities to the test he will capitalize on them and provide himself with an adequate income. And so we *see* him totally mobilized for a long life, prepared always to exploit the vein even to the point of depletion of both mine and miner. At about the same time another slave to work, Michelangelo, is undertaking projects only to desert them in disgust and leave them unfinished.

Tintoretto *always* finishes things with the terrible application of a man bent on finishing his statements come what may; even death stood aside for him at San Giorgio, where it allowed him to apply the finishing touches to his last canvas, or at least to give final instructions to his collaborators. Never during his entire life did he allow himself an indulgence, a dislike, a preference, or even the comfort of a dream. During periods of exhaustion he must have repeated to himself this principle: "To refuse a commission is to hand it over to my colleagues."

He has to produce at any cost. Here the will of a man and that of city coalesce. A hundred years earlier Donatello had scolded Uccello for sacrificing creativity to experimentation and for carrying the love of painting to the point of ceasing to paint pictures;* but that was in Florence, and the Florentine artists had just begun to risk experimentation with *perspective;* by applying to painted objects the laws of geometrical optics, they were trying to construct a new plastic space. Other times, other customs. In Venice, under the leadership of Titian, everyone shares the opinion that painting has just reached the peak of perfection, that further advances are impossible: Art is dead, long live life. The supreme barbarity begins with Aretino's foolish statements: "How realistic it is! How true to life! You *would never believe it is painted!*" In short, it is time for painting to disappear in the face of *realizations;* inspired merchants want something beautiful and useful. A work ought to please the lover of art, dazzle Europe with the pageantry of the Republic, awe the people. And still today we stand in awe, we the little tourists, before the Venetian cinema-scope and

---

* Paolo Uccello (1397-1475) first exhibited a heroic sense of design and helped to create the Renaissance superman. His rigorous application of linear perspective during a later period is generally assumed to represent a paradoxical return to Gothic Traditions.

prattle about one of Titian's realizations, one of Paolo Cagliari's productions, one of Pordenone's performances, one of Vincentino's stagings. Jacopo Robusti shares the prejudices of his age, and our experts stress the point. How many times have I heard them say, "Tintoretto, bah! Just like the movies." And still, no one else in the world, either before or after him, has carried so far the passion for research. With Titian, painting flowers and dies, a victim of its own perfection; Jacopo sees in its death the necessary condition for a resurrection: everything is to have a new beginning, to be done over—a theme to which we shall return. But—and this is his major contradiction—he will never allow his experiments to restrict his productivity. So long as there remains in Venice one barren wall, the painter's task is to cover it; morals prohibit transforming a studio into a laboratory. Art is in its entirety a serious profession and a battle to the death against intruders. Like Titian, like Veronese, Jacopo will produce exquisite cadavers. With one difference: his cadavers are racked by fever, and we do not know at first whether this is the aftermath of life or the onset of putrefaction. And if the comparison with movie-making is pressed, he resembles the cinematographer in *this* respect: he accepts imbecile scenarios but imbues them with his obsessions. He has to fool the buyer, to give him something for his money; the buyer will have his Catherine, his Theresa, his Sebastian; for the same price he will have on the same canvas, if there is sufficient room, his wife and his brothers. But underneath it all, behind the sumptuous and banal façade of the *realization* he pushes forward his experimentation. Each of his great works has a double meaning; its strict utilitarianism disguises an unending quest. Fitting his research into the frame of the paid commission, he is obliged to revolutionize painting even while respecting the stipulations of his client. Such is the inner motivation of his excessive activity, and such will later be the reason for his perdition.

He also has to win commissions. We have already seen that he succeeds. But let us re-examine his actions; now they will appear in a new light. Tintoretto's rebellion has various repercussions. Having rebelled against the politics of the melting-pot, he is forced to infringe upon corporate regulations or practices. The government, unable to eliminate competition and aware of its advantages, takes pains to channel it through contests. The powerful and the rich, if their taste is the deciding factor, will preserve public order by practicing bland protectionism in the form of directed competition.

Are they sincere? Doubtless, and all would be perfect if we were certain of their abilities but we have only their word. Sometimes harmony reigns—and then they choose Vincentino. Tintoretto always avoids their contests. Does he deny their competence? Certainly not! He simply refuses them the right to treat a native in the same way as an intruder. But contests do exist, and by shunning them, our rebel is trying deliberately to destroy protectionism. He is trapped in a corner. Since the officials pretend to base their judgment on merit, and since he challenges their right to judge him, he has either to renounce painting or to win recognition through the quality of his works. He loses no time in bringing his works to their attention. Seizing upon every opportunity, he takes his competitors by surprise, confronts his jurors with the accomplished fact, and utilizes all his cunning and speed, all the diligence of his collaborators in establishing a system of mass production which breaks every record and allows him to sell his canvases at rock-bottom prices, and at times to give them away. Two secondhand shops face each other on a Roman avenue; the shop-keepers, I imagine, have conspired to simulate a merciless struggle that will not cease until both shops are brought under a single proprietor; through their eternal confrontation the shop-windows suggest a tragic comedian bent on contrasting the two sides of his nature. One is covered with gloomy slogans: "*Prezzi disastrosi!*" The other contains multicolored placards which announce: "*Prezzi da ridere! da ridere! da ridere!*" This has been going on for years, and whenever I see the shops they make me think of Tintoretto. Had he chosen laughter or tears? Both, I think—depending on the client. We can even surmise that he chuckled privately and complained publicly that he was being robbed; in any case, in his studio, every day was like a year-end clearance sale, and clients were willing to meet the judicious prices set at his liquidation sales. Having set out to commission a medallion, they ended by turning over to him every wall in their house. He was the first to break the strained bonds of friendship within the confraternity. For this unlabeled Darwinist, colleague meant personal enemy, and he discovered before Hobbes the meaning of absolute competition: *Homo homini lupus.* Venice trembles. Unless a vaccine can be found to combat the virus Tintoretto, the good old corporate system will fall apart and all that remains will be smoldering antagonisms, molecular solitudes. The Republic condemns his new methods, brands them felonies, speaks of slipshod work, of cut-rate sales, of monopoly. Later, much later, other cities will honor his methods in another language, using terms like *struggle for life, mass production, dumping, trust*, etc. For a while this man of bad character will lose on one canvas all that he gains on another. Through hook or crook he will win commissions—but not acceptance. Through a strange reversal he, the *native*, the one-hundred-percent Rialtan, is an intruder, almost a pariah in his own city. The inevitable consequence is that he will perish unless he establishes a family. First, to stifle competition within his studio. This champion of liberalism reverses the Biblical precept; he will have others never do to him what he does to them. Moreover, he needs steadfast loyalty; outside collaborators can be frightened and discouraged by all the scandals circulated about him, and much time will be wasted if he has to reassure them. None of the scandals will permanently damage his reputation. Why does he need disciples? He wants other hands, other pairs of arms, nothing more. From absolute competition to exploitation of the family—that is his course. In 1550 he marries Faustina dei Vescovi and immediately starts producing children. Just as he produces pictures: without let or hindrance. His brood has only one shortcoming: there are too many girls. Too bad! He will put all of them except two in the convent: Marietta, whom he retains as his helper, and Ottavia, whom he marries to a painter. "Lightning Tintoretto" will persist until Faustina gives birth to two sons, Domenico and Marco. Before their arrival he has already begun to teach the craft to his oldest daughter, Marietta. A woman painter is something extraordinary in Venice. He must have been very impatient. Finally, around 1575, his operation is completed; the new staff includes Sebastiano Casser, his son-in-law, Marietta, Domenico and Marco. The symbol of a domestic association is the *domus* which protects and imprisons the group. At about the same date Jacopo buys a house, which he will never abandon. In this small lazaret the leper will live half-quarantined with his family, loving them more and more as he witnesses the swelling of the ranks of the *others* who hate him. On observing him *in his home*, at work, in his relations with his wife and children, we discover another side of his personality—that of the austere moralist. Was there not more than a trace of Calvinism in his life? We see here pessimism and work, the profit motive and devotion to the family. Human nature is vitiated by original sin; men are divided by self-interest. The Christian must seek salvation through his works; he must struggle for survival, labor unceasingly to improve the Earth that God has entrusted to him; he will find the mark of divine favor in the material success of his undertaking. As for the promptings of his heart, they should be reserved for the flesh of his flesh, for his children. Was Venice feeling the influence of the reformed Religion? We know that in the second half of the century there was in Venice an odd person, Fra Paolo Sarpi, who was popular among the patricians, hostile to Rome, and familiar with foreign Protestant movements. But in all probability the petty bourgeoisie knew nothing about the tendencies, discernible in certain intellectual quarters, that seemed vaguely to favor the Reform. It would be more accurate to say that the Republic reformed itself. And by Tintoretto's time this reform has been going on for a long time. Venetian merchants owe their living to credit; they can not accept the sentence pronounced by the Church on those whom it insists on labeling usurers, and they scorn Roman obscurantism in favor of science, especially when practical. The State has always affirmed the domination of civil authority and will not change its basic doctrine. The State has the upper hand over its clergy and, when Pope Pius V takes it upon himself to remove ecclesiastics from the jurisdiction of lay tribunals, the Senate pointedly refuses to recognize the removal. Furthermore, the government has many reasons for considering the Holy See a temporal and military power rather than a spiritual power. All this does not prevent the authorities from currying the Pope's favor, if the interest of the Republic is at stake, or pursuing heretics, or organizing a sumptuous feast in honor of St. Bartholomew to flatter a very Christian monarch. Tintoretto's pseudo-Calvinism is transmitted to him by his city; the painter unknowingly assimilates the benign Protestantism found at that time in every great capitalist stronghold.* The artist's position is then highly equivocal, especially in Venice. But let us press our advantage; this very ambiguity may well enable us to understand Jacopo's puritanical passion.

We read that "the Renaissance attributed to the artist the traits which Antiquity reserved for the man of action and which the Middle Ages had used to adorn its saints." This is not untrue, but to me the opposite observation seems at least equally true: "[During the sixteenth century] painting and sculpture were still looked upon as manual arts; all the honors were reserved for poetry. That explains the attempts to put the figurative arts on the same footing with literature."† We know that Aretino, the Petronius of the poor and the Malaparte of the rich, was the arbiter of taste and elegance for the snobs of the Venetian patriciate and that Titian was honored by his friendship, for the artist, with all his fame, was not the poet's equal. And Michelangelo? He made the mistake of imagining that he was of noble birth, and this illusion ruined his life. As a youth he wanted to cultivate the humanities, to write, in the belief that a nobleman deprived of his sword could take up the pen without degrading himself. Forced to take up the chisel, he was never able to console himself. From his dais of shame he looked down upon sculpture and painting, deriving what empty, shriveled joy he could from feeling superior to what he was doing. Forced to remain silent, he sought to provide a lan-

---

* The very same one that inoculated Italian towns against the Lutheran sickness and encouraged Italy to carry out its own religious revolution under the name of Counter Reformation.

† Eugenio Battista, in an excellent article on Michelangelo, published in *l'Epoca* (August 25, 1957).

guage for the mute arts, to multiply allegories and symbols; he wrote a book on the ceiling of the Sistine Chapel and tortured marble to force it to speak.

What are we to conclude? Are the Renaissance painters heroes and gods, or are they manual workers? Everything is relative, depending on the clientele and the mode of remuneration. Or rather painters are primarily manual workers. They may become employees of the court or remain local masters. It is up to them to choose—or to be chosen. Raphael and Michelangelo are court appointees. Proud but dependent, they will be dumped in the street if on the slightest pretext they meet with disfavor; against this, the sovereign guarantees their fame. This sacred person accords to the elect a portion of his supernatural powers; the glory of his throne falls upon them like a ray of sunshine, and they reflect it upon the people; the divine right of kings gives painters divine rights. The result: daubers changed into supermen. Just who are these ordinary men whom a giant has snatched from the petty bourgeoisie and suspended between heaven and earth, these satellites whose borrowed splendor is overpowering? Are they anything other than ordinary men raised above humanity? They are heroes, yes—intercessors, intermediaries. Today still, nostalgic republicans worship in them, under the guise of genius, the light from the dead star of Monarchy.

Tintoretto is of another ilk. He works for merchants, for officials, for parish churches. Not that he is uneducated. He was enrolled in school at the age of seven and probably ended his schooling at twelve, after he had learned to write and reckon; besides, and more important still, we would surely have to class as education the patient cultivation of the senses, of manual and mental faculties, and of the traditional empiricism still associated with studio painting around 1530. But he will never acquire the trappings of the court painters. Michelangelo writes sonnets; Raphael is supposed to have been versed in Latin; and Titian himself finally acquired a veneer through associating with intellectuals. Compared to these worldlings, Tintoretto seems like a dunce; he will never have the leisure or the taste for toying with ideas and words. He ridicules the humanism of men of letters. Venice has few poets and still fewer philosophers, but for him these are too many and he has nothing to do with any of them. Not that he shies away from them; he simply ignores them. He is willing to admit their social superiority. Aretino has every right to congratulate him with condescending benevolence; this high-ranking person has been *received* in Venice and is a member of the inner circle; patricians who would never dream of greeting a painter in the street invite him to their table. But does Tintoretto have to envy him, too? Does he have to envy him *because he writes?* To him the creations of the mind acquire an utterly immoral air because they are gratuitous. God placed us on the earth to earn our bread by the sweat of our brow; but writers do not sweat. Do they really work? Jacopo never opens a book with the exception of his missal; he would never be so foolish as to force his talent for the sake of competing with literature. His paintings include everything but *mean* nothing; they are as mute as the world. All that he really values, this son of an artisan, is physical effort, manual creation. What fascinates him in the profession of painting is that here professional ability is pushed to the point of prestidigitation and the delicacy of the merchandise reduced to its quintessence. The artist is the supreme worker; he exhausts himself and his material in order to produce and sell visions.

That would not prevent him from working for princes if he liked them. He does not and that is the crux of the matter.

They frighten him without inspiring him. He never tries to approach them or to make himself known to them. He seems to take pains to confine his reputation within the walls of Venice. During his whole life he left Venice only once, when he was in his sixties, to go just outside the city to Mantua. Even then he had to be begged to go. His clients wanted him to hang up his own canvases, but he refused to go without his wife. This stipulation not only affords proof of his conjugal sentiments; it leaves no doubt about his horror of travel. And it would be wrong to think that his Venetian colleagues share his horror, for they leave no road untraveled. A century earlier Gentile Bellini was sailing the seas. What adventurers! But Jacopo is a mole, happy only within the network of his molehills. Whenever he tries to imagine the outside world, he is gripped by terror; still, if he has a choice, he prefers to risk his skin rather than his paintings. He accepts foreign commissions—and for him anything beyond Padua is foreign—but does not solicit them. What a contrast between his frenzied behavior in the Doge's Palace, the Scuola San Rocco, the home of the Crociferi, and this indifference! He entrusts the execution of foreign commissions to his collaborators, surveys from afar their serial productions, takes care not to interfere, as if fearful of allowing the tiniest spangle of his talent to venture beyond his native soil—European distribution rights are available for only his B pictures. In the Uffizi, the Prado, the National Gallery, the Louvre, in Munich, and in Vienna, we find Raphael, Titian, a hundred others. Every painter, or almost every painter, except Tintoretto. He fiercely guarded his works for his fellow citizens and the only way to find out anything about him is to search for him in his native city for the very good reason that he did not *want* to leave Venice.

But we must be specific. In Venice itself he has two distinct clienteles. He besieges public officials and, naturally, puts his whole studio to work, including the head of the family, if the Senate gives him a commission. Still visible in the Doge's Palace, under a lighting system that shows them off to advantage, are the works of a strong collective personality that bore the name of Tintoretto. But if you are interested in Jacopo Robusti you will have to abandon the Piazzetta, cross the Piazza San Marco, ride a donkey across bridges that span the canals, turn down a labyrinth of dark, narrow streets, enter still darker churches. There you will find him. At the Scuola San Rocco you will find him in person, without Marietta or Domenico or Sebastiano Casser; there he works alone. A grimy haze darkens the canvases, or perhaps the lighting is at fault; wait patiently until your eyes become adjusted; finally you will see a rose in the darkness, a genius in the penumbra. And who paid for these paintings? Sometimes the faithful of the parish, sometimes the members of the Brotherhood—middleclass men, great and small; they are his true public, the only public that he loves.

This huckster-painter has none of the qualities of a God-hero. With a little luck he will become notorious, famous, but never glorious; his profane clientele lacks the power to crown him. Of course the renown of his august colleagues honors the whole profession and he, too, scintillates somewhat. Does he covet their glory? Perhaps. But he meets none of the requirements for acquiring glory; he rejects the favor of princes because it would reduce him to servitude. Jacopo Robusti takes pride in remaining a petty chief, a peddler of Fine Arts made to order, the master of his own studio. He makes no difference between the economic independence of the producer and the freedom of the artist; his activities prove that he has a secret desire to reverse the laws of marketing, to create demand by supplying goods. Did he not create slowly and patiently within the Brotherhood of San Rocco a demand for art—a certain kind of art—which he alone could satisfy? His independence is preserved to an even greater degree when he works for associations—*consorterie*, parishes—and when these great bodies make their decisions by majority vote.

Michelangelo, a pseudo-noble, and Titian, the son of peasants, are directly exposed to the attraction of the monarchy. Tintoretto's heritage is that of the independent craftsman and worker. The artisan is an amphibian; as a manual worker, he is proud of his hands, and as a member of the petty bourgeoisie, he is attracted by the ruling bourgeoisie. By fostering competition the ruling bourgeoisie allows fresh air to circulate within a stifling protectionism. At that time there is in Venice *a bourgeois hope*. Only a glimmer, for the aristocracy has long since taken precautions; in their stratified world, rich men are *made*, patricians are born. But restrictions are placed on the wealthy; not only are businessmen and industrialists restricted to their own class but they are also denied entrance into the most lucrative professions; the State restricts the concession of the *appalto* (shipping franchise) to the aristocracy. Sad, dreamy bourgeoisie! Everywhere else in Europe members of the bourgeoisie are hastening to disown their past and buy titles and castles. In Venice everything is denied them, even the humble blessing of betrayal. Betrayal will therefore take the form of dreams. Giovita Fontana, originally from Piacenza, moves into the business world, accumulates gold and spends it in building a palace on the Canale Grande; an entire existence is summed up in these brief words: a voracious desire, satiated, is finally turned into dreamy snobbery, a merchant dies and is reborn as an imaginary patrician. Rich commoners dance in a ring and hide their nocturnal fantasies; grouped into associations they outdo themselves in charitable works, their melancholy austerity contrasting sharply with the melancholy orgies of a disenchanted patriciate.

For the Republic is no longer mistress of the seas. Gradually the aristocracy begins to decline, failures multiply, the number of poor noblemen increases, the others lose their spirit of enterprise. The sons of the merchant princes buy land and live on their income. Soon ordinary "citizens" replace them in certain functions; ships eventually come under the control of men from the bourgeoisie. But the bourgeoisie is still not ready by any stretch of the imagination to consider itself the rising class. It even harbors the notion that it may one day insure the resurgence of the fallen nobility; we should say rather that an obscure agitation took hold of it, making its condition less tolerable and resignation to it more difficult.

Tintoretto does not dream. Never. If ambition is dependent on opportunities for social advancement, then the most ambitious commoners in Venice are the members of the petty bourgeoisie, for they still have the opportunity to rise above their class. But the painter is aware of his deep-seated affinities with his clients. He appreciates their attitude toward work and morality, their good common sense. He likes their nostalgia and, especially, he shares their profound desire for freedom; all of them need freedom, if only to produce and to buy and sell. These are the clues to his opportunism; his is a need for air which comes from the summits. A troubled sky, a distant, invisible ascent opens to him a vertical future; like a balloon he is borne aloft, filled with the new spirit, for since childhood his outlook has been that of the bourgeoisie. But the contradictions within the class of his origin are to limit his ambitions: as a peddler, he hopes always to outdo himself; as a laborer he pretends to work with his hands. That is enough to determine his position. There are in Venice approximately 7,600 patricians, 13,600 citizens, 127,000 artisans, workers and small businessmen, 1,500 Jews, 12,900 domestics and 550 beggars. Ignoring the Jews and nobles, beggars and domestics, Tintoretto is interested only in the imaginary barrier that separates the commoners into two groups, 13,600 on the one hand and 127,000 on the other. He wants to be first in the second group and last in the first—in short, the most humble of the rich and the most distinguished of the tradesmen. This makes the artisan, in the heart of troubled Venice, a pseudo-bourgeois more true than a true bourgeois. In him and on his canvases the Brotherhood of San Rocco will admire the embellished image of a bourgeoisie untainted by betrayal.

Michelangelo has reservations about working for the Sovereign Pontiff; his contempt sometimes makes him recoil, for this nobleman looks down on art. Tintoretto is just the opposite; he outstrips himself; without art, what would he be? A dyer. Art is the force that lifts him above his natal condition, and his dignity is the thing that sustains him. He has to work or to fall back to the bottom of the well. Recoil from art? Keep away from it? How? He has no time to raise questions about painting. Who knows whether he even gives it a second thought? Michelangelo thinks too much; he is a gentleman, an intellectual. Tintoretto does not meditate—he paints.

So much for his opportunism. His destiny is to incarnate bourgeois puritanism in an aristocratic Republic during its decline. Elsewhere this somber humanism would take root; in Venice it will disappear before being recognized for what it is, but not before arousing the distrust of an aristocracy always on guard. The moroseness that official and bureaucratic Venice manifests toward Tintoretto is the same as that which the patriciate evidences toward the Venetian bourgeoisie. These cantankerous merchants and their painter pose a danger to the Establishment and have to be kept under surveillance.

Man At Bay

There is something superb about Tintoretto's stubborn refusal to compete: "I acknowledge no rival and accept no judge." Michelangelo would probably say that. The bad part is that Tintoretto does not. Quite the opposite: when invited to present a sketch, he will lose no time in accepting. Afterwards, we know that he releases his bolts of lightning. Yes, somewhat in the same manner that a cuttle-fish scatters its ink. Blinded by lightning, spectators are unable to see his picture clearly. Everything is arranged, moreover, so that they need never study it or—more important still—appreciate it. When they come out of their stupor, the canvas is in place, the offer under seal, and they will have seen only the flash. Either I am badly mistaken or he is being evasive; he seems to be afraid to come face to face with his adversaries. Would he waste all this ingenuity if he felt certain that his talent would suffice? Would he deign to astound his contemporaries through the quantity of his output if they had no reservations about its quality?

And then rivalry brings to the fore his mania for self-affirmation through self-effacement; this is his strong point, his trademark. The slightest criticism upsets him, offends him. In 1559 the San Rocco church commissioned the *Healing of the Paralytic* to balance a canvas by Pordenone. No one asks him to imitate the style of his predecessor. There is no cause for rivalry,* for Antonio di Sacchis has been dead for twenty years; and if it was once possible for him to influence the younger painter, that time has passed, for Jacopo has mastered his art. Still, he is unable to resist the temptation; he has to paint in the style of Pordenone. Attention has been focused on the way in which he "exaggerates the baroque violence of their gestures . . . by contrasting his monumental figures with the architecture inside which they are compressed" and "achieved this effect by lowering the ceiling . . . and using the columns themselves . . . to immobilize the gestures, freeze their violence." He shudders at the notion of being forever imprisoned in an inert confrontation: "Compare, if you like, one Pordenone with the other; I, Jacopo Robusti, am leaving." He has, of course, taken pains to have the spurious Di Sacchis outshine the real Di Sacchis. His retreat is not a rout; he issues a parting challenge: "Old or young, I take them all on and beat them on their own ground." But this is precisely the thing that arouses suspicion. Why would he need to play their game and submit to their rules if he could outshine them all by being himself? What resentment in his insolence! This Cain assassinates every Abel preferred over him: "You like this Veronese? Well, I can do much better when I deign to imitate him; you take him for a man and he is nothing but a technique." And what humility. From time to time this pariah slips into the skin of another person in order to enjoy in his turn the delight of being loved. And then at times it would seem that he lacks the courage to manifest his scandalous genius; disheartened, he leaves his genius in semidarkness and tries to prove it *deduc-*

---

* Ridolfi, deceived by the resemblance of their styles, declared that the canvas was painted "in concurrenza con it Pordenone."

tively: "Since I paint the best Veroneses and the best Porde-
nones, just imagine *what I am capable of painting* when I allow
myself to be me." As a matter of fact, he almost never takes
the liberty of being himself unless someone builds up his confidence and leaves him alone in an empty room. This lack of
self-confidence has its origin, of course, in the hostility manifested toward him by others. But the painter's timidity and his
fellow citizens' bias have their source in the same disease; in
1548, in Venice, under Tintoretto's attack against patricians,
connoisseurs and aesthetes, *painting is in jeopardy.*

A long evolution has begun—an evolution which will substitute everywhere the profane for the sacred. Cold, glittering,
rimy, the diverse branches of human activity emerge one after
the other from mellow divine promiscuity. Art has its turn, and
from the settling mists emerges a sumptuous disenchantment,
painting. It still recalls the time when Duccio and Giotto were
showing God his Creation just as it had left his hands, after
he had recognized it as his work, put the world in its frame
for all eternity, and closed the books of the whole affair. Into
the picture, the fief of the Sun and the supreme Eye, monks
and prelates sometimes slipped their transparency; they came
tiptoeing in to view what God was viewing, then excused
themselves and went away. Finished: the Eye is closed, Heaven
blind. What is the result? First a change of clientele. As long as
the work was done for the clergy, all went well; but the day the
biggest of the Florentine bankers had the ridiculous notion of
using frescos to beautify his house, The Omnipotent One, dis-
mayed, began to buttress his claim to the role of Lover of Souls.
Then, too, there was the Florentine affair, the conquest of perspective. Perspective is profane; sometimes even, it is a profa-

nation. Observe Mantegna's Christ lying feet first and head remote; do you think that the Father is satisfied with a foreshortened Son?* God is absolute proximity, universal envelopment by love; can He be shown *from a distance* the Universe that He has created and that He is at each instant saving from annihilation? Is Being to conceive and produce Non-Being? The Absolute to engender the Relative? Light to contemplate Shadow? Reality to be taken for Appearance? No, this would be a renewal of the eternal story: Ingenuity, the Tree of Knowledge, Original Sin and Expulsion. This time the Apple is called perspective. But the Florentine Adamites nibble at it rather than eat it, thereby avoiding immediate discovery of their Fall. During the middle of the Quattrocento, Uccello thinks that he is still in Paradise, and poor Alberti, the theoretician of the "perspectivists," is still trying to present geometrical optics as an Ontology of Visibility; he is rather ingenuous in asking the Divine Look to guarantee convergent lines. Heaven has failed to heed this absurd request, relegating man to the nothingness which is properly his and which he has just rediscovered once again; distance, isolation, separation—these negations set our bounds; only man has a horizon. Alberti's window opens on a measurable universe, but this rigid miniature depends wholly on the point that defines both concentration and dispersion—the eye. In Piero della Fra Francesca's *Annunciation*, between the Angel and the Virgin we see retreating columns; this is an illusion, for in themselves and for their Creator none of these inert white columns, identical and incomparable, have ever stirred in their sleep. Perspective is an act of violence which

---

* Andrea Mantegna (1431-1506) began at an early age to experiment with traditional subjects. His most daring achievement is the unorthodox image of Christ in the ungainly position from which medical students might have viewed his deathly pallor and open wounds.

human weakness is forcing upon God's little world. A hundred years later in the Netherlands Being will be rediscovered at the very heart of appearing and appearance will reclaim the dignity of apparition; painting will have new aims and will acquire new meaning. But before Vermeer can give us the sky, the stars, day and night, the moon and the earth in the form of a tiny brick wall, the bourgeoisie from the North must win their greatest victories and forge their humanism.

In sixteenth-century Italy faith still burns in the artists' hearts, combatting the atheism of their hands and eyes. In their attempt to get a firmer grasp on the Absolute, they perfect techniques which force upon them a Relativism which they detest. These mystified dogmatists can neither push forward nor retrace their steps. If God no longer looks at the images that they paint, who will replace Him? Their images are but the reflection of man's impotence; what will validate them? If the sole aim of painting is to gauge our myopia, it is not worth one hour's labor. To reveal man to the Omnipotent One who deigned to raise him from the clay was an act of thanksgiving, a sacrifice. But why reveal man to man? Why reveal him *as he is not?* The artists born near the end of the century, around 1480—Titian, Giorgione, Raphael—pay lip service to heaven. More about this later. And then the wealth and efficacy of means still disguise the sinister indetermination of ends. Furthermore, we can surmise that Raphael had a presentiment of those ends; he mocked everyone and everything, caroused with women, sold chromos, and through his *Schadenfreude* incited his collaborators to produce obscene engravings. Insincerity means suicide. At any rate the serenity of painting vanishes with these sacred monsters. In the second quarter of the century painting runs amuck as a result of its own perfection. In the barbaric taste which contemporaries evidenced for great "realizations," a certain uneasiness is manifested; the public demands that the painter utilize all the pomp of realism to conceal his subjectivity, that he efface himself before life, blot out all memory of himself; ideally it should be as if one came upon the pictures by surprise, somewhere in the forest, and saw persons springing from the canvas and splinters from the broken frame flying at the throats of passers-by. The object should reabsorb its visibility, contain it, turn attention away from it by continuously appealing to all the senses, and particularly to the sense of touch; every artifice should be employed to replace the *representation* by a hollow participation of the spectator in the spectacle, so that horror and tenderness would thrust men against their images and, if possible, into their midst, so that desire, burning all the fires of perspective, would discover the *ersatz* of divine ubiquity—the immediate presence of flesh; the logic of the heart. What is desired is *the thing itself* and its destruction: bigger than nature, more real, more beautiful—Terror. But Terror is a disease of rhetoric. Art will slink away, ashamed, once it has lost its letters of credit. Fettered, kept under surveillance, subjected to restrictions imposed by the State, the Church and taste, more sought after and honored, perhaps, than ever before, the artist for the first time in history becomes conscious of his solitude. Who gave him this mandate? What is the source of the right which he arrogates to himself? God has gone out, Darkness reigns. How can he paint in the dark? And *whom?* And *what?* And *why?* The object of art is still the world, that Absolute, but *Reality* steals away, reversing the relation between the finite and the infinite. A vast plenitude has been supporting the wretchedness of bodies and their fragility; now fragility becomes the sole plenitude, the unique surety. The Infinite is emptiness, darkness, inside and outside the creature;

the Absolute is absence, it is God sequestered in human souls, it is desertion. It is too late to *portray*, too early to *create*; the painter is in hell; something comes to birth: a new damnation—genius, that uncertainty, that foolish desire to traverse the world's darkness and contemplate it from without, to crush it against walls and canvases, to sift out its unknown splendors. Genius—a new word in Europe, a conflict between the Relative and the Absolute, between a finite presence and an infinite absence. For the painter knows full well that he will not leave the world, that even if he could, he would bear with him everywhere the Nothingness that transpierces him; he can not transcend perspective without first acquiring the right to create other plastic spaces.

Michelangelo dies obsessed, summing up his despair and scorn in these two words: original sin. Tintoretto says nothing; he practices deceit, for if he acknowledged his solitude, he would find it unbearable. But for that very reason we can understand that he suffers from it more than anyone else; our spurious bourgeois, working for the bourgeoisie, lacks even the alibi of glory. In the pit of vipers the little dyer thrashes about, infected with the moral neurosis which Henri Jeanson so aptly named "the frightening moral robustness of the ambitious"; he sets modest objectives for himself: to rise above his father through the judicious exploitation of his talents, to corner the market by flattering public taste. Light-hearted opportunism, cunning, speed, talent—nothing is lacking and everything is undermined by a vertiginous void, by Art without God. This Art is ugly, mean, dark; it is the imbecile passion of the part for the whole, an icy, tenebrous wind blowing through perforated hearts. Drawn by the void, Jacopo sets out on a motionless voyage from which he will never return.

Genius does not exist; it is the scandalous audacity of

Nothingness. He, the Little Dyer, exists and knows his limitations; this level-headed boy wants simply to mend the rent. All he asks is a modest plenitude; how can Infinity concern him? And how is he to know that one stroke of his brush is enough to confound his judges? His mean, stubborn ambition will be unleashed in the Darkness of Ignorance. After all, it is not his fault if painting is a lost dog with no collar; later there will be fools who will rejoice over their Abandonment; in mid-sixteenth century Italy, the first victim of monocular perspective seeks to hide his. To work alone and for nothing is to die of fear. One must have arbiters. At any price. God has died away, Venice remains—Venice which can fill up holes, seal cavities, plug outlets, stop hemorrhages and leaks. In the Doge's Republic good subjects have to consider the State in all their activities; painters must paint to beautify the city. Jacopo places himself at the disposal of his fellow citizens; they formulate a certain academic notion of Art which he is quick to adopt. All the more so since he has always had the same notion; it was explained to him when he was a small child, and he believed it: an artisan's worth is measured by the number and importance of the commissions that he receives, the honors that he is accorded. He will hide his genius under his opportunism and consider social success the sole obvious sign of a mystical victory. His deception blinds others; on the earth he plays poker and cheats; and then he gambles on heaven, without deception. If he wins down here with all the aces that he pulls from his sleeve, he dares to pretend that he will win up there; if he sells his canvases, this means that he has snared the world. But who could blame him for his malice? It is the nineteenth century that pronounced the divorce of the artist and the public; in the sixteenth, it is *true* that painting is running amuck; it has ceased to be a religious sacrifice; but it is *equally true* that it is being rationalized—it is becoming a social service. Who then would dare to say, in Venice: "I paint for myself, serve as my own witness"? And as for those who say this today, are we sure that they are telling the truth? Everyone is a judge, no one is; make what you will of that. Tintoretto is more to be pitied than blamed; his Art cuts through his age like a flaming sword, but he can see it only through the eyes of his time. Besides, he has chosen his own hell; thereupon the Finite again closes up over the Infinite, ambition over genius, Venice over her painter who will never again emerge. But captive Infinity gnaws away at everything; Jacopo's calculated opportunism turns to a frenzy; now he has not only to succeed but also to *prove*. A voluntary culprit, the unfortunate painter has made himself party to an endless trial; acting as his own attorney, he has made each painting a witness for the defense and has never ceased to plead his case. There is a city to convince, with its magistrates and its bourgeoisie whose verdict, to be rendered solely by them and not subject to appeal, will determine his mortal future and his immortality. He and he alone is responsible for the strange amalgam; he has to choose between drawing up a code for his own court of last resort and transforming the Republic of Venice into a supreme tribunal. He makes the only choice possible under the circumstances. Unfortunately for him. How well I understand his indifference toward the rest of the universe! He is not concerned with the opinion of the Germans or even the Florentines. Venice is the most beautiful, the richest; she has the best painters, the best critics, the most enlightened patrons of art. *Here*, inside the brick walls, between a tiny patch of sky and still water, under the flamboyant absence of the Sun, Eternity will be won, lost, in a single lifetime, forever.

Well and good. But why cheat? Why deck himself out in

the trappings of Veronese? If he wants his genius to arouse admiration, why does he smother it so frequently? And why does he name judges only to corrupt them and deceive them?

Why? Because the court is prejudiced, his cause lost, his sentence set, and he knows it. In 1548 he asks Venice to bear witness to the Infinite; she becomes frightened and refuses. What a destiny! Abandoned by God, he has to practice deceit in choosing judges; having found them, he has to cheat in order to have his case adjourned. Throughout his life he will keep them in suspense, sometimes fleeing, sometimes turning on them and blinding them. Everything has its place: suffering and ill-humor, arrogance, flexibility, tremendous effort, rancor, implacable pride, and the humble desire to be loved. Tintoretto's painting is first and foremost a passionate love affair between a man and a city.

A Mole in the Sun

In this senseless romance the city is apparently even more foolish than the man. She has not failed to honor all her other painters. Then why evidence toward this one, the greatest of them all, sullen distrust, moroseness? For the simple reason that she is in love with someone else.

The Republic of Venice is hungry for prestige. Her ships have long accounted for her glory; tired and threatened with decline, she flaunts an artist. Titian alone is worth a fleet. From tiaras and crowns he has stolen flakes of fire to fashion for himself a halo. His adopted land admires him *first and foremost* because of the respect that he inspires in the Emperor; in the sacred light, awesome but perfectly harmless, which encircles his cranium, Venice pretends to recognize her own glory. The painter of kings can be nothing less than the king of painters; the Queen of the Seas acknowledges him as her son and through him recovers a trace of majesty. She has at once given him a profession, a reputation; but when he works for kings, he is suffused with divine light which seeps through walls and spreads as far as San Marco; then she knows that he is repaying a hundredfold what he has received from her. He is a National Asset. Furthermore, this man has the longevity of trees; he endures for a century and unobtrusively becomes an Institution. The presence of an academy consisting of one member born before them and determined to survive them is demoralizing to young artists; it exasperates them and stunts their ambitions. They imagine that their city has the power to immortalize the living and that Venice has reserved this favor for Titian alone. A victim of this misunderstanding, Tintoretto—under the fallacious pretext "I am entitled to it"—demands the same recognition as his illustrious predecessor. But worth is not subject to litigation; one cannot demand from a Republic something which belongs by right to a hereditary monarchy. Jacopo is wrong in upbraiding the Doge's City for focusing all reflectors toward the baobab of the Rialto; the reverse is true. A pencil of light whose source is Rome or Madrid—outside the walls, at any rate—strikes the ancient trunk and reflects onto Venice, eliminating the shadows through a sort of indirect lighting. And I, too, was about to make a mistake, for I first thought of entitling this chapter "In Titian's Shadow." The truth is that *Titian cast no shadow*. Weigh this carefully: on the day of Jacopo's birth the old man is forty; he is seventy-two when his young rival first tries to assert himself. That would be the moment for him to step down, to fade away gracefully. Nothing doing! The indomitable monarch reigns on for twenty-seven years. When he finally disappears, the centenarian has the supreme good fortune of leaving an unfinished *Pietà—like* a youthful dream cut short. For more than half a century Tintoretto the Mole burrows in a labyrinth whose walls are splattered with glory; until the age of fifty-eight the nocturnal beast is hemmed in by sunlight, blinded by the implacable celebrity of an Other. When the light is finally extinguished, Jacopo Robusti is old enough to die but insists on surviving the tyrant. He will gain nothing thereby, however, for Titian is adroit enough to combine two contradictory functions and to serve as an employee of the Court without relinquishing his independence as a petty employer—a happy circumstance not often found in history, and certainly not in the case of Tintoretto, who has put all his eggs in one basket. Visit both tombs and you will see the price he is still paying for his sacrifice to his country. The radioactive corpse of the Grand Old Man lies buried under a mountain of embellishments at Santa Maria dei Frani, a veritable cemetery of Doges; Tintoretto's corpse rests beneath a slab in the murky darkness of a parish church. To me, this is well and good. Titian has the garnish, the sugar and spice, and this is poetic justice; I even wish that he had been buried in Rome beneath Victor Emmanuel's monument, the most hideous in all Italy except for Milan's Grand Central Station. Against this, Jacopo has the horror of naked stone; his name is sufficient. But since this is strictly a personal opinion, I can understand why an irritated traveler would ask Venice for an explanation: "Ungrateful town, is that the best you could do for the best of your sons? Mean city, why do you put floodlights around Titian's *Assumption* and stint on electricity for Robusti's canvases?" I know the explanation; it appeared in 1599 in Aretino's correspondence: "If Robusti wants to be honored, why doesn't he paint like Vecellio?" Jacopo will hear the same refrain every day of his life; it will be repeated before his canvases after his death as well as before, and it is still heard today: "Why does he paint like this? Why does he stray from the Royal Way prepared for him? Our great Vecellio has carried painting to such heights of perfection that no further progress is possible; newcomers will have to follow in the Master's footsteps or Art will fall back into barbarism." Fickle Venetians! Inconsequential bourgeois! Tintoretto is *their* painter; he portrays what they see and feel; this they can not endure. Titian ridicules them, and they worship him.* Titian spends most of his time soothing princes, reassuring them through his canvases that everything is for the best in this best of all possible worlds. Discord is but an illusion, archenemies are secretly reconciled by the colors of their cloaks. Violence? only a ballet danced half-heartedly by spurious he-men with downy beards. Such is his method of depreciating wars. The painter's art borders on the apologetic, becomes a theodicy: suffering, injustice, evil do not exist; nor does mortal sin; Adam and Eve sinned only in order that they might have the opportunity to know and to make known to us that they were naked. In a magnificent quadruple gesture God, noble and benevolent, leaning out from his Heaven, stretches out His arms toward the upraised arms of supine Man. Order reigns; quelled and enslaved, perspective respects hierarchies; discreet accommodations assure kings and saints of preferred positions. If someone is lost in the distance, shrouded by the haze that envelops vague terrain or obscured by smoke from remote lamps, this is never by accident. The indistinctness of the figure corresponds to the obscurity of his condition; besides, it helps to focus attention on the patches of light in

---

* Titian Tiziano Vecellio (c. 1477-1576) owed his enormous success as a portraitist to his ability to paint each subject's ideal of himself.

the foreground. The artist pretends with his brush to relate an event or record a ceremony; by sacrificing movement to order and contrast to unity, he makes his brush caress bodies rather than copy them. Not one of the bearded persons witnessing the Assumption is individualized. First come several legs and upraised arms—a flaming bush; then the substance is impregnated with an element of differentiation and engenders fleeting figures scarcely distinguishable from the collective background which can at any moment reabsorb them—such is the condition of the underlings; Titian reserves individuality for the Great. Even here, however, he is careful to round off their angles; sharp lines isolate, create distance, signify pessimism; the courtier, who is a professional optimist, directs a symphony of colors proclaiming God's glory, which he epitomizes and mitigates. Titian then applies the finishing touches; he scrapes and polishes, applies lacquers and varnishes. Sparing no effort to hide his labor, he manages finally to remove every trace of himself from the canvas. The stroller enters an unobstructed area, walks among flowers under a proper sun; the proprietor is dead; the stroller is so lonely that he forgets himself and disappears. The result is treason of the worst sort: the betrayal of Beauty.

For once the traitor has the excuse of believing in what he is doing. He is not a townsman but a transplanted peasant; when he arrives in Venice, he comes as a rustic child of the middle ages. The country youth has long nurtured a popular, reverent love for the nobility; he makes his way through the bourgeoisie without even seeing it and rejoins his true masters at the summit, all the more certain of pleasing them because they have his sincere respect. We frequently hear that he secretly considered himself their equal; this, I think, is completely false. What would have been the source of his light? He is a vassal;

raised to the peerage through the glory that only kings can dispense, he owes to them everything, even his pride; why would he choose to turn against them? He looks upon his haughty serenity, the hierarchy of power and the beauty of the world as complementary reflexes; in the best possible faith he puts the bourgeois techniques of the Renaissance to the service of feudalism—he has stolen their tool.

Yet he is admired by both the bourgeoisie and the patriciate. He provides the Venetian technocrats with an alibi by speaking of happiness, glory and preordained harmony at the time they are making laudable efforts to obscure their decline. Every merchant, whether a nobleman or a commoner, is captivated by the sanctimonious canvases that reflect the tranquility of kings. If all is for the best, if evil is but a beautiful illusion, if each keeps forever his hereditary place in the divine and social hierarchy, then this means that nothing has happened for the last hundred years: the Turks have not taken Constantinople, Columbus has not discovered America, the Portuguese have not even dreamed of dumping spices or the continental powers of forming a coalition against the Republic of Venice. People had thought that the Barbary pirates were threatening the seas, that the African source of precious metals had been exhausted, that the scarcity of money had slowed down transactions during the first half of the century and that then suddenly an outpouring of Peruvian gold from the Spanish waterworks had reversed the tide, raised prices, flooded the market—but that was only a dream. Venice still reigns over the Mediterranean; she is at the pinnacle of her power, wealth and grandeur. In other words, they want Beauty, these uneasy souls, because it is reassuring. I understand them, for I have boarded a plane two hundred times without ever becoming reconciled to it. I am too earthbound to consider flying normal; occasionally fear surges up—especially when my companions are as ugly as I; but if there is on board a beautiful woman or a handsome boy or a charming couple in love, my fear vanishes; ugliness is a prophecy—it trails a certain element of extremism which seeks to carry negation to the point of horror. Beauty seems indestructible; its sacred image protects us; so long as we have it in our presence, no catastrophe will occur. The same is true of Venice; she is beginning to fear that she will sink into the mire of her lagoons; imagining that she will find salvation through Beauty, the supreme levity, she makes a pretense of transforming her palaces and canvases into buoys and floats. Those responsible for Titian's success are the very ones who desert the sea, who try to escape their disenchantment through orgies, who prefer the security of ground rent to profit from commerce.

Tintoretto is born in a troubled town; he breathes Venetian uneasiness, is consumed by Venetian uneasiness, can paint nothing but Venetian uneasiness. If they were in his place, his severest critics would behave no differently. But they are not; they can not escape uneasiness but wish not to have it brought to their attention; they condemn paintings that *represent* it. Fate has decreed that Jacopo unwittingly expose an age which refuses to recognize itself. Now we understand the meaning of his destiny and the secret of Venetian malice. Tintoretto displeases everyone: patricians because he reveals to them the puritanism and fanciful agitation of the bourgeoisie; artisans because he destroys the corporate order and reveals, under their apparent professional solidarity, the rumblings of hate and rivalry; patriots because the frenzied state of painting and the absence of God discloses to them, under his brush, an absurd and unpredictable world in which anything can occur, *even* the death of Venice. It would seem that this painter who has assimilated bourgeois culture might at least find favor with the class that he has adopted. Not so. The bourgeoisie will accept him only with reservations; it always finds him fascinating, but often it finds him terrifying. The reason is that it has not recognized itself for what it is. Signor de Zigninoni must have dreamed of betrayal; he was searching covertly for a means of acceding to the patriciate, of escaping from the bourgeois reality that he was helping in spite of himself to create. What he finds most distasteful in Robusti's paintings is their radicalism and their "demystifying" virtues. In short, it is necessary at any price to refute Tintoretto's testimony, to make it seem that he has failed in his venture, to deny the originality of his research, *to get rid of him.*

Consider the charges brought against him: *first,* that he works too fast and leaves his imprint everywhere. People want smooth, finished work, especially *the impersonal element;* if the painter portrays himself, he is subjecting himself to interrogation and thereby putting the public on trial. Venice imposes on her artists the maxim of the puritans: "No personal remarks." She is careful to equate Jacopo's lyricism with the callous haste of a jaded contractor. Then comes Ridolfi's charge that Tintoretto wrote on the walls of his studio: "The color of Titian combined with the drawing of Michelangelo." The charge is baseless; the statement first appears in 1548 in the writings of a Venetian art critic and does not refer to Robusti. The latter, in fact, could have known the works of Michelangelo only through reproductions by Daniele de Volterra—consequently, *not before* 1557. And could anyone take those words at face value? Is it conceivable that he would try *seriously* to follow the absurd formula? The legend is but a dream of his age; confronted by the Spanish menace, the Northern states and the Central states dream of forming an alliance—too late.

But the awakening of a national consciousness, though brief, can not fail to have a transient influence on the Fine Arts. "Michelangelo and Titian" means Florence and Venice. How nice for painting to be unified!

Nothing serious, obviously. The dream is inoffensive so long as it is everyone's dream. But those who pretend to see in it the obsession of Robusti *alone* must have wanted to destroy the artist by lodging in the heart of his art an explosive nightmare. Color is Jake laughing; drawing, Jake crying. In the first instances unity, in the second the risk of disorder. On the one hand the harmony of the spheres, on the other abandonment. The two Titans of the century throw themselves on each other, embrace each other, try to stifle each other—Jacopo is the theater of operations. And sometimes Titian wins by a hair and sometimes Michelangelo barely manages to claim the match. In either case, the loser is strong enough to spoil the winner's triumph, and the result of the Pyrrhic victory is a botched picture. Botched through excess. Tintoretto seems to his contemporaries like an insane Titian, devoured by Buonarroti's somber passion, shaken by St. Vitus's dance—possessed, a freakish split-personality. In one sense Jacopo exists only as a battlefield; in another sense he is a monster, a fraud. Vasari's fable becomes crystal clear: Adam Robusti wanted to taste the fruits of the tree of knowledge and Archangel Tiziano, pointing his finger and flapping his wings, chased him out of Paradise. To have bad luck or to bring bad luck is still one and the same in Italy. If you have recently had financial troubles or an automobile accident, if you have broken your leg or lost your wife, do not expect to be invited to dinner; a hostess would not wittingly expose her other guests to premature baldness, a head cold or, in extreme cases, to a broken neck caused by a fall on her stairway. I knew a Milanese who had the evil eye;

this was discovered last year; he no longer has a single friend, and he dines alone, at home. Such is Jacopo: a caster of spells because a spell was cast on him. Or perhaps on his mother when she was carrying him. The spell actually has its source in Venice: uneasy, accursed, she has produced a troubled soul and placed a curse on his uneasiness. The unfortunate victim loves a despairing and uncompromising town to the point of despair, and his love horrifies the beloved. When Tintoretto passes by, people step aside: he smells of death. Exactly. But what other odor is given off by patrician festivities and bourgeois charity and the docility of the people? Pink houses with flooded cellars and walls crisscrossed by rats? What odor is given off by stagnant canals with their urinous cresses and by grey mussels fastened with squalid cement to the underside of quays? In the depths of a river a bubble is clinging to the mud; broken loose by the eddies formed by gondolas, it rises through murky water, breaks through the surface, spins around, glistens and bursts; everything crumbles away when the blister bursts—bourgeois nostalgia, the grandeur of the Republic, God and Italian painting.

Tintoretto was the chief mourner for Venice and a way of life, but when he died there was no one to act as his chief mourner; then silence fell, and hypocritically pious hands hung crepe over his canvases. When we remove this black veil, we find a portrait, started anew a hundred times. The portrait of Jacopo? The portrait of the Queen of the Seas? As you will: the city and her painter have one and the same face.

2. THE QUEST FOR
THE ABSOLUTE

A glance at Giacometti's antediluvian face reveals his arrogance and his desire to place himself at the beginning of time. He ridicules Culture and has no faith in Progress—not in the Fine Arts, at least. He considers himself no further "advanced" than his adopted contemporaries, the men of Eyzies and Altamira.* Then, when nature and men were in their prime, there was neither ugliness nor beauty, neither taste nor dilettantes nor criticism. The man who first had the notion of carving a man from a block of stone had to start from zero.

His model: man. Neither a dictator nor a general nor an athlete, primitive man still lacked the dignity and charm that would seduce future sculptors. He was nothing more than a long, indistinct silhouette walking across the horizon. But his movements were perceptibly different from the movements of things; they emanated from him like first beginnings and impregnated the air with signs of an ethereal future. They must be understood in terms of their ends—to pick a berry

---

* That the paleolithic hunters of southern France and Northern Spain had a keenly developed aesthetic sense is attested by many artifacts preserved in limestone caves near Eyzies-de-Tayac and Altamira.

or push aside a briar—not their origins. They could never be isolated or localized.

I can separate a bent branch from a tree but never an upraised arm or a clinched fist from a man. The *man* raises his arm, the *man* clinches his fist, the man is the indissoluble unit and the absolute source of his movements. Furthermore, he is an enchanter of signs; they cling to his hair, shine in his eyes, dance between his lips, perch on his fingertips. He speaks with his whole body; when he runs he speaks, when he talks he speaks, and when he falls asleep his sleep is speech.

His substance: a rock, a lump of space. From mere space Giacometti therefore had to fashion a man, to inscribe movement in total immobility, unity in infinite multiplicity, the absolute in pure relativity, the future in the eternal present, the loquacity of signs in the tenacious silence of things. The gap between substance and model seems unbridgeable, yet exists only because Giacometti has gauged its dimensions. I am not sure whether he is a man bent on imposing a human seal on space or a rock dreaming of human qualities. Or perhaps he is both and mediates between the two.

The sculptor's passion is to transform himself completely into extensity so that from its fullness can spill the statue of a man. He is haunted by thoughts of stone. Once he was terrified by the void; for months he walked to and fro, accompanied by an abyss—his emptiness in the process of achieving awareness of its desolate sterility. On another occasion it seemed to him that objects, spiritless and dead, were no longer touching the ground; he lived in a fluctuating universe, knowing in his flesh and even to the point of martyrdom that there is neither height nor depth nor length nor real contact between things; but at the same time he was aware that the sculptor's task is to carve from the infinite archipelago a face filled with the only being that can *touch* other beings.

I know no one else who is as sensitive as he to the magic of faces and gestures. He looks at them with passionate envy, as if they were from another kingdom. At his wit's end he has at times tried to mineralize his equals: to envision crowds advancing blindly toward him, rolling across boulevards like stones in an avalanche. Thus each of his obsessions was a task, an experience, a means of experiencing space.

"He's crazy," people say. "Sculptors have been carving away for three thousand years—and nicely, too—without such rigmaroles. Why doesn't he try to produce impeccable works according to tested techniques instead of pretending to ignore his predecessors?"

The truth is that for three thousand years sculptors have been carving only cadavers. Sometimes they are shown reclining on tombs; sometimes they are seated on curule chairs or perched on horses. But a dead man on a dead horse does not make even half a living creature. He deceives the rigid, wide-eyed people in the Museum. His arms pretend to move but are held fast by iron shanks at each end; his rigid outlines can hardly contain infinite dispersion; mystified by a crude resemblance, the spectator allows his imagination to imbue the eternal sinking of matter with movement, heat and light.

It is therefore necessary to start again from zero. After three thousand years the task of Giacometti and of contemporary sculptors is not to glut galleries with new works but to prove that sculpture is possible by carving. To prove that sculpture is possible just as by walking Diogenes proved to Parmenides and Zeno the possibility of movement. It is necessary to go the limit and see what can be done. If the undertaking should end in failure, it would be impossible to decide under even the most favorable circumstances whether this meant the failure of the sculptor or of sculpture; others would come along, and they would have to begin anew. Giacometti himself is forever beginning anew. But involved here is more than an infinite progression; there is a fixed boundary to be reached, a unique problem to be resolved: how to make a man out of stone without petrifying him. All or nothing: if the problem is solved, the number of statues is of little consequence.

"If I only knew how to make one," says Giacometti, "I could make them by the thousands. . . ." Until he succeeds, there will be no statues at all but only rough hewings that interest Giacometti only insofar as they bring him closer to his goal. He shatters everything and begins anew. From time to time his friends manage to save from destruction a head, a young woman, an adolescent. He raises no objection and again takes up his task. In fifteen years he has had but one exposition.

He consented to the exposition because he had to make a living, but even then he had misgivings and wrote by way of excusing himself: "It is mainly because I was goaded by the terror of poverty that these sculptures exist in this state (bronzed and photographed), but I am not quite sure of them; still, they were almost what I wanted. Almost."

What bothers him is that these impressive works, always mediating between nothingness and being, always in the process of modification, perfection, destruction and renewal, have begun to exist independently and in earnest, and have made a start, far from him, toward a social career. He prefers simply to forget about them. The remarkable thing about him is his intransigence in his quest for the absolute.

This active, determined worker is displeased by the resistance of stone, which slows down his movements. He has chosen a weightless substance which is also the most ductile, perishable and spiritual of all substances—plaster. He hardly feels it at his fingertips; it is the impalpable reflex of his movements.

One first notices in his studio strange scare-crows made of white daubs that coagulate around long reddish strings. His experiences, his ideas, his desires and his dreams project themselves for a moment on his plaster men, give them a form and pass on, and their form passes on with them. Each of these nebulous creatures undergoing perpetual metamorphosis seems like Giacometti's very life transcribed in another language.

Maillol's statues insolently fling in our eyes their heavy eternity. But the eternity of stone is synonymous with inertia; it is the present forever solidified. Giacometti never speaks of eternity, never thinks of eternity. I was pleased by what he had said to me one day concerning some statues that he had just destroyed: "I was happy with them, but they were made to last only a few hours."

A few hours—like the dawn, like sadness, like ephemera. And his creations, because they were destined to perish on the very night of their birth, are the only ones among all the sculptures that I know to retain the ineffable charm of transiency. Never was substance less eternal, more fragile, more nearly human. Giacometti's substance—this strange flour that slowly settles over his studio and buries it, that seeps under his nails and into the deep wrinkles on his face—is the dust of space.

But space, even if naked, is still superfluity. Giacometti is terrified by the infinite. Not by Pascalian infinity, not by what is infinitely great. The infinity that runs through his fingers is of a more subtle and secretive type. In space, says Giacometti, there is a superfluity. This *superfluity* is the pure and simple coexistence of juxtaposed elements. Most sculptors have allowed themselves to be deceived; they have confused the proliferation of space with generosity, they have put too much into their works, they have been captivated by the plump contour of a marble bosom, they have unfolded, stuffed and distended the human gesture.

Giacometti knows that there is nothing superfluous about a living person because everything is function. He knows that space is a cancer that destroys being, that devours everything. For him, to sculpture is to trim the fat from space, to compress it and wring from it all its exteriority. The attempt may well seem hopeless, and I believe that on two or three occasions Giacometti has reached the verge of despair. If sculpturing entails carving and patching in this incompressible medium, the sculpture is impossible. "And yet," he said, "if I begin my statue, like others, at the tip of the nose, it will not be too great an infinity of time before I reach the nostril." Then it was that he made his discovery.

Consider Ganymede on his pedestal. If you ask me how far away he is, I will tell you that I don't know what you are talking about. By "Ganymede" do you mean the youth carried away by Jupiter's eagle? If so, I will say that there is no *real* distance between us, that no such relation exists because he does not exist. Or are you referring to the block of marble that the sculptor fashioned in the image of the handsome lad? If so, we are dealing with something real, with an existing mineral, and can draw comparisons.

Painters have long understood all that since in pictures the unreality of the third dimension necessarily entails the unreality of the two other dimensions. It follows that the distance between the figures and my eyes is *imaginary*. If I advance, I move nearer to the canvas, not to them. Even if I put my nose on them, I would still see them twenty steps away since for me they exist once and for all at a distance of twenty steps. It follows also that painting is not subject to Zeno's line of reasoning; even if I bisected the space separating the Virgin's foot from St. Joseph's foot, and the resulting halves again and again to infinity, I would simply be dividing a certain length on the canvas, not flagstones supporting the Virgin and her husband.

Sculptors failed to recognize these elementary truths because they were working in a three-dimensional space on a real block of marble and, although the product of their art was an imaginary man, they thought that they were working with real dimensions. The confusion of real and unreal space had curious results. In the first place, instead of reproducing what they *saw*—that is, a model ten steps away—they reproduced in clay what *was*—that is, the model itself. Since they wanted their statue to give to the spectator standing ten steps away the impression that the model had given them, it seemed logical to make a figure that would be for him what the model had been for them; and that was possible only if the marble was *here* just as the model had been *out there.*

But what exactly is the meaning of being *here* and *out there?* Ten steps away from her, I form a certain image of a nude woman; if I approach and look at her at close range, I no longer recognize her; the craters, crevices, cracks, the rough, black herbs, the greasy streaks, the lunar orography in its entirety simply can not be the smooth, fresh skin I was admiring from a distance. Is that what the sculptor should imitate? There would be no end to his task, and besides, no matter how close he came to her face, he could always narrow the gap still further.

It follows that a statue truly resembles neither what the model *is* nor what the sculptor *sees.* It is constructed according to certain contradictory conventions, for the sculptor represents certain details not visible from so far away under the pretext that they exist and neglects certain others that do exist under the pretext that they are unseen. What does this mean other than that he takes the viewpoint of the spectator in order to reconstruct an acceptable figure? But if so, my relation to Ganymede varies with my position; if near, I will discover details which escaped me at a distance. And this brings us to the paradox: I have *real* relations with an illusion; or, if you prefer, my true distance from the block of marble has been confused with my imaginary distance from Ganymede.

The result of all this is that the properties of true space overlay and mask those of imaginary space. Specifically, the real divisibility of marble destroys the indivisibility of the person. Stone and Zeno are the victors. Thus the classical sculptor flirts with dogmatism because he thinks that he can eliminate his own look and imbue something other than man with human nature; but the truth is that he does not know what he is doing since he does not reproduce what he sees. In his search for truth he encounters convention. And since the net result is to shift to the visitor the responsibility for breathing life into his inert images, his quest for the absolute finally makes his work depend on the relativity of the angles from which it is viewed. As for the spectator, he takes the imaginary for the real and the real for the imaginary; he searches for indivisibility and everywhere finds divisibility.

By reversing classicism, Giacometti has restored to statues an imaginary, indivisible space. His unequivocal acceptance of relativity has revealed the absolute. The fact is that he was the first to sculpture man as he is seen—from a distance. He confers *absolute distance* on his images just as the painter confers absolute distance on the inhabitants of his canvas. He creates a figure "ten steps away" or "twenty steps away," and do what you will, it remains there. The result is a leap into the realm of the unreal since its relation to you no longer depends on your relation to the block of plaster—the liberation of Art.

A classical statue must be studied or approached if it is continuously to reveal new details; first, parts are singled out, then parts of parts, etc. with no end in sight. You can't approach one of Giacometti's sculptures. Don't expect a belly to expand as you draw near it; it will not change and you on moving away will have the strange impression of marking time. We have a vague feeling, we conjecture, we are on the point of seeing nipples on the breasts; one or two steps closer and we are still expectant; one more step and everything vanishes. All that remains are plaits of plaster. His statues can be viewed only from a respectful distance. Still, everything is there: whiteness, roundness, the elastic sagging of a beautiful ripe belly. Everything except matter. From twenty steps we only think we see the wearisome desert of adipose tissue; it is suggested, outlined, indicated, but not given.

Now we know what press Giacometti used to condense space. There could be but one—distance. He placed distance within our reach by showing us a distant woman who keeps her distance even when we touch her with our fingertips. The breasts that we envisioned and anticipated will never be exposed, for they are but expectancy; the bodies that he creates have only enough substance to hold forth a promise.

"That's impossible," someone might say. "The same object can't be viewed from close range and from afar." But we are not speaking of the same object; the block of plaster is near, the imaginary person far away.

"Even so, distance would still have to compress all three dimensions, and here length and depth are affected while height remains intact." True. But it is also true that each man in the eyes of other men possesses absolute dimensions. As a man walks away from me, he does not seem to grow smaller; his qualities seem rather to condense while his "figure" remains intact. As he draws near me, he does not grow larger but his qualities expand.

Admittedly, however, Giacometti's men and women are closer to us in height than in width—as if they are projecting their stature. But Giacometti purposely elongated them. We must understand that his creatures, which are wholly and immediately what they are, can neither be studied nor observed. As soon as I see them, I know them; they flood my field of vision as an idea floods my mind; the idea has the same immediate translucidity and is instantaneously wholly what it is. Thus Giacometti has found a unique solution to the problem of unity within multiplicity by simply suppressing multiplicity.

Plaster and bronze are divisible, but a woman in motion has the indivisibility of an idea or an emotion; she has no parts because she surrenders herself simultaneously. To give perceptible expression to pure presence, to surrender of self, to instantaneous emergence, Giacometti has recourse to elongation.

The original movement of creation—the timeless, indivisible movement so beautifully epitomized by long, gracile legs—shoots through his Greco-like bodies and lifts them toward the heavens. In them even more than in one of Praxiteles' athletes I recognize man, the first cause, the absolute source of movement. Giacometti succeeded in giving to his substance the only truly human unity—unity of action.

Such is the type of Copernican revolution that Giacometti has attempted to introduce into sculpture. Before him men thought that they were sculpturing *being*, and this absolute dissolved into an infinite number of appearances. He chose to sculpture *situated* appearance and discovered that this was the path to the absolute. He exposes to us men and women as *already seen* but not as already seen by himself alone. His figures are already seen just as a foreign language that we are trying to learn is already spoken. Each of them reveals to us man as he is seen, as he is for other men, as he emerges in interhuman surroundings—not, as I said earlier for the sake of simplification, ten or twenty steps away, but at a man's distance. Each of them offers proof that man *is* not at first in order to be *seen* afterwards but that he is the being whose essence is in his existence for others. When I perceive the statue of a woman, I find that my congealed look is drawn to it, producing in me a pleasing uneasiness. I feel constrained, yet know neither why nor by whom until I discover that I am constrained to see and constrained by myself.

Furthermore, Giacometti often takes pleasure in adding to our perplexity—for example by placing a distant head on a nearby body so that we no longer know where to begin or exactly how to behave. But even without such complications his ambiguous images are disconcerting, for they upset our most cherished visual habits. We have long been accustomed to smooth, mute creatures fashioned for the purpose of curing us of the sickness of having a body; these guardian spirits have watched over the games of our child-hood and bear witness in our gardens to the notion that the world is without risks, that nothing ever happens to anyone and, consequently, that the only thing that ever happened to them was death at birth.

Against this, something obviously has happened to Giacometti's bodies. Are they emerging from a concave mirror, from a fountain of youth or from a deportation camp? We seem at first glance to be confronted by the emaciated martyrs of Buchenwald. But almost immediately we realize our mistake. His thin, gracile creatures rise toward the heavens and we discover a host of Ascensions and Assumptions; they dance, they *are* dances, made of the same rarefied substance as the glorious bodies promised us. And while we are still contemplating the mystical upsurge, the emaciated bodies blossom and we see only terrestrial flowers.

The martyred creature was only a woman but she was *all* woman—glimpsed, furtively desired, retreating in the distance with the comic dignity of fragile, gangling girls walking lazily from bed to bathroom in their high-heeled shoes and with the tragic horror of scarred victims of a holocaust or famine; all woman—exposed, rejected, near, remote; all woman—with traces of hidden leanness showing through alluring plumpness and hideous leanness mollified by suave plumpness; all woman—in danger here on earth but no longer entirely on earth, living and relating to us the astounding adventure of flesh,*our* adventure. For she chanced to be born, like us.

Nevertheless, Giacometti is dissatisfied. He could win the match promptly simply by deciding that he has won. But he can't make up his mind and keeps putting off his decision from hour to hour, from day to day. Sometimes, during the course of a night's work, he is ready to acknowledge his victory; by morning everything has been shattered. Is he afraid of the boredom that lurks beyond his triumph, the boredom that beset Hegel after he had imprudently stapled together his system? Or perhaps matter seeks revenge. Perhaps the infinite divisibility that he eliminated from his work keeps cropping up between him and his goal. The end is in sight, but to reach it he must improve.

Much has been done but now he must do *a little* better. And then *just a little* better still. The new Achilles will never catch the tortoise; a sculptor must in some way be the chosen victim of space—if not in his work, then in his life. But between him and us, there must always be a difference of position. He knows what he wanted to do and we don't; but we know what he has done and he doesn't. His statues are still largely incorporated in his flesh; he is unable to see them. Almost as soon as they are produced he goes on to dream of women that are thinner, taller, lighter, and it is through his work that he envisions the ideal by virtue of which he judges it imperfect. He will never finish simply because a man always transcends what he does.

"When I finish," he says, "I'll write, I'll paint, I'll have fun." But he will die before finishing. Are we right or is he right? He is right because, as Da Vinci said, it is not good for an artist to be happy. But we are also right—and ours is the last word. Kafka as he lay dying asked to have his books burned and Dostoevski, during the very last moments of his life, dreamed of writing a sequel to *The Brothers Karamazov*. Both may have died dissatisfied, the former thinking that he would depart from the world without even making a mark on it and the latter that he had not produced anything good. And yet both were victors, regardless of what they might have thought.

Giacometti is also a victor, and he is well aware of this fact. It is futile for him to hoard his statues like a miser and to procrastinate, temporize and find a hundred excuses for borrowing more time. People will come into his studio, brush him aside, Carry away all his works, including the plaster that covers his floor. He knows this; his cowed manner betrays him. He knows that he has won in spite of himself, and that he belongs to us.

3. THE PAINTINGS OF GIACOMETTI*

From the back of the room where I was sitting at the Sphinx, I could see several nude women. The distance that separated us (the glossy wood floor seemed insuperable even though I wanted to walk across it) impressed me as much as did the women.†

The result: four inaccessible figurines balanced on the edge of a vertical background formed by the floor. Giacometti painted them as he saw them—*from a distance*. Still, the four women have an arresting presence. They seem to be poised on the floor, ready at any moment to drop down upon him like the lid on a box.

---

* Alberto Giacometti (1901-) belongs to an artistic Swiss family. Unchanged by success, he has worked since 1927 in a two-room studio in the industrial section of Paris. His paintings are for the most part studies of himself, his wife Annette and his brother Diego. His best known sculptures are probably *Three Men Walking* (1949), *Walking Quickly Under the Rain* (1949), and *Man Crossing a Square on a Sunny Morning* (1950). Known primarily as a surrealist in the early 1930's, he went through a long period of experimentation and emerged in the 1940's as one of the world's most controversial sculptors. Defining art as "an absurd activity," he has evolved elongated figures expressing nihilism and despair, terror and doom.

† Letter to Matisse (November, 1950).

I have often seen them, especially in the evening, in a little place on the Rue de l'Echaudé, very close and menacing.

Distance, far from being an accident, is in his eyes part and parcel of every object. These whores, twenty steps away—twenty impossible steps away—are forever outlined in the light of his hopeless desire. His studio is an archipelago, a conglomeration of irregular distances. The Mother Goddess against the wall retains all the nearness of an obsession. When I retreat, she advances; when I am far away, she is closest. The small statue at my feet is a man seen in the rear-view mirror of an automobile—in the act of disappearing; moving closer to the statue is to no avail, for the distance cannot be traversed. These solitudes repel the visitor with all the insuperable length of a room, a lawn, or a glade that none would dare to cross. They stand as proof of the paralysis that grips Giacometti at the sight of his equal.

It does not follow, however, that he is a misanthropist. His aloofness is mixed with fear, often with admiration, sometimes with respect. He is distant, of course, but man creates distance while distance has no meaning outside human space. Distance separates Hero from Leander and Marathon from Athens but not one pebble from another.

I first understood what distance is one evening in April, 1941. I had spent two months in a prison camp, which was like being in a can of sardines, and had experienced absolute proximity; the boundary of my living space was my skin; night and day I felt against my body the warmth of a shoulder or a bosom. This was not incommodious, for the others were *me*.

That first evening, a stranger in my home town, having not yet found my old friends, I opened the door of a café. Suddenly I was frightened—or almost; I could not understand how these squat, corpulent buildings could conceal such deserts. I was lost; the scattered patrons seemed to me more distant than the stars. Each of them could claim a vast seating area, a whole marble table while I, to touch them, would have had to cross over the "glossy floor" that separated us.

If they seemed inaccessible to me, these men who were scintillating comfortably in their bulbs of rarefied gas, it was because I no longer had the right to place my hand on their shoulders and thighs or to call one of them "knucklehead." I had re-entered middle-class society and would have to learn once again to live "at a respectable distance." My attack of agoraphobia had betrayed my vague feeling of regret for the collective life from which I had been forever severed.

The same applies to Giacometti. For him distance is not a voluntary isolation, nor even a withdrawal. It is something required by circumstances, a ceremony, a recognition of difficulties. It is the product—as he himself said*—of forces of attraction and forces of repulsion. He cannot walk a few steps across the glossy floor that separates him from the nude women because he is nailed to his chair by timidity or by poverty; and he feels at this point that the distance is insuperable because he wants to touch their lush flesh. He rejects promiscuity, the fruit of close proximity, because he wants friendship, love. He dares not take for fear of being taken.

His figurines are solitary, but when placed together, no matter how, they are united by their solitude and transformed into a small magical society:

> On observing the figures which, to clear away
> the table, had been set at random on the floor, I

---

* Letter to Matisse (1950).

> discovered that they formed two groups which
> seemed to correspond to what I was looking for.
> I mounted the two groups on bases without the
> slightest change. . . .

One of Giacometti's scenes is a crowd. He has sculptured men crossing a public square without seeing each other; they pass, hopelessly alone and yet *together*; they will be forever lost from each other, yet would never lose each other if they had not sought each other. He defined his universe better than I possibly could when he wrote, concerning one of his groups, that it reminded him of

> a part of a forest observed during the course of
> many years . . . a forest in which trees with bar-
> ren, slender trunks seemed like people who had
> stopped in their tracks and were speaking to each
> other.

What is this circular distance—which only words can bridge—if not negation in the form of a *vacuum?* Ironic, defiant, ceremonious, and tender, Giacometti sees space everywhere. "Not everywhere," you will say, "for some objects are in contact." But Giacometti is sure of nothing, not even that. Week after week he was captivated by the legs of a chair: they were not touching the floor. Between things, between men lie broken bridges; the vacuum infiltrates everything, each creature creates its own vacuum.

Giacometti became a sculptor because of his obsession with emptiness. About one statuette he wrote: "Me, rushing down a street in the rain." Sculptors rarely fashion their own busts. Those who do attempt "self-portraits" study themselves from without, in a looking glass. They are the true prophets of objectivity. But imagine a lyrical sculptor: what he tries to reproduce is his inner feeling, the boundless vacuum that surrounds him, leaving him defenseless and exposing him to the storm. Giacometti is a sculptor because he wears his vacuum as a snail its shell, because he wants to explain all its facets and dimensions. And sometimes he finds compatible the modicum of exile that he carries everywhere—and sometimes he finds it horrifying.

A friend once moved in with him. Pleased at first, Giacometti soon became upset: "I opened my eyes one morning and found his trousers and his jacket *in my space*." At other times, however, he grazes walls and skirts ramparts; the vacuum all around him portends a catastrophe, untoward events, avalanches. In any case he must bear witness to its presence.

Can he do this through sculpture? By kneading plaster, he creates a vacuum *from a plenum*. The figure when it leaves his fingers is "ten steps away," and no matter what we do, it remains there. The statue itself determines the distance from which it must be viewed, just as courtly manners determine the distance from which the king must be addressed. The situation engenders the surrounding no man's land. Each of his figures is Giacometti himself producing his little local vacuum. Yet all these slight absences that are as much a part of us as our names, as our shadows, are not enough to make a world. There is also the Void, the universal distance between all things. The street is empty, drinking in the sun; suddenly, in this empty space a human being appears.

Sculpture can create a vacuum *from a plenum*, but can it show the plenum arising from what was previously a vacuum? Giacometti has tried a hundred times to answer this question. His composition *La Cage* represents his "desire to abolish the

socle and have a *limited* space for creating a head and face."
That is the crux of his problem, for a vacuum will forever ante-
date the beings that inhabit it unless it is first surrounded by
walls. The "Cage" is "a room that I have seen. I have even seen
curtains behind the woman. . ." On another occasion he made
"a figurine in a box between two boxes which are houses." In
short, he builds a frame for his figures, with the result that they
remain at a certain distance away from us but live in the closed
space imposed on them by their individual distances, in the
prefabricated vacuum which they cannot manage to fill and
which they endure rather than create.

And what is this framed and populated vacuum if not a painting? Lyrical when he sculptures, Giacometti becomes objective
when he paints. He tries to capture the features of Annette or of
Diego just as they appear in an empty room or in his deserted
studio. I have tried elsewhere to show that he approaches sculpture as a painter since he treats a plaster figurine as if it were a
person in a painting. He confers on his statuettes a fixed, imaginary distance. Inversely, I can say that he approached painting as a sculptor since he would like to have us assume that the
imaginary space enclosed by a frame is a *true* void. He would
like to have us perceive through thick layers of space the woman
that he has just painted in a sitting position; he would like for
his canvas to be like still water and for us to see the figures *in* the
painting as Rimbaud saw a room in a lake—as a transparency.

Sculpturing as others paint, painting as others sculpture, is
he a painter? Is he a sculptor? Neither, both. Painter and sculptor
because his era does not allow him to be both sculptor and architect; sculptor in order to restore to each his circular solitude and
painter in order to replace men and things in the world—that is,
in the great universal void—he finds it convenient to model what

he had at first hoped to paint.* At times, however, he knows that only sculpture (or in other instances only painting) will allow him to "realize his impressions." In any case two activities are inseparable and complementary. They allow him to treat from every aspect the problem of his relations with others, whether distance has its origin in them, in him, or in the universe.

How can one paint a vacuum? Before Giacometti it seems that no one had made the attempt. For five hundred years painters had been filling their canvases to the bursting point, forcing into them the whole universe. Giacometti begins by expelling the world from his canvases. For example, he paints his brother Diego all alone, lost in a hangar, and that is sufficient.

A person must also be separated from everything around him. This is ordinarily achieved by emphasizing his contours. But a line is produced by the intersection of two surfaces, and an empty space cannot pass for a surface. Certainly not for a volume. A line is used to separate the container from the content; a vacuum, however, is not a container.

Is Diego "outlined" against the partition behind him? No, the "foreground-background" relation exists only when surfaces are relatively flat. Unless he leans back against it, the distant partition cannot "serve as a background" for Diego; in short, he is in no way connected with it. Or rather he is only because man and object are in the same painting and must therefore maintain appropriate relations (hues, values, proportions) for conferring on the canvas its unity. But these cor-

---

* For example, his *Nine Figures* (1950): "I had wanted very much to paint them last spring."

respondences are at the same time erased by the vacuum that interposes itself between them.

No, Diego is not outlined against the gray background of a wall. He is there, the wall is there, that is all. Nothing encloses him, nothing supports him, nothing contains him; he *appears* all alone within the vast frame of empty space.

With each of his paintings Giacometti takes us back to the moment of creation *ex nihilo*. Each painting restates the old metaphysical question: Why is there something rather than nothing? And yet there is something: this stubborn, unjustifiable, superfluous apparition. The painted person is hallucinatory because presented in the form of an interrogative apparition.

But how can the artist place a figure on his canvas without confining it? Will it not explode in empty space like a fish from the depths on the surface of the water? Not at all. A line represents arrested flight, a balance between the external and the internal; it fastens itself around the shape adopted by an object under the pressure of outside forces; it is a symbol of inertia, of passivity.

Giacometti does not think of finitude as an arbitrary limitation, however. For him the cohesion of an object, its determination are but one and the same effect of its inner power of affirmation. "Apparitions" affirm and confine themselves while defining themselves. Somewhat as the strange curves studied by mathematicians are both encompassing and encompassed, the object encompasses itself.

One day when he had undertaken to sketch me, Giacometti expressed surprise: "What density," he said, "what lines of force!" And I was even more surprised than he since I believe my features to be weak and ordinary. But the reason is that he saw each feature as a centripetal force. A face is forever changing, like a spiral. Turn around: you will never find a contour—only a plenum. The line is the beginning of negation, the passage from being to non-being. But Giacometti holds that reality is pure positivity, that there *is* being and then suddenly there no longer is any, but that there is no conceivable transition from being to nothingness.

Notice how the multiple lines that he draws are *inside* the form depicted. See how they represent intimate relations between being and itself; the fold in a garment, the wrinkle in a face, the protruding of a muscle, the direction of a movement—all these lines are centripetal. They tend to confine by forcing the eye to follow them and leading it always to the center of the figure. The face seems to be contracting under the influence of an astringent substance, giving the impression that in five minutes it will be the size of your fist, like a shrunken head. Still, demarcation of the body is missing. At times the heavy mass of flesh is demarcated vaguely, slyly by a blurred brown nimbus somewhere under the tangly lines of force—and sometimes it is literally unbounded, the contour of an arm or a hip being lost in a dazzling play of light.

We are shown without warning an abrupt dematerialization. For example, a man is shown crossing his legs; as long as I looked only at his head and bust, I was convinced that he had feet. I even thought that I could see them. If I look at them, however, they disintegrate, disappear in a luminous haze, and I no longer know where the void begins and where the body ends. And do not think that this is the same as one of Masson's attempts to disintegrate objects and give them a semblance of ubiquity by scattering them over the whole canvas. If Giacometti fails to demarcate a shoe, the reason is not that he believes it to be unbounded but that he counts on us to add its bounds. They are actually there, these shoes, heavy and dense. To see them, we need only refrain from viewing them in their entirety.

To understand this procedure we need only examine the sketches that Giacometti sometimes makes for his sculptures. Four women on a socle—fine. But let us examine the drawing. First we see the head and neck sketched in bold strokes, then nothing, then an open curve encircling a fixed point—the belly and navel; we also see the stump of a thigh, then nothing, and then two vertical lines and, further down, two others. That is the whole thing. A whole woman. What did we do? We used our knowledge to re-establish continuity, our eyes to join together these *disjecta membra*. We *saw* shoulders and arms on a white paper; we saw them because we had *recognized* a head and torso.

The members were indeed there, though not represented by lines. In the same way we sometimes apprehend lucid, complete ideas that are not represented by words. The body is a current flowing between its two extremities. We are face to face with the absolute reality, the invisible tension of blank paper. But does not the blankness of the paper also represent empty space? Certainly, for Giacometti rejects both the inertia of matter and the inertia of absolute nothingness. A vacuum is a distended plenum, a plenum and oriented vacuum. Reality fulgurates.

Have you noticed the superabundance of light strokes that striate his torsos and faces? Diego is not solidly stitched but merely basted, in the language of dressmakers. Or could it be that Giacometti wishes "to write luminously on a dark background"? Almost. The emphasis is no longer on separating a plenum from a vacuum but on painting plenitude itself. And since it is at once unity and diversity, how can it be differentiated unless divided? Dark strokes are dangerous, for they risk effacing being, marring it with fissures. If used to outline an eye or encircle a mouth they may create the impression that there are fistules of empty space at the heart of reality. The white striae are there to serve as unseen guides. They guide the eye, determine its movements, dissolve beneath its gaze. But the real danger lies elsewhere.

We are aware of the success of Arcimboldo—his jumbled vegetables and cluttered fish. Why do we find his artifice so appealing? Is it perhaps because the procedure has long been familiar to us? In their own way, have all painters been Arcimboldos? Have they not fashioned, day after day, face after face, each with a pair of eyes, a nose, two ears and thirty-two teeth? Wherein lies the difference? He takes a round cut of red meat, makes two holes in it, sets in each of them a white marble, carves out a nasal appendage, inserts it like a false nose under the ocular spheres, bores a third hole and provides it with white pebbles. Is he not substituting for the indissoluble unity of a face an assortment of heterogeneous objects? Emptiness insinuates itself everywhere: between the eyes and eyelids, between the lips, into the nostrils. A head in its turn becomes an archipelago.

You say that this strange assemblage conforms to reality, that the oculist can remove the eye from its orbit or the dentist extract the teeth? Perhaps. But what is the painter to paint? Whatever is? Whatever we see? And what do we see?

Take the chestnut-tree under my window. Some have depicted it as a huge ball, a trembling unity; others have painted its leaves individually, showing their veins. Do I see a leafy mass or a multitude of leaves? I must say that I see both, but neither in its entirety, with the result that I am constantly shifting from one to the other. Consider the leaves: I fail to see them in their entirety, for just as I am about to apprehend them they vanish. Or the leafy mass: just as I am about to apprehend it, it disintegrates. In short I see a swarming cohesion, a writhing dispersion. Let the painter paint that.

And yet Giacometti wants to paint what he sees just as he sees it. He wants the figures at the heart of their original vacuum on his motionless canvas forever to fluctuate between continuity and the discontinuity. He wants the head to be at once isolated because sovereign and reclaimed by the body to serve as a mere periscope of the belly in the sense that Europe is said to be a peninsula of Asia. The eyes, the nose, the mouth—these he wants to make into the leaves of a leafy mass, isolated from each other and blended all together. He succeeds, and this is his supreme triumph.

How does he succeed? By refusing to be more precise than perception. He is not *vague;* he manages rather to suggest through the lack of precision of perception the absolute precision of being. In themselves or for others with a better view, for angles, his faces conform rigidly to the principle of individuation. A glance reveals that they are precise down to the most minute detail; furthermore, we immediately recognize Diego or Annette. That in itself would be sufficient, if required, to cleanse Giacometti of any taint of subjectivism.

At the same time, however, we cannot look at the canvas without uneasiness. We have an irrepressible urge to call for a flashlight or at least a candle. Is it a haze, the fading light of day, or our tired eyes? Is Diego lowering or raising his eyelids? Is he dozing? Is he dreaming? Is he spying? It happens of course that the same questions are asked at popular exhibitions, in front of portraits so bland that any answer is equally appropriate and none mandatory.

The awkward indetermination of popular painters has

nothing in common with the calculated indetermination of Giacometti, which might more appropriately be termed over-determination. I turn back toward Diego and see him alternately asleep and awake, looking at the sky, gazing at me. Everything is true, everything is obvious; but if I bend my head slightly, altering my viewpoint, this truth vanishes and another replaces it. If after a long struggle I wish to adopt one opinion, my only recourse is to leave as quickly as possible. Even then my opinion will remain fragile and probable.

When I discover a face in the fire, for example, or in an ink-blot, or in the design of a curtain, the shape that has abruptly appeared becomes rigid and forces itself upon me. Even though I can see it in no other way than this, I know that others will see it differently. But the face in the fire has no truth while in Giacometti's paintings we are provoked and at the same time bewitched by the fact that *there is* a truth and that we are certain of it. It is there, right under my nose, whether I look for it or not. But my vision blurs, my eyes tire, I give up. Then I begin to understand that Giacometti overpowers us because he has reversed the facts in stating the problem.

A painting by Ingres is also instructive. If I look at the tip of the odalisk's nose, the rest of the face is light and soft, like pinkish butter interrupted by the delicate red of the lips; and if I shift my attention to the lips, they emerge from the shadows, moist and slightly parted, and the nose disappears, devoured by the absence of differentiation in the background. I am not bothered by its disappearance, however, for I am secure in the knowledge that I can always recreate it at will.

The reverse holds true in the case of Giacometti. To make a detail seem clear and reassuring all I need do is refrain from centering my attention on it. My confidence is reinforced by what I see through the corner of my eye. The more I look at

Diego's eyes the less they communicate to me; but I notice slightly sunken cheeks, a peculiar smile at the corners of the mouth. If my obsession with truth draws my attention down to his mouth, everything immediately escapes me. What is his mouth like? Hard? Bitter? Ironical? Wide-open? Sealed? Against this, *I know* that his eyes, which are almost beyond my range of vision, are half-closed. And nothing prevents me from continuing to turn, obsessed by the phantom face that is constantly being formed, deformed and reformed behind me. The remarkable part is its credibility. Hallucinations also make their appearance on the periphery only to disappear when viewed directly. But on the other hand, of course. . . .

These extraordinary figures, so perfectly immaterial that they often become transparent and so totally, so fully real that they can be as positive and unforgettable as a physical blow, are they appearing or disappearing? Both. They seem so diaphanous at times that we do not even dream of questioning their features; we have to pinch ourselves to learn whether they really exist. If we insist on examining them, the whole canvas becomes alive; a somber sea rolls over them, leaving only an oil-splotched surface; and then the waves roll back and we see them glistening under the water, white and naked. But their reappearance is marked by a violent affirmation. They are like muffled shouts rising to the top of a mountain and informing the hearer that somewhere someone is grieving or calling for help.

The alternation of appearance and disappearance, of flight and provocation, lends to Giacometti's figures a certain air of coquetry. They remind me of Galatea, who fled from her lover under the willows and desired at the same time that he should see her. Coquettish, yes, and graceful because they are pure action, and sinister because of the emptiness that surrounds them, these creatures of nothingness achieve a plenum of existence by eluding and mystifying us.

Every evening an illusionist has three hundred accomplices: his audience and their second natures. He attaches to his shoulder a wooden arm in a bright red sleeve. His viewers expect him to have two arms in identical sleeves; they see two arms, two sleeves, and are satisfied. Meantime a real arm, clothed in black and invisible, produces a rabbit, a card, an explosive cigarette.

Giacometti's art is similar to that of the illusionist. We are his dupes and his accomplices. Without our avidity, our gullibility, the traditional deceitfulness of the senses and contradictions in perception, he could never make his portraits live. He is inspired not only by what he sees but also, and especially, by what he thinks we will see. His intent is not to offer us an exact image but to produce likenesses which, though they make no pretense at being anything other than what they are, arouse in us feelings and attitudes ordinarily elicited by the presence of real men.

At the Grévin Museum one may feel irritated or frightened by the presence of a wax guardian. Nothing would be easier than to construct elaborate farces by capitalizing on that fact. But Giacometti is not particularly fond of farces. With one exception. A single exception to which he has consecrated his life. He has long understood that artists work in the realm of the imaginary, creating illusions, and he knows that "faked monsters" will never produce in spectators anything other than factitious fears.*

---

* Sartre's first philosophical work was a study of the imagination, published in France in 1936.

In spite of his knowledge, however, he has not lost hope. One day he will show us a portrait of Diego just like all others in appearance. We shall be forewarned and know that it is but a phantom, a vain illusion, a prisoner in its frame. And yet on that day, before the mute canvas we shall feel a shock, a very small shock. The very same shock that we feel on returning late and seeing a stranger walking toward us in the dark.

Then Giacometti will know that through his paintings he has brought to birth a real emotion and that his likenesses, without ever ceasing to be illusory, were invested for a few instants with *true* powers. I hope that he will soon achieve this memorable farce. If he does not succeed, no one can. In any case, no one can surpass him.

4. THE MOBILES OF CALDER*

The sculptor is supposed to imbue something immobile with movement, but it would be wrong to compare Calder's art with the sculptor's. Calder captures movement rather than suggests it; he has no intention of entombing it forever in bronze or gold, those glorious, asinine materials that are by nature immobile. With vile, inconsistent substances, with tiny slivers of bone or tin or zinc, he fashions strange arrangements of stems and branches, of rings and feathers and petals. They are resonators or traps; they dangle at the end of a fine wire like a spider at the end of its silk thread or settle on a pedestal, wan, exhausted, feigning sleep; a passing tremor strikes them, animates them, is canalized by them and given a fugitive form—a *Mobile* is born.

A Mobile: a small local festival, an object defined by its movement and nonexistent apart from it, a flower that withers as soon as it stops moving, a free play of movement, like coruscating light. Sometimes Calder amuses himself by imitating a new form. For example, he once presented me with a bird of paradise with iron wings; a wisp of air brushing it while escap-

---

* Alexander Calder achieved recognition as a sculptor some twenty years ago when the Museum of Modern Art exhibited his works. His mobiles are today found in such diverse places as New York's Chase Manhattan Bank, a hotel in Cincinnati, an airport in Pittsburgh, and UNESCO headquarters in Paris. He maintains two studio-homes, one near Saché, France, and the other near Roxbury, Connecticut.

ing through the window is enough to rouse the bird; it clicks, stands erect, spins, nods its crested head, rolls and pitches and then, as if in sudden obedience to an unseen signal, executes a slow turn with its wings spread. But most of the time it imitates nothing, and I know no other art less deceptive than his.

Sculpture suggests movement, painting depth or light. Calder suggests nothing; he captures and embellishes true, living movements. His mobiles signify nothing, refer to nothing other than themselves; they simply are, they are absolutes.

In his mobiles chance probably plays a greater part than in any other creation of man. The forces at work are too numerous and too complicated for any human mind, even that of their creator, to foresee all possible combinations. For each of them Calder establishes a general scheme of movement, then abandons it; the time, the sun, heat and wind will determine each particular dance. Thus the object is always midway between the servility of statues and the independence of natural events. Each of his evolutions is an inspiration of the moment; it reveals his general theme but permits a thousand personal variations. It is a little hot-jazz tune, unique and ephemeral, like the sky, like the morning; if you miss it, you will have lost it forever.*

Valéry said that the sea is a perpetual renewal. One of Calder's objects is like the sea—and equally spellbinding: ever changing, always new. A passing glance is not enough; one must live with it and be bewitched by it. Then the imagination can revel in pure, ever-changing forms—forms that are at once free and fixed.

The movements of the object are intended only to please

---

* In Sartre's earliest novel, *Nausea* (first published in 1938), jazz enables the central character to escape momentarily from the pervasive, overpowering feeling of nausea that engulfs him.

us, to titillate our eyes, but they have a profound, metaphysical meaning. The reason is that the mobiles have to have some source of mobility. Previously Calder used an electric motor; he now abandons his mobiles in the midst of nature; in a garden or near an open window, they vibrate in the wind like aeolian harps. Fed on air, they respire and draw their life from the tenuous life of the atmosphere. Thus their mobility is of a very peculiar kind.

Although they are human creations, they never have the precision and efficiency of movement of Vaucanson's automatons.* But the charm of the automaton resides in the fact that it agitates a fan or plays a guitar like a man, yet moves its hand with the blind, persistent rigor of purely mechanical translations. Against this, Calder's mobiles move and hesitate, as if correcting a mistake by starting anew.

I have seen in his studio a beater and a gong suspended high overhead; the slightest gust caused the beater to pursue the gong as it turned round; it would take aim, lash out at the gong, miss it by a hair, like an awkward hand, and then when least expected, strike and hit it squarely in the center, producing a frightening noise. But the movements are too artistically contrived to be compared with those of a ball rolling on an uneven plane and changing its course solely on the basis of irregularities encountered. They have a life of their own.

One day when I was talking with Calder in his studio, a model which until then had remained at rest was seized, right in my presence, by a violent agitation. I retreated until I thought I was beyond its reach. Suddenly, just when the agitation had ceased and the model seemed lifeless, its long, majes-

---

* * Jacques de Vaucanson (1709-1782) devised mechanisms that brought him considerable fame. Among his most celebrated automatons were his *Flute Player* and *Duck*.

tic tail, which had not moved previously, indolently roused, as if regretfully, rotated in the air and grazed my nose.

Their hesitations, revivals, gropings, fumblings, abrupt decisions, and especially their marvelous swan-like nobility make of Calder's mobiles strange creatures, halfway between matter and life. Sometimes their movements seem to have a purpose and sometimes they seem to have lost their purpose along the way and to have lapsed into imbecile fluctuations. My bird flies, wavers, swims like a swan, like a frigate; he is a bird, a single bird and then, suddenly, he falls apart and all that remains are slivers of metal traversed by vain little tremors.

Calder's mobiles, which are neither completely living nor completely mechanical and which constantly change but always return to their original position, are like aquatic plants bent low by a stream, the petals of the sensitive plant, the legs of a headless frog, or gossamer caught in an updraft. In short, although Calder has no desire to imitate anything—his one aim is to create chords and cadences of unknown movements—his mobiles are at once lyrical inventions, technical, almost mathematical combinations and the perceptible symbol of Nature: great elusive Nature, squandering pollen and abruptly causing a thousand butterflies to take wing and never revealing whether she is the blind concatenation of causes and effects or the gradual unfolding, forever retarded, disconcerted and thwarted, of an Idea.

BIBLIOGRAPHY

I. WORKS BY SARTRE

A. Philosophy

1936. *L'Imagination* (Presses Universitaires). *Imagination* (University of Michigan, 1962).

1937. "La transcendance de l'Ego," *Recherches Philosophiques* VI (1936-1937). *Transcendence of the Ego* (Noonday, 1957).

1939. *Esquisse d'une théorie des émotions* (Hermann). *The Emotions, Outline of a Theory* (Philosophical Library, 1948).

1940. *L'Imaginaire, psychologie phénoménologique de l'imagination* (Gallimard). *Psychology of Imagination* (Philosophical Library, 1948).

1943. *L'Etre et le Néant* (Gallimard). *Being and Nothingness* (Philosophical Library, 1956).

1960. *Critique de la raison dialectique*, I (Gallimard).

B. Fiction

1938. *La Nausée* (Gallimard). *Nausea* (New Directions, 1949).

1939. *Le Mur* (Gallimard). *The Wall and Other Stories* (New Directions, 1948).

1945-49. *Les Chemins de la liberté* (*Roads to Freedom*). I—*L'Age de raison;* II—*Le Sursis;* III—*La Mort dans l'âme* (Gallimard). Published by Knopf: *Age of Reason* (1947); *The Reprieve* (1947); *Troubled Sleep* (1951).

C. Drama

1943. *Les Mouches* (Gallimard). In *No Exit and The Flies* (Knopf, 1947).

1944. *Huis-clos* (Gallimard). In *No Exit and The Flies* (Knopf, 1947).

1946. *Morts sans sépulture* (Gallimard). *The Victors*, in *Three Plays* (Knopf, 1949).

1947. *Les Jeux sont faits* (Nagel). *The Chips Are Down* (Lear, 1948).

1948. *Les Mains sales* (Gallimard). *Dirty Hands*, in *Three Plays* (Knopf, 1949).

1949. *L'Engrenage* (Nagel). *In the Mesh* (Dakers, 1954).

1951. *Le Diable et le Bon Dieu* (Gallimard). In *The Devil and the Good Lord and Two Other Plays* (Knopf, 1960). Published in England as *Lucifer and the Lord* (Hamilton, 1952).

1954. *Kean* (Gallimard). *Kean*, in *The Devil and the Good Lord and Two Other Plays* (Knopf, 1960).

1955. *Nekrassov* (Gallimard).

1960. *Les Séquestrés d'Altona* (Gallimard).

D. Essays and Autobiographical Works

1946. *Descartes* (Trait). Introduction and selected texts.

1947. *L'Existentialisme est un humanisme* (Nagel). *Existentialism* (Philosophical Library, 1947).

1947. *Situations* I (Gallimard). Selections in *Literary and Philosophical Essays* (Philosophical Library, 1957).

1947. *Baudelaire* (Gallimard). *Baudelaire* (Horizon, 1949).

1947. *Réflexions sur la question juive*, ed. Paul Morihien (Gallimard). *Anti-Semite and Jew* (Schocken, 1948).

1948. *Situations* II (Gallimard). Contains articles published in *Qu'est-ce que la littérature?*

1948. *Qu'est-ce que la littérature?* (Gallimard). *What Is Literature?* (Philosophical Library, 1947).

1948. *Visages* (Seghers).

1949. *Situations* III (Gallimard). Selections in *Literary and Philosophical Essays* (Philosophical Library, 1957).

1949. *Entretiens sur la politique* [in collaboration with David Rousset and Gerard Rosenthal] (Gallimard).

1952. *Saint-Genêt, comédien et* martyr (Gallimard). *Saint Genet, Actor and Martyr* (Braziller, 1963).

1964. *Les Mots* (Gallimard). *The Words* (Braziller, 1964).

II. SIGNIFICANT ARTICLES BY SARTRE

Most of the articles published by Sartre in *N.R.F.* (1938-1949), in *Cahiers du Sud* (1943-1944), in *Europe* (1939), in *Poésie 44* (1944), in *Figaro* (1945), and in *Les Temps Modernes* beginning in 1946, have been republished in three volumes, *Situations* I, II, and III. Below are listed only those that have not been republished.

"L'Ange du morbide," *Revue sans titre* (1923).

"Légende de la vérité," *Bifur* (1931).

"La Structure intentionnelle de l'image," *Revue de Métaphysique et de Morale* (September, 1938).

"Discussion sur le péché," *Dieu Vivant* IV.

"Introduction aux Ecrits intimes de Baudelaire," *Confluences* (January-February, 1945).

"Présence noire," *Présence Africaine* (Paris-Dakar, November-December, 1947).

"Les communistes et la paix," *Les Temps Modernes:* I (July, 1952); II (October-November, 1952); III (August 1954).

"Réponse à Albert Camus," *Les Temps Modernes* (August, 1952).

"Réponse à Claude Lefort [on Marxism]," *Les Temps Modernes* (April, 1953).

"Le colonialisme est un systérne," *Les Temps Modernes* (March-April, 1956).

"Sur les évenéments de Hongrie," *L'Expres* (9 November 1956).

"Le fantôme de Staline," *Les Temps Modernes* (January 1957).

"Vous êtes formidables," *Les Temps Modernes* (May 1957).

"Questions de méthode," *Les Temps Modernes* XIII (1957). *Search for a Method* (Knopf, 1963).

"Nous sommes tous des assassins," *Les Temps Modernes* (March, 1958).

III. WORKS DEVOTED TO THE WRITINGS OF JEAN-PAUL SARTRE

Robert Campbell. *Jean-Paul Sartre ou une littérature philosophique* (Editions Pierre Ardent, 1945).

D. Troisfontaines. *Le Choix de J.-P. Sartre* (Aubier, 1945).

Pierre Boutang and Jean Pingaud. *Sartre est-il un possédé?* (La Table Ronde, 1946).

Francis Jeanson. *Le Probléme moral et la pensée de Jean-Paul Sartre* (Editions du Myrte, 1947).

Marc Beigbeder. *L'Homme Sartre* (Bordas, 1947).

Jean Kanapa. *L'existentialisme n'est pas un humanisme* (Editions Sociales, 1947).

Simone de Beauvoir. *The Ethics of Ambiguity*. Trans. by Bernard Frechtman (Philosophical Library, 1948).

Jean-Marie Grévillot. *Les Grands Courants de la pensée contemporaine* (Beauchesne, 1948).

Gilbert Varet. *L'ontologie de Sartre* (Presses Universitaires, 1948).

P.-H. Simon. *L'homme en procès* (Neuchâtel: La Baconniére, 1950).

Régis Jolivet. *Le probléme de la mort chez Heidegger et chez Sartre* (Ed. de Fontenelle, 1950).

Pierre de Boisdeffre. *Métamorphoses de la littérature* (Editions Alsatia, 1951) II, pp. 209-307.

Iris Murdoch. *Sartre: Romantic Rationalist* (Yale University Press, 1953).

Pierre de Boisdeffre. *Des Vivants et des Morts* (Editions Universitaires, 1954).

Charles Moeller. *Littérature du XXe siécle* (Albin Michel, 1955).

Cahiers de la Compagnie Madeleine-Jean-Louis Barrault XIII. *Connaissance de Sartre* (Julliard, 1955).

Francis Jeanson. *Sartre par lui-meme* (Editions du Seuil, 1956).

Robert Champigny. *Stages on Sartre's Way* (Indiana University Press, 1959).

John D. Wild. *The Challenge of Existentialism* (Indiana University Press, 1959).

Wilfrid Desan. The Tragic Finale: *An Essay on the Philosophy of Jean-Paul Sartre* (Harvard University Press, 1960).

Justus Streller. *Jean-Paul Sartre: To Freedom Condemned.* Trans. Wade Baskin (Philosophical Library, 1960).

René Marill Albérès. *Jean-Paul Sartre: Philosopher Without Faith.* Trans. Wade Baskin (Philosophical Library, 1961).

Frederic Jameson. *Sartre: The Origins of a Style* (Yale University Press, 1961).

E. G. Kern (ed.). *Sartre, A Collection of Critical Essays* (Prentice-Hall, 1962).

Jacques Salvan. *To Be or Not To Be* (Wayne State University Press, 1962).

M. W. Cranston. *Jean-Paul Sartre* (University of Michigan Press, 1963).

Ronald Davis Laing and D. G. Cooper. *Reason and Violence: A Decade of Sartre's Philosophy, 1950-1960* (Tavistock Publications, 1964).

IV. SIGNIFICANT ARTICLES ON THE WRITINGS OF JEAN-PAUL SARTRE

(Only a few of the most important articles are listed.)

Marcel Arland. "Compte rendu de la Nausée," *N.R.F.* (July 1938).

Maurice Merleau-Ponty. "Compte rendu des Mouches," *Confluences* XXV (September-October, 1943).

Gaëtan Picon. "Jean-Paul Sartre et le roman contemporain," *Confluences VIII* (October, 1945).

Maurice Blanchot. "Les Romans de Sartre," *L'Arche* X (October, 1945).

Gabriel Marcel. "Les Chemins de la liberté," *La Nef* XIII (December, 1945).

Jean-José Marchand. "Sartre et les Temps Modernes," *Le Magasin du Spectacle* I (April, 1946).

Claude Cuénot. "Littérature et philosophie chez J.-P. Sartre," *Renaissances* XXI (May, 1946).

Raymond Polin. "Introduction à philosophie de J.-P. Sartre," *Revue de Paris* XLV (1946).

Claude Roy. "Descriptions critiques," *Poésie* XXXVII (1947).

Georges Blin. "Jean-Paul Sartre et Baudelaire," *Fontaine* LIX (1947).

Yale French Studies. I:1 (1948).

Thierry Maulnier. "Jean-Paul Sartre et le suicide de la littérature," *La Table Ronde* II (February, 1948).

André Blanchet. "Comment Jean-Paul Sartre se représente le Diable et le Bon Dieu," *Etudes* (September, 1951).

Claude Lefort. "Le marxisme et Sartre," *Les Temps Modernes* (April, 1953).

Henri Magnan. "Interview," *Le Monde* (1 July, 1955).

Yale French Studies. *Foray Through Existentialism* XVI (Winter 1955-1956).

Maurice Nadeau. "Sartre et l'affaire Hervé," *Les Lettres Nouvelles* (April, 1956).

Frederic Will. "Sartre and the Question of Character in Literature," *Publications of the Modern Language Association* LXXVI (1961).

Michael Wreszin. "Jean-Paul Sartre: Philosopher as Dramatist," *Tulane Drama Review* V (1961).

Jean-Marie Domenach. "Sartre et l'Europe," *Esprit* IV, V (1961-1962).

Mikel Dufrenne. "La critique de la raison dialectique," (*Esprit* IV 1962).

Alphonse de Waelhens. "Sartre et la raison dialectique," *Revue philosophie de Louvain* LX (1962).

Madeleine Fields. "*De la Critique de la raison dialectique aux Séquestrés d'Altona,*" *Publications of the Modern Language Association* LXXVIII (1963).

INDEX

EBOOKS BY JEAN-PAUL SARTRE

FROM PHILOSOPHICAL LIBRARY
AND OPEN ROAD MEDIA

Available wherever ebooks are sold

Philosophical Library's mission is to reintroduce readers to **books of lasting value** by the intellectual icons of the twentieth century, including Albert Einstein, Jean-Paul Sartre, Kahlil Gibran, and André Gide.

FIND OUT MORE AT

WWW.PHILOSOPHICALLIBRARY.COM

FOLLOW US:

@PhilLibrary
Facebook.com/PhilosophicalLibrary
PhilosophicalLibrary.Tumblr.com

Philosophical Library is one of a select group of publishing partners of Open Road Integrated Media, Inc.

Open Road Integrated Media is a digital publisher and multimedia content company. Open Road creates connections between authors and their audiences by marketing its ebooks through a new proprietary online platform, which uses premium video content and social media.

Videos, Archival Documents, and New Releases

Sign up for the Open Road Media newsletter and get news delivered straight to your inbox.

Sign up now at
www.openroadmedia.com/newsletters

CPSIA information can be obtained
at www.ICGtesting.com
Printed in the USA
FFOW04n2124150116
20471FF